Photoshop®

CS

Accelerated

YJ IT Publishing Team

Manager: **Suzie Lee**
Chief Editor: **Angelica Lim**
Developmental Editor: **Colleen Wheeler Strand**
Production Editor: **Patrick Cunningham**
Editor: **Sas Jacobs**
Proofreader: **Semtle**
Book Designer: **Semtle**
Production Control: **Ann Lee**
Indexer: **Adam Barrett**

ISBN: 89-314-3505-3

Printed and bound in the Republic of Korea.

How to contact us

E-mail: support@youngjin.com
        feedback@youngjin.com.sg
Address: Youngjin.com
1623-10, Seocho-dong, Seocho-gu, Seoul 137-878, Korea
Telephone: +65-6327-1161
Fax: +65-6327-1151

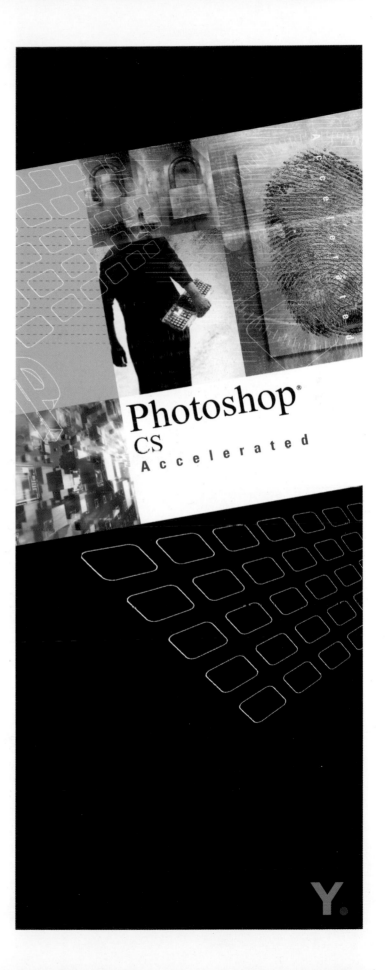

Photoshop®
CS
Accelerated

Y.

contents

Chapter 1

Welcome to Photoshop CS / 8

The Basics of Photoshop / 10

Chapter 2

Making Selections / 30

Selection Tools / 32

Exercise 1   Selecting and Changing a Color / 42
Exercise 2   Adding a Motion Effect / 44
Exercise 3   Creating a Reflection / 46
Exercise 4   Using the Quick Mask Mode to Create a Selection / 48

Chapter 3

Essential Image Editing Skills / 50

Basic Tools and Commands / 52

Exercise 1   Blending Pictures / 60
Exercise 2   Modifying a Portrait / 63
Exercise 3   Creating a Shadow / 67
Exercise 4   Making a Transparent Image for a Web Page / 72

Chapter 4

Retouching Images / 74

An Overview of Retouching Tools / 76

Exercise 1   Removing Red Eyes / 84
Exercise 2   Removing Fine Lines and Correcting Skin Tone / 86
Exercise 3   Applying a Pattern to an Uneven Surface / 89
Exercise 4   Using the Art History Brush to Create a Painting Effect / 91

Chapter 5

Painting and Image Editing / 94

The Essentials of Painting and Image Editing / 96

Exercise 1   Adding Color to Line Drawings / 116
Exercise 2   Coloring Black-and-White Images / 122
Exercise 3   Creating a CD-ROM Cover Insert / 126

Chapter 6

Paths and Vector Tools / 132

Introduction to Paths and Vectors / 134

Exercise 1   Using Paths to Frame Pictures / 146
Exercise 2   Using Paths to Create Neon Lights and Fireworks / 150
Exercise 3   Working with Cartoon Characters / 154

Chapter 7

Color Correction / 158

Color Correction Options / **160**

Exercise 1   Brightening Dark Images / **179**
Exercise 2   Correcting Overexposed Pictures / **181**
Exercise 3   Changing Image Composition and Correcting a Faded Image / **183**
Exercise 4   Adding Color to Black-and-White Pictures / **186**
Exercise 5   Adding TV Scan Lines to an Image / **189**

Chapter 8

Working with Layers / 192

What Is a Layer? / **194**

Exercise 1   Using Layer Blend Modes to Create Luminosity / **217**
Exercise 2   Using Layer Masks to Blend Images - Example 1 / **220**
Exercise 3   Using Layer Masks to Blend Images - Example 2 / **224**
Exercise 4   Making a Water Droplets Image / **230**

Chapter 9

Channels / 236

About Channels / **238**

Exercise 1   Creating Text with a Stitching Effect / **244**
Exercise 2   Applying Texture to 3D Text / **250**
Exercise 3   Creating a Gold Coin / **256**

Chapter 10

Filters / 266

The Filter Menu / **268**

Exercise 1   Making New Pictures Look Old / **345**
Exercise 2   Creating a Pencil Sketch / **349**

Appendix

Configuring the Photoshop Environment / 352

Photoshop CS Menus / 358

contents

Installing Photoshop CS › › ›

The following section provides step-by-step instructions for installing Photoshop CS on your system. The procedure for installing the 30-day trial version of Photoshop CS is similar. You can download the trial version from Adobe's Web site.

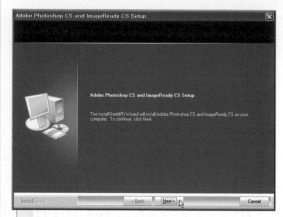

1 Double-click CD-ROM\PS CS\Setup.exe to start the installation. When you see the dialog box shown above, click [Next] to continue.

2 When you see the dialog box shown here, close all Adobe applications and click [OK].

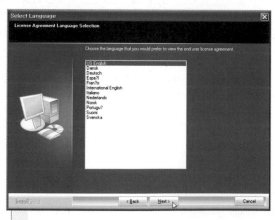

3 Select US English and click [Next].

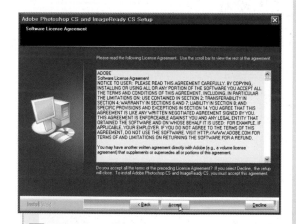

4 Before you can install the file, you will be asked to accept the license agreement. Click the [Accept] button to accept the agreement and carry on with the installation. If you click [Decline], the installation will end.

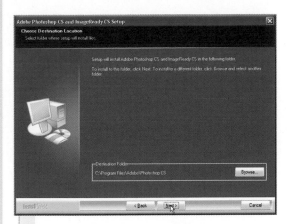

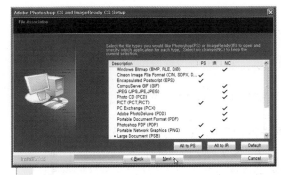

5 In this step, you will decide where to install the program. Click [Next] to install Photoshop CS in the Programs folder, or use the [Browse] button to choose a different location.

6 You will then be asked which file types you want to associate with Photoshop or ImageReady.

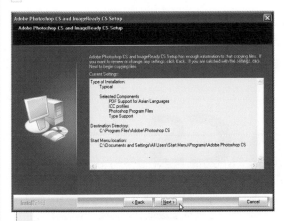

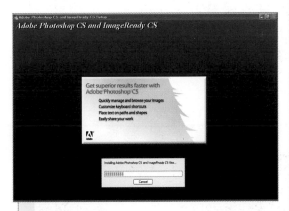

7 Click [Next] to begin installing or click [Back] to change your settings. You will need to go back to change the target drive if it does not have enough disk space.

8 Once you've clicked [Next], the installation will begin.

9 When the installation has finished, you will see a message stating that the installation is compete. Click the [Finish] button to close the dialog box.

Chapter 1

Welcome to Photoshop CS

Photoshop CS is the latest version of Photoshop, Adobe's powerful image-editing program. It's part of Adobe's Creative Suite, a package of design programs for people working with both print and Web graphics. Among the new features in Photoshop CS are a range of productivity enhancements and exciting options for photographers. Photoshop CS also includes the ImageReady CS program, which integrates closely with Photoshop CS to facilitate the creation of Web graphics.

The Basics of Photoshop

Before you start working with Photoshop, it is important to cover some of the basic skills and become familiar with the Photoshop interface. In this chapter, you will learn to use some of the basic functions in Photoshop, including Photoshop tools and palettes, by creating and saving an image.

The Photoshop Work Area

The Photoshop work area contains pull-down menus, a toolbox, and palettes.

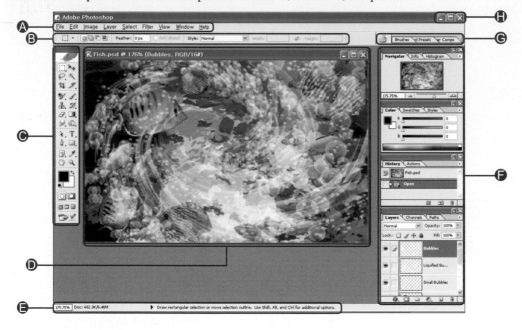

Ⓐ Menu Bar: Photoshop provides nine pull-down menus across the top of the screen named File, Edit, Image, Layer, Select, Filter, View, Window, and Help.

Ⓑ Tool Options Bar: When a tool is selected in the toolbox, the tool options bar provides the options for working with that tool.

Ⓒ Toolbox: The toolbox is a collection of the tools used most frequently in Photoshop.

Ⓓ Image Window: The image window contains the current images. Each image has a title bar that displays the file name, magnification, and color mode.

Ⓔ Status Bar: The status bar shows information about the current file, including the magnification and file size and how to use the selected tool.

Ⓕ Palettes: The palettes are used for a variety of functions. Each group contains palettes that perform similar functions.

ⓖ Palette Well: The well contains frequently-used palettes. You can drag any of the palettes into the well to make them easy to access. In most cases, the well displays the File Browser and Brushes palette.

ⓗ Minimize, Maximize, and Close Buttons: These buttons are used to minimize, maximize, and close the Photoshop window.

Working with Tools

The toolbox contains the Photoshop tools that you will use when working with an image. There is an icon for each tool. If you place your pointer over an icon, you will see a tool tip containing the tool name and shortcut key. To use a tool, click on the icon. You can set the options for the selected tool in the tool options bar.

There are also some hidden tools in the toolbox. If you see a small triangle in the lower-right corner of a tool icon, this means that there are similar tools hidden behind this icon. To see the hidden tools, click and hold down the mouse button on the tool icon.

The Toolbox

Let's look at the functions of all the tools in the toolbox. The shortcut key for each of these tools is indicated in the brackets beside the tool name.

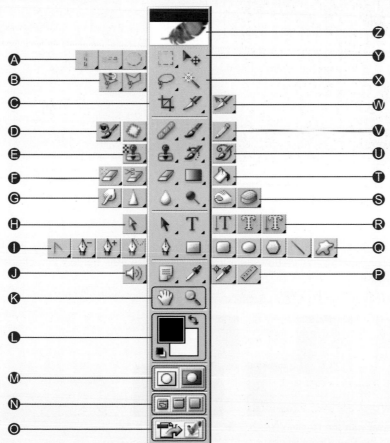

Ⓐ Selection Tools

- Rectangular Marquee Tool [M] 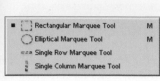: Makes a rectangular or square selection.
- Elliptical Marquee Tool [M] < >: Makes an elliptical or circular selection.
- Single Row Marquee Tool < >: Makes a horizontal 1-pixel selection.
- Single Column Marquee Tool < >: Makes a vertical 1-pixel selection.

◀ Making a Selection with the Rectangular Marquee Tool

Ⓑ Lasso Selection Tools

- Lasso Tool [L] < >: Makes a selection by drawing freehand lines.
- Polygonal Lasso Tool [L] < >: Makes a selection in the shape of a polygon by drawing connected straight lines.
- Magnetic Lasso Tool [L] < >: Makes a selection by snapping to an object's border like a magnet.

◀ The Lasso tool is great for selecting irregular shapes.

Ⓒ Crop Tool [C] < >: Cuts out a portion of the image.

◀ Using the Crop Tool to Cut Out a Rectangular Section

Ⓓ Correction Tools

- Healing Brush Tool [J] < >: Removes flaws by copying and blending another area into the selected area.
- Patch Tool [J] < >: Removes flaws like the Healing Brush tool, but lets you choose a healing patch with more flexibility.
- Color Replacement Tool [J] < >: Replaces image colors.

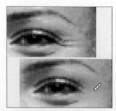  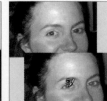 

▲ Removing Flaws with the Healing Brush Tool (Left) and the Patch Tool (Right)

▲ Changing a Color with the Color Replacement Tool

Ⓔ Clone Tools

- Rubber Stamp Tool [S] : Clones another area and stamps it on a selection.
- Pattern Stamp Tool [S] <>: Stamps a pattern on an image.

◀Using the Rubber Stamp Tool and the Pattern Stamp Tool

Ⓕ Eraser Tools

- Eraser Tool [E] <>: Erases an image.
- Background Eraser Tool [E] <>: Erases a background to make it transparent.
- Magic Eraser Tool [E] <>: Erases areas similar to the area that was clicked with the tool.

  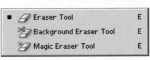

▲From Left: Using the Eraser Tool, Background Eraser Tool, and Magic Eraser Tool

Ⓖ Sharpness Tools

- Blur Tool [R] <>: Blurs an image.
- Sharpen Tool [R] <>: Sharpens the edges of an image.
- Smudge Tool [R] <>: Smudges an image.

▲From Left: Applying the Blur Tool, the Sharpen Tool, and the Smudge Tool

Ⓗ Path Selection Tools

- Path Selection Tool [A] <>: Selects paths.
- Direct Selection Tool [A] <>: Selects part of a path for editing.

◀Using the Path Selection Tool

● Path Tools
- Pen Tool [P] 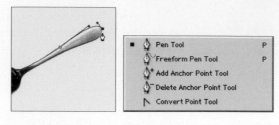: Creates lines and curves in a path.
- Freeform Pen Tool [P] < >: Draws freeform paths.
- Add Anchor Point Tool < >: Adds anchor points to a path.
- Delete Anchor Point Tool < >: Removes anchor points from a path.
- Convert Point Tool < >: Edits points on a path.

◀Drawing a Path with the Pen Tool

● Notes Tools
- Notes Tool [N] < >: Adds text notes to images.
- Audio Annotation Tool [N] < >: Adds audio notes to images.

◀Adding a Text Note to an Image

ⓚ Viewing Tools
- Hand Tool [H] < >: Moves the image around so that you can see the parts that are outside the screen.
- Zoom Tool [Z] < >: Zooms in on an image. Using the tool with the [Alt] key zooms out from an image.

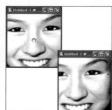

◀Using the Hand Tool (Left) and the Zoom Tool (Right)

● Color Swatches
- Foreground Color Swatch <■>: Shows the current foreground color. Click on the swatch to open the Color Picker dialog box and select a new foreground color. The [Alt]-[Delete] shortcut fills the image with the foreground color.
- Background Color Swatch < >: Shows the current background color. Click the tool to open the Color Picker dialog box and select a new background color. The [Ctrl]-[Delete] shortcut fills the image with the background color.
- Switch Foreground and Background Colors [X] < >: Switches the foreground and background colors.
- Default Foreground and Background Colors [D] < >: Sets the foreground color to black and the background color to white.

14

Ⓜ Editing Modes
- Standard Mode [Q] <▣>: The standard Photoshop editing mode.
- Quick Mask Mode [Q] <▣>: Used to create and edit selections by adding a temporary mask to the image. Areas that are not masked appear red.

Ⓝ Screen Modes
- Standard Screen Mode [F] <▣>: The standard Photoshop window that shows the toolbox, palettes, and menus.
- Full Screen Mode with Menu Bar [F] <▣>: The image is centered in the window without the menu bar or title bar.
- Full Screen Mode [F] <▣>: Shows the image in full screen mode.

◉ Edit in ImageReady ([Shift]-[Ctrl]-[M]) <▣>: Opens file in ImageReady.

Ⓟ Sampling and Measuring Tools
- Eyedropper Tool [I] <▣>: Samples color to use for the foreground color.
- Color Sampler Tool [I] <▣>: Defines a color sample in the RGB (Red, Green, and Blue) color mode.
- Measure Tool [I] <▣>: Measures distance, position, and angles.

▲Using the Eyedropper Tool (Left) and the Measure Tool (Right)

◉ Shape Tools
- Rectangle Tool [U] <▣>: Draws rectangular and square shapes.
- Rounded Rectangle Tool [U] <▣>: Draws rectangular and square shapes with rounded corners.
- Ellipse Tool [U] <▣>: Draws circles or ellipses.
- Polygon Tool [U] <▣>: Draws polygons or stars.
- Line Tool [U] <▣>: Draws lines or arrows.
- Custom Shape Tool [U] <▣>: Draws a variety of custom shapes.

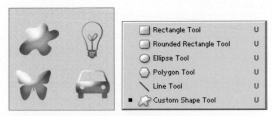

▲One of the Predefined Shapes You Can Draw with the Custom Shape Tool

® Type Tools
- Type Tool [T] <T>: Adds horizontal text.
- Vertical Type Tool [T] <T>: Adds vertical text.
- Horizontal Type Mask Tool [T] <T>: Adds a horizontal selection in the shape of text.
- Vertical Type Mask Tool [T] <T>: Adds a vertical selection in the shape of text.

▲Using the Horizontal Type Tool (Left) and the Horizontal Type Mask Tool (Right)

ⓢ Brightness and Saturation Tools
- Dodge Tool [O] <🔍>: Lightens an area.
- Burn Tool [O] <✋>: Darkens an area.
- Sponge Tool [O] <🧽>: Increases or decreases the color saturation of an area.

▲From Left: Applying the Dodge Tool, the Burn Tool, and the Sponge Tool

ⓣ Fill Tools
- Gradient Tool [G] <▣>: Creates a color gradient.
- Paint Bucket Tool [G] <🪣>: Fills an image using the foreground color or pattern.

▲Using the Gradient Tool (Left) and the Paint Bucket Tool (Right)

ⓤ History Brushes
- History Brush Tool [Y] <🖌>: Restores an image to a previous state picked from the History palette.
- Art History Brush Tool [Y] <🖌>: Similar to the History Brush tool, but includes artistic effects.

◀Using the Art History Brush Tool
for an Artistic Effect (Right)

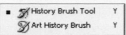

▲Restoring a Selected Color to the Previous State with the History Brush Tool (Left)

Ⓥ Painting Tools

- Brush Tool [B] <>: Creates brush stroke drawings.
- Pencil Tool [B] <>: Draws pencil lines.

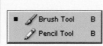

▲Using the Brush Tool (Left) and the Pencil Tool (Right)

Ⓦ Slice Tools

- Slice Tool [K] <>: Slices an image into smaller pieces.
- Slice Select Tool [K] <>: Selects or moves a slice.

▲Slicing an Image (Left) and Moving a Slice (Right)

Ⓧ Magic Wand Tool [W] <>

Selects adjacent colors similar to the color that was clicked with the tool.

◀Using the Magic Wand Tool to Select Areas with Similar Colors

Ⓨ Move Tool [V] <>

Moves a selection, layer, or guide.

◀Moving a Selection with the Move Tool

17

②Adobe Online <  **>**

Connects to the Adobe Web site for file updates and new product information.

<< note

Using Shortcut Keys to Select Tools

A tool can be activated by pressing its shortcut key(s). If you hold down the [Shift] key while pressing a shortcut key, you will toggle among the hidden tools of the selected tool group.

Working with Palettes

Palettes contain options for working with images. Palettes with similar functions are grouped together for convenience.

The Navigator Palette

This palette is used to zoom in and out of an image and to move to another position within the image.

The Info Palette

The Info palette displays color values, angles, and coordinates of a point or selection.

The Histogram Palette

The Histogram palette displays a bar graph of image color information.

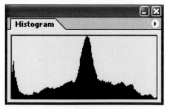

The Color Palette

This palette is used to mix and select colors.

The Swatches Palette

The Swatches palette contains commonly used colors. Colors can be added and removed from this palette and new swatches can be loaded.

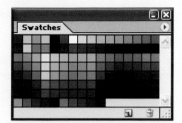

The Styles Palette

The Style palette contains pre-made layer styles.

The History Palette

This palette shows a list of all the steps that you have carried out in your work. You can use this palette to undo many steps and go back to a previous state.

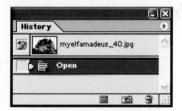

The Actions Palette

The Actions palette can be used to save and work with common actions.

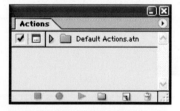

The Tool Presets Palette

The Tool Presets palette contains any tools that you have configured specifically for the current tool.

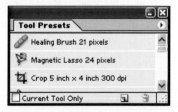

The Layers Palette

The Layers palette is used to manage and edit layers.

The Channels Palette

This palette is used to manage and edit color channels.

The Paths Palette

The Paths palette is used to manage and edit paths created with the Pen tool.

The Character Palette

The Character palette is used to set text options.

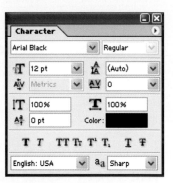

The Paragraph Palette

The Paragraph palette is used to change the paragraph options of text.

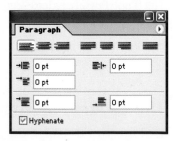

The Brushes Palette

The Brushes palette contains brush properties.

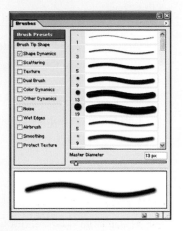

The New Dialog Box

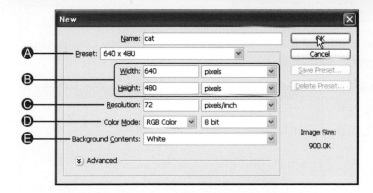

Ⓐ Preset: Select an image size from the preset sizes.
- Custom: The user determines the image size.
- Clipboard: Uses the size of the last object that you copied.
- Default Photoshop Size: The default image size of a Photoshop image is 7 inches by 5 inches at 72 pixels/inch.
- Image Formats: Includes Letter (8.5" × 11"), Legal (8.5" × 14"), and Tabloid (11" × 17").
- Photograph Size: Standard photograph sizes.
- TV Screen Resolutions: The most commonly used TV screen resolutions.
- Paper Size: Includes sizes A4, A3, B5, B4, and B3.

Ⓑ Width and Height

You can specify width and height using these units of measurement: pixels, inches, centimeters, points (1 point = 1/72 inch), picas (1 pica = 12 points), and columns. You can set the size of 1 column by selecting [File] - [Preferences] - [Units & Rulers] - [Column Size] from the menu bar.

Ⓒ Resolution

The higher the resolution of an image, the more details it includes. However, increasing the resolution will also increase the file size of the image. Web images normally use a resolution of 72 pixels/inch and printed images use 300 pixels/inch.

Ⓓ Color Modes: Here is a brief explanation of color modes; you will learn more about color modes later in this chapter.

- Bitmap: Images that contain only black and white.
- Grayscale: Uses only shades of gray.
- RGB Color: In this mode, 16,700,000 colors are defined using combinations of the colors Red, Green, and Blue.
- CMYK Color: Specifies color for print using a combination of Cyan, Magenta, Yellow, and Black.
- Lab Color: A color made up of a luminance component and two color elements (a: Green to Red, b: Blue to Yellow).

Ⓔ Background Contents

- White: White background
- Background Color: Uses the current background color from the color picker.
- Transparent: The background layer is transparent

Creating a New Image

In this section, you will learn how to create new image files. When you create a new file, you can choose the size of the image, the background color, and the image resolution.

1. Select [File] - [New] to create a new document or image file. In the New dialog box, enter **cat** for the Name, set the width to 640 pixels, and the height to 480 pixels.

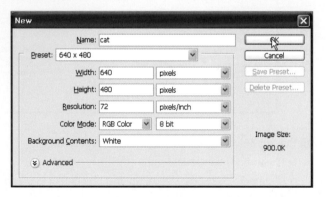

2. Click OK to create the image. Click and hold on the Brush tool icon in the toolbox and select the Pencil tool 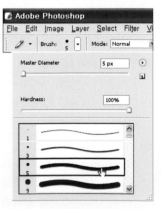.

3. In the Tool Options bar, click on the Brush Preset picker and select Hard Round 5 pixels.

4. Use the Pencil tool to make a simple drawing. Make sure there are no spaces in the image outline, as it will be filled with color. The title bar displays the image name as cat, the magnification as 100%, and shows that it is an 8-bit RGB image.

<< **tip**

Undoing Mistakes

If you make a mistake in your drawing, select [Edit] - [Step Backward] to undo the previous step. You can use this command to undo several steps.

5. Click and hold on the Gradient tool and select the Paint Bucket tool < >from the toolbox. Drag the R, G, and B slider bars in the Color palette to select a fill color for the drawing, or select a color from the color bar below.

6. Click inside your drawing to fill the image with the selected color.

Saving an Image File

1. Select [File] - [Save]. In the Save As dialog box, choose the image location and click [Save]. The image will be named cat. Select JPEG (∗.JPG, ∗.JPEG, ∗.JPE) from the drop-down Format menu.

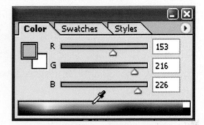

[File] - [Save] Options
- **Save**: This command saves the current file using the current filename, format, and location. If the file has not been saved before, the Save As dialog box will be shown.
- **Save As**: The Save As command allows the file name, location, and file format to be selected. You can use it to save a different version of an existing file.
- **As a Copy**: Creates a backup of the image file. This saves a copy of the image without affecting the file that is currently open.

2. When an image is saved in JPEG format, the JPEG Options dialog box will appear. This dialog box is used to set the compression rate for the image. The lower the Quality setting, the smaller the file size. However, the image quality will decline as the Quality setting is lowered. Enter a Quality of 8 and click OK.

3. The image has been saved. Select [File] - [Exit] to close Photoshop.

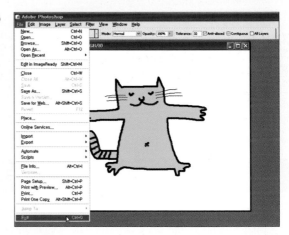

Understanding Color and Image Modes

A color mode determines how colors make up an image. Let's have a look at each of the color modes available in Photoshop.

- **Bitmap**: Only the colors black and white can be used in bitmap images.

<< note

Color in Bitmap Images

Although bitmaps created in Photoshop can only display black and white, you can save color images in the bitmap file format while retaining their color.

24

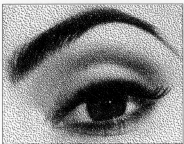

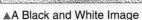
▲A Black and White Image

▲Magnifying the image makes it possible to see the black and white pixels.

- **Grayscale**: Grayscale mode uses up to 256 shades of gray. The color black is given a value of 0 and all numbers between 1 and 254 are increasingly lighter shades of gray. White has a value of 255.

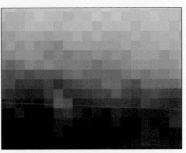

▲Image Displayed in Grayscale Mode

▲Magnifying the image makes it possible to see the gray pixels.

- **RGB Color**: The RGB color mode uses the three primary colors - red, green, and blue - and is the format that is used on computer monitors. Within this color mode, up to 16.7 million different colors can be displayed. RGB color is normally used for color images as all file formats and filters within Photoshop support this mode.

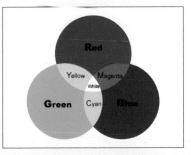

- **CMYK Color**: The CMYK color mode is used primarily for printing. Within this mode, colors are given a percentage value for each of the process inks - cyan, magenta, yellow, and black. When working with print images, the editing is often done within RGB mode and the mode is changed to CMYK as the final step.

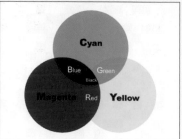

• **Lab Color**: The Lab color mode uses lightness as well as two color axes - the A-axis (shades from green to magenta) and the B-axis (shades from blue to yellow). Photoshop uses lab color to convert an image from one color mode to another.

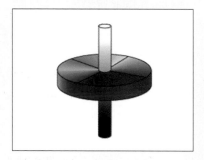

• **HSB Color**: The HSB color mode uses hue, brightness, and saturation to determine color.

  - *Hue*: Hue is the color of the object and uses a measurement between 0 and 360.

  - *Brightness*: Represents the lightness or darkness of a color and is measured in a percentage between 0% (black) to 100% (white).

  - *Saturation*: Saturation is also called chroma and is the strength or purity of the color. It is measured in a percentage from 0% (gray) to 100%. Higher saturations create colors that are closest to the primary colors. A saturation of 100% red would be referred to as a pure red color.

Selecting the Color Mode
The color mode can be changed at any time using the [Image] - [Mode] menu. It is important to select the color mode according to the purpose of the image. The Bitmap color mode is used for line art images in black and white. Grayscale color mode is used for images that contain only black, gray, and white. The RGB color mode is used for images that will be displayed on a monitor, for example on a Web page or in a screen presentation. CMYK color is used for print images.

Photoshop File Formats

Photoshop supports a variety of file formats so that you can create images for different purposes and share them with other programs. You can specify the file format when you use the [File] - [Save] or [Save As] commands to save an image. Photoshop supports the following file formats.

- **PHOTOSHOP (*.PSD, *.PDD)**

  This format is the Photoshop native file format. It cannot be used with other programs, but it allows the greatest flexibility when working with images. It supports all color modes and features such as alpha channels, paths, and layers.

  Although this file format compresses the image file, the file is still larger than compressed files of other formats. Increasing the number of layers and channels within the image will increase the file size. This file format is usually used to create and edit the image, and a final copy is saved in another format for use in Web pages, print, or multi-media presentations.

- **BMP (*.BMP, *.RLE, *.DIB)**

  The bitmap format is the most basic graphic file format. When you save a bitmap file, you will need to specify the operating system, either Windows or OS/2, and configure the depth of the image up to a value of 32 bits. Channels and layers cannot be saved in this format.

- **CompuServe GIF (*.GIF)**

  The GIF (Graphic Interchange Format) format was developed as a way to compress image sizes. It is used for Internet images, animations, and images with transparent sections. The GIF format supports up to 256 colors (8 bit) and is not suitable for complex images such as photographs. RGB images, as well as those in Bitmap, Grayscale, and Indexed color modes, can be saved as GIF files.

- **Photoshop EPS (*.EPS)**

  The EPS (Encapsulated PostScript) format, used for vector or bitmap images, is appropriate when importing images to an editing program, such as Illustrator, PageMaker, or QuarkXpress. The EPS format is normally used in the print process, so images will often need to be changed to CMYK mode. This format saves the paths within an image but does not save alpha channels.

- **Photoshop DCS1.0 (*.EPS), Photoshop DCS2.0 (*.EPS)**

  When CMYK images are saved in EPS format, the DCS (Desktop Color Separations) format saves the file as 4 individual files and 1 master file. The DCS2.0 format includes spot channels and can be used for images with customized colors.

- **JPEG (*.JPG, *.JPEG *.JPE)**

  The JPEG (Joint Photographic Experts Group) format is another compressed file format that is widely used on the Internet. JPEGs can display up to 24 bits of color and are used for saving images with continuous color, such as photographs. The compression rate can be changed as needed. Higher compression rates result in smaller files, but will also lower the quality of an image.

- **PCX (*.PCX)**

  The PCX format was created for exchange of files with Zsoft's PC Paintbrush. This file format is rarely used.

- **Photoshop PDF (*.PDF, *.PDP)**

The Photoshop PDF (Portable Document Format) format was created for compatibility with Adobe Acrobat. This format allows Photoshop to read PDF documents.

- **PICT (*.PCT, *.PICT)**

This format is the standard graphics format for Macintosh computers. RGB images saved as PICT files can use either 16 or 32 bits. JPEG compression is possible at 32 bits.

- **Pixar (*.PXR)**

The Pixar format is a special format that was developed by Pixar, an animation company. This format supports RGB and grayscale images with a single alpha channel.

- **PNG (*.PNG)**

The PNG (Portable Network Graphic) format is a compressed file format that can be used to create transparent images. This format can be saved in 8-bit or 24-bit. PNG is a newer file format that provides compression without loss of image quality. However, PNG files are larger compared with JPEG-compressed files. Older web browsers may have difficulty displaying these images.

- **Raw (*.RAW)**

The Raw file format contains raw pixel information and is a flexible format for transferring images between programs and computer types.

- **Scitex CT (*.SCT)**

The Scitex CT (Scitex Continuous Tone) file format is for file transfer with Scitex computers.

- **TGA (*.TGA, *.VDA, *.ICB, *.VST)**

The TGA (Targa) format was developed by Truevision for their Targa and Vista video board. This format can be used on PCs and Macs and supports 24-bit color, as well as 32-bit Web color.

- **TIFF (*.TIF, *.TIFF)**

The TIFF (Tagged Image File Format) format was developed to allow for sharing of images between programs and between Macintosh computers and PCs. It includes LZW compression, which does not affect the quality of an image file. This format preserves channels and produces smaller file sizes compared with the EPS file format. TIFF also supports ZIP compression and preserves transparent frames.

Choosing the Right File Format

Photoshop supports many different file formats. Each format is used for a different purpose and should be selected depending on how your image will ultimately be used.

- **Incomplete Files or Files Requiring Modification**

  If you need to continue to work on an image file, it is most useful to save it in Photoshop (PSD) format. This will preserve the layers, paths, and channels within the image.

- **DTP for Printing**

  If you are going to use Photoshop images in a desktop publishing program, they should be saved in EPS format. This allows image properties such as paths to be made available.

- **Web Images**

  GIF and JPEG formats are used on Web pages because they compress the image file size. The GIF format allows you to save images with transparent backgrounds without loss of quality. Within the JPEG format, you can specify your own compression rate to determine the final file size and image quality. The JPEG format is suitable for photographs.

Chapter | 2

Making Selections

Using Photoshop, you can create and edit many types of images including hand-drawn line art, scans, and photographic collages. To work with images, you will often need to focus on and adjust specific areas. There are a variety of selection techniques and tools that can be used and it is important to learn these, as it will make creating your own images much easier.

Selection Tools

In this chapter, let's look at some of the tools and commands that can be used to select parts of an image, including the Marquee, Lasso, and Magic Wand tools. You'll be able to practice working with these tools in the examples at the end of the chapter.

The Marquee Tools

The marquee tools make image selections in the shape of a rectangle or square (Rectangular Marquee tool); ellipse or circle (Elliptical Marquee tool); a single row of pixels (Single Row Marquee tool); or a single column of pixels (Single Column Marquee tool).

The Rectangular Marquee tool ( ) and the Elliptical Marquee tool ( ) are used by clicking and dragging the tool in the image. Hold down the [Shift] key at the same time to create a perfect square or circle.

▲Using the Rectangular
Marquee Tool

▲Using the Elliptical
Marquee Tool

The Single Row Marquee tool ( ) and the Single Column Marquee tool ( ) are used by clicking the mouse at the point where the selection will begin.

▲Using the Single Row
Marquee Tool

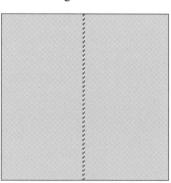

▲Using the Single Column
Marquee Tool

<< tip

**The Single Row/
Column Marquee Tools**

Selections made with the Single Row Marquee tool and the Single Column Marquee tool are one pixel high or wide. You will need to zoom in on the image to see where the selection will be made.

The Marquee Tool Options Bar

When a marquee tool is selected, the tool options bar at the top will display the tool's options. The options will differ depending on which marquee tool is selected. Options for the marquee tool must be set before you make a selection.

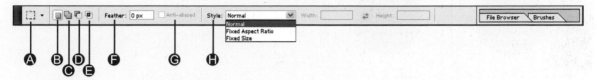

Ⓐ Tool Preset Picker

The Tool Preset picker allows you to save tools with the options that you frequently use. Once the tool has been saved, you can select it from the Tool Preset picker.

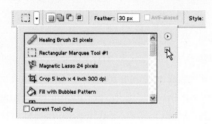

<< tip

Current Tool Only

Checking the Current Tool Only option will display only the tool presets defined for the current tool.

To save a tool, set the options and click the Tool Preset picker. In the Preset Picker palette, click the [Add Preset] button. Enter a name for the tool preset and click OK.

Ⓑ **New selection** (▣): A new selection will be made each time the tool is used. Any existing selection will be cleared first.

Ⓒ **Add to selection** (▣): Each time you make a selection, it will be added to the current selection. You can also hold down the [Shift] key to add to the selection.

Ⓓ **Subtract from selection** (▣): Each time you make a selection, the area will be removed from the current selection. This is the same as holding down the [Alt] key as you make a selection.

Ⓔ **Intersect with selections** (▣): Each time you make a selection, only the areas that intersect with the current selection will be selected. This is the same as holding down the [Shift]-[Alt] keys as you make a selection.

Ⓕ **Feather:** Feather softens the edges of a section using values from 0 to 250 pixels. A higher Feather value produces wider feathered areas and softer selections.

<< tip

Softening Edges

Feathering is often used to soften and blend the edges when combining images.

▲From Left: The Effects of Feather Values of 0, 5, and 20

ⓖ Anti-aliased: This option is only available with the Elliptical Marquee tool. Checking this option softens the edges of the selection.

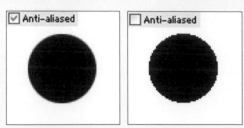

▲The Effect of Checking (Left) and Unchecking (Right) the Anti-Aliased Option

<< tip

Pixels and Anti-Aliasing

Images are made up of small squares called pixels. You can see pixels as you zoom into an image. When you can see the jagged pixel outlines at the edge of a selection, this is called aliasing. The Anti-aliased option smoothes these edges.

ⓗ Style: With the Normal style selected, dragging the mouse over an image makes a freeform selection. The Fixed Aspect Ratio style uses fixed width and height proportions for the selection. For example, setting the width to 2 and the height to 1 will result in selections where the width is always twice the height. The Fixed Size setting allows you to enter a width and height for the selection.

The Lasso Tools

There are three types of lasso tools: the Lasso tool, the Polygonal Lasso tool, and the Magnetic Lasso tool. The Lasso tool (⬚) makes selections by drawing with the mouse.

▲Click and drag the mouse without releasing the mouse button to define the selected area.

▲When you release the mouse button, a blinking border will indicate that you have made a selection.

The Polygonal Lasso tool (⬚) is useful for making selections with straight edges. To use the tool, click points around the image. Each time you click a straight line will be created between the new point and the previous point. Before the selection is completed, the [Delete] key allows you to erase the line segments in reverse order, while the [Esc] key deletes all line segments. To complete the selection, click the starting point or double-click.

▲Click the tool on a corner to create the starting point. Release the mouse and click the next point to create a straight line.

▲Click the final point or double-click to complete the selection.

The Magnetic Lasso tool (⬚) is used for making selections in images with contrasting borders. The tool automatically selects the edges based on color contrast. Click to create the first point. Dragging the mouse creates fastening points along the border. The fastening points will anchor the border to the edges. If the border doesn't snap correctly, you can click once to add a manual fastening point.

Click the first point or double-click the mouse to finish the selection. Before the selection is completed, the [Delete] key can be used to erase recent sections.

▲Click the mouse on the starting point and move it along the image edge to make the selection.

<< tip

Closing a Selection

While using the Magnetic Lasso tool, you can close a selection with a straight line by holding down the [Alt] key and double-clicking.

The Lasso Tools and the [Alt] key

- Holding down the [Alt] key with the Lasso tool allows it to be used like the Polygonal Lasso tool.
- Holding down the [Alt] key with the Polygonal Lasso tool, allows it to be used like the Lasso tool.
- Holding down the [Alt] key with the Magnetic Lasso tool allows it to be used like the Lasso tool or the Polygonal Lasso tool.

Saving and Loading Selections

❶ You can save a selection so that you can use it again. After creating the selection, choose [Select] - [Save Selection]. Enter a name for the selection and click OK.

❷ You can load a saved selection by choosing [Select] - [Load Selection]. Locate the selection to be loaded in the Channel drop-down menu and click OK.

▲Save Selection Dialog Box

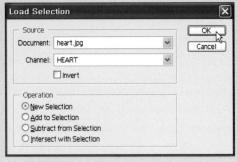
▲Load Selection Dialog Box

The Lasso Tool Options Bar

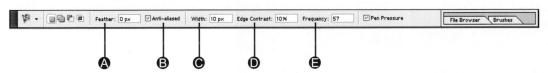

Ⓐ **Feather**: Adjust the Feather value to soften the edges of the selection.

Ⓑ **Anti-aliased**: Check to use anti-aliasing.

Ⓒ **Width**: Specify the detection width of the Magnetic Lasso tool from 1 to 256 in pixels. Edges will only be detected within the chosen pixel distance from the mouse pointer. Turn on the [Caps Lock] key with the Magnetic Lasso tool to show the detection width as a circle around the mouse pointer.

▲Width 10 Pixels

▲Width 15 Pixels

<< note

The Precise Mouse Cursor

The [Caps Lock] key is used to turn on the precise cursor (⊹) so that the mouse pointer is easier to use.

D Edge Contrast: The edge contrast is a value between 1% and 100%. It determines how much of a contrast is required for the edge to be detected by the Magnetic Lasso tool. When larger values are used, only high contrast edges will be found.

▲Edge Contrast 100% ▲Edge Contrast 10%

E Frequency: Frequency affects the rate at which the lasso sets fastening points. A higher value anchors the selection border in place more quickly.

▲Frequency 57　　　▲Frequency 100

<< tip

Frequency Value

Although decimal fractions such as 10.5 can be used for the feather, width, and edge contrast settings, the frequency value should be an integer between 0 and 100.

The Magic Wand Tool

The Magic Wand tool (🔧) creates a selection based on the color of the pixel that is clicked. For example, if you click a red pixel within an image, all matching colored pixels will be selected. Photoshop uses a color range, or tolerance, to decide which pixels to select. As you increase the tolerance value, more colors will be included in the selection. The Magic Wand tool is useful for images that are made up of simple colors or shadows.

The Magic Wand tool cannot be used on an image in Bitmap mode.

▲Tolerance 32　　　　▲Tolerance 150

The Magic Wand Tool Options Bar

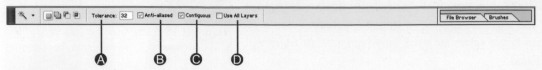

Ⓐ Tolerance: Tolerance adjusts the color range of the selection (0-255). The default tolerance value is 32. As you increase this value, a wider range of colors will be included in the selection.

Ⓑ Anti-aliased: Check to use anti-aliasing on the selection edges.

Ⓒ Contiguous: When this option is checked, the selection is restricted to adjacent areas in the image. If this option is not checked, the selection will include all the areas in the image that have the same color.

▲Contiguous Option Checked   ▲Contiguous Option Unchecked

Ⓓ Use All Layers: This option allows you to make selections from any layer within the image, including layers that are hidden by other layers. You will learn more about layers in Chapter 8.

▲Layer 1, which contains the torch image, is selected in the Layers palette.

▲When Use All Layers is checked, the blue area on the Background layer is also selected.

▲When Use All Layers is unchecked, only the blue area on Layer 1 is selected.

The Select Menu

To make accurate selections, you should use the selection tools together with the Select command on the menu bar. Let's look at some of the commands available on the Select menu.

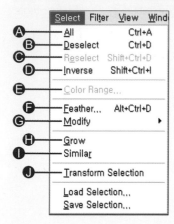

A All: Selects the entire image.

B Deselect: Deselects the current selection.

C Reselect: Reselects the deselected selection.

D Inverse: Inverts the selection. The current selection is deselected and the selection is created from the previously unselected areas.

E Color Range: Selections are created based on color. The Eyedropper tool can be used to select the appropriate color.

F Feather: Set the feather value for the current selection.

G Modify: Modifies the current selection.
   Border: Use the border of the current selection.
   Smooth: Clean up stray pixels left inside or outside a color-based selection.
   Expand: Expand a selection by a specified number of pixels.
   Contract: Contract a selection by a specified number of pixels.

H Grow: Expand to include adjacent pixels within the tolerance range specified in the Magic Wand option.

I Similar: Include pixels anywhere in the image that fall within the tolerance range.

J Transform Selection: Transform the shape of the selection.

Selections can be created according to colors within an image. Choose [Select] - [Color Range] to open the Color Range dialog box. Click the Eyedropper tool (image) on the image to select a color. Change the Fuzziness option to add or remove from the selection. You can also use the Add (image) and Subtract (image) Eyedropper tools.

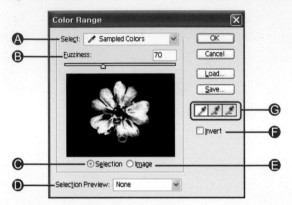

Ⓐ Select: Selections will be made based on the color chosen.

Ⓑ Fuzziness: Increasing fuzziness increases the size of the selection area.

Ⓒ Selection: Displays the image in black and white. White areas are the selected regions.

Ⓓ Selection Preview: Shows a preview of the image.

Ⓔ Image: Displays the image.

Ⓕ Invert: Inverts the selection colors.

Ⓖ Preview Screen: Use the Eyedropper to add and remove from the selection in the preview screen.

Other Ways of Making a Selection

There are many other ways to make selections in addition to the tools covered at the beginning of this section.

Quick Mask Mode

The [Quick Mask Mode] icon (⬚) is found at the bottom of the toolbox and it is used to create irregular selections. In Quick Mask mode, you create a selection by masking the areas that need to be protected or deselected. Masked areas are colored in a red overlay that does not show when printed. The areas that are not colored are the selected areas.

You can either work with an existing selection or create the selection entirely in Quick Mask mode. The Quick Mask can be modified using virtually any Photoshop tool or filter. You can also use selection tools to modify the mask.

Quick Mask Mode Options

Double-click the [Quick Mask Mode] icon (⬚) to open the Quick Mask Options dialog box.

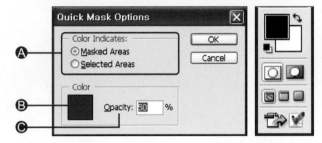

Ⓐ **Color Indicates**

Masked Areas: Choosing the Masked Areas option shows masked areas as opaque and the selected areas as transparent. Painting with the color black adds to the mask whereas painting with white adds to the selection. This is the default option and, when selected, the [Quick Mask] button in the toolbox appears as a white circle on a gray background (⬚).

Selected Areas: Choose the Selected Areas option to have masked areas appear transparent and selected areas appear opaque. With this setting, painting with white increases the masked area while painting with black increases the selection. When this option is selected, the [Quick Mask] button in the toolbox appears as a gray circle on a white background (⬚).

Ⓑ **Color**: Click on the color swatch to select a new mask color.

Ⓒ **Opacity**: Determines the mask color's opacity. If the Opacity is set to 100%, parts of a masked image will be completely hidden. It is often easier to use the default setting of 50%.

<< tip

Saving Masks as Selections

To save masks permanently as selections, return to Standard mode and select [Select] - [Save Selection]. The selection will be saved as an Alpha Channel. You will learn more about channels in Chapter 9.

Selecting and Changing a Color

Original Image   Final Image

Project File
• Lip.jpg

Final File
• Lip_end.jpg

Features Used
• Magic Wand Tool, Lasso Tool, Color Balance

In this exercise, you will create a selection and use it to change the color of lipstick on a woman's face. This example will help you practice adding to and subtracting from a selection.

<< note
Resource Files

Remember to copy the resource files on the CD-ROM to your hard drive before you start each exercise in this book.

1 Open \Sample\Chapter2\Lip.jpg. Select the Magic Wand tool ( ) from the toolbox and click on the upper lip.

<< note
Tolerance and the Magic Wand Tool

The Tolerance option affects the selection made by the Magic Wand tool. The default Tolerance value is 32 and a value between 0 and 255 can be used. As you increase the value, a larger area will be selected.

2 Click the [Add to selection] icon (⬛) in the tool options bar and click on the lower lip. With the Add to selection option selected, you will add to the selection as you click on the lower lip.

3 The Magic Wand tool (🪄) will not select colored areas outside the Tolerance value. Use the Lasso tool to add the unselected area on the bottom lip to the selection.

<< tip
Using the [Shift] Key

You can also add to a selection by holding down the [Shift] key as you click each area.

<< note
Feather Value

To make an accurate selection, the Feather value must be set to the default value of 0 when using the Lasso tool (🪄). Make sure this option is selected before using the tool.

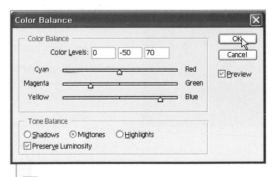

4 To remove areas from the selection, click the [Subtract from selection] icon (⬛⬛⬛⬛). Use the Lasso tool with the add and subtract options until you are satisfied that you have selected the lips perfectly.

5 To adjust the color of the lips, select [Image] - [Adjustments] - [Color Balance]. Move the second slider bar towards Magenta to select a value of -50. Move the third slider bar towards Blue to set a value of 70. Click OK. You will get the final image as shown on the previous page.

<< tip
Using the [Alt] Key

You can also subtract from the selection area by holding down the [Alt] key when you use a tool.

<< note
Preview Option

Make sure that the Preview option is checked so that you can see the effect of the changes on the original image.

2

Adding a Motion Effect

Original Image

Final Image

Project File
└─ ● Wind.jpg

Final File
└─ ● Wind_end.psd

Features Used
└─ ● Lasso Tool, Radial Blur, Layer via Copy

In this example, you will create a selection that will be used to add a motion effect to the blades of a fan. The [Filter] - [Blur] - [Radial Blur] command adds motion effects for objects that use circular motion. A motion effect can be added to objects that move in a straight line with the [Filter] - [Blur] - [Motion Blur] command.

<< note
Resource Files

Remember to copy the resource files on the CD-ROM to your hard drive before you start each exercise in this book.

1 Open \Sample\Chapter2\Wind.jpg. Select the Lasso tool () and set the Feather value to 30. Drag a selection around the fan as shown above. Because you applied a Feather value before making the selection, the selection appears very smooth. Click OK.

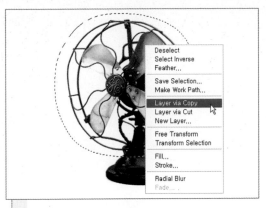

2 Right-click the image and select Layer via Copy ([Ctrl]-[J]). This will create a copy of the selected part of the image on a new layer. This selection is made prior to applying the Radial Blur command on the image so that only the blades of the fan will appear blurred after the command is applied.

3 In the Layers palette, you can see that the image has been copied to Layer 1. To select the contents of Layer 1, hold down the [Ctrl] key and click the Layer 1 layer in the Layers palette.

<< **tip**

Selecting a Layer

The easiest way to select the contents of a layer is to [Ctrl]-click the layer name in the Layers palette. Any layer, except the Background layer, can be selected in this way.

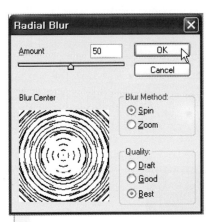

4 With the selection active, choose [Filter] - [Blur] - [Radial Blur]. Set the Amount to 50, the Blur Method to Spin, the Quality to Best, and click OK.

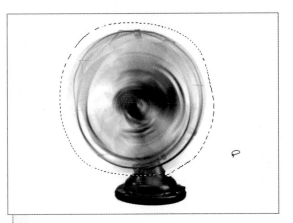

5 The blur effect will be applied to the area within the selection, making it look as if the fan is spinning. Clear the selection by clicking somewhere on the image or by pressing [Ctrl]-[D].

6 In the Layers palette, change the Opacity value of Layer 1 to 70%. This will make Layer 1 slightly transparent, reducing the Radial Blur effect and allowing the background image to be seen through the blurred image. The completed image is shown on the previous page.

3   Creating a Reflection

Original Image

Final Image

Project File
Window.jpg

Final File
Window_end.jpg

Features Used
Magnetic Lasso Tool, Lasso Tool, Copy, Paste, Move Tool, Soft Light

Can you tell the difference between the two images above? The second image shows the reflection of the man in the window. In this exercise, you will learn how to work with opacity and blend modes to create a reflection.

<< **note**

Resource Files

Remember to copy the resource files on the CD-ROM to your hard drive before you start each exercise in this book.

1 Open \Sample\Chapter2\Window.jpg. Use the Magnetic Lasso tool (🔲) and set the Feather value to 5 in the tool options bar. Click on the edge of the man's face and drag around the man's head and shoulders. When you return to the starting point, you will see a circle and you should click to close the selection.

2 Select [Edit] - [Copy] to copy the selection and choose [Edit] - [Paste] to paste the copied selection. The Layers palette will show a new layer, Layer 1.

3 Select the Move tool (⊹) from the toolbox and drag the image to the window.

4 In the Layers palette, set the Opacity of the Layer 1 layer to 70%. Since only the upper part of the man should be reflected in the window, all other parts of the image must be erased. Select the Lasso tool (⌀) and set the Feather value to 5. Select the parts of the image that will not be reflected in the window.

5 Press [Delete] to remove the selection and choose [Select] - [Deselect] to clear the selection.

6 To make a natural reflection, you will use the blend mode in the Layers palette. Select Soft Light from the drop-down box at the top of the Layers palette. The completed image is shown above.

4

Using the Quick Mask
Mode to Create a Selection

Original Image   Final Image

In this exercise, you'll use the Quick Mask mode to select the image of a woman from the background.

Project File
  - Summer.jpg

Features Used
  - Rectangular Marquee Tool,
    Quick Mask Mode, Paint Brush Tool,
    Erase Tool

<< note
Resource Files

Remember to copy the resource files on the CD-ROM to your hard drive before you start each exercise in this book.

1 Open \Sample\Chapter2\Summer.jpg. Drag the Rectangular Marquee tool () to make a selection as shown.

48

2 Click on the ⬛ icon at at the bottom of the toolbox to enter Quick Mask mode. The areas not selected are masked in red.

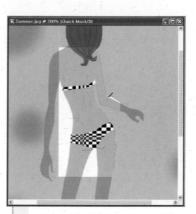

3 Set the foreground color to black and use the Paint Brush tool (🖌) to paint over the background areas that will be excluded from the selection. You may need to zoom into the image.

4 Use the Eraser tool (🖌) to erase the red mask over the woman.

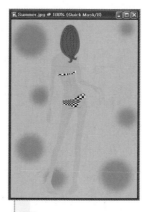

5 Continue to color and erase around the edges. Zoom to 100% to view the final mask.

6 Click the [Edit in Standard Mode] icon (⬛) in the toolbox to return to Standard mode. The image of the woman should be selected.

Chapter | 3

Essential Image Editing Skills

Whether you are creating images for print or for use in Web pages, it is important to develop key skills that allow you to work with the image as a whole. These essential skills include moving, cropping, transforming, and resizing images. In this chapter we'll cover these basic skills, so that, in later chapters, you'll have the proper foundation for more advanced Photoshop techniques.

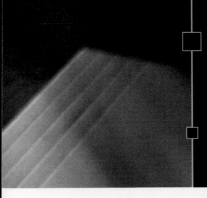

Basic Tools and Commands

In this chapter, you will learn about the Move, Crop, and Slice tools. You will also learn how to transform an image and resize both the image and image canvas. This chapter also includes some useful exercises that will allow you to practice these skills.

The Move Tool

The Move tool (🔸), which is found right at the top of the toolbox, is used to move a selected part of an image (or a guide). If you have another tool selected, you can access the Move tool temporarily by holding down the [Ctrl] key. The mouse pointer will change shape and you can use the tool until you release the [Ctrl] key.

▲Holding the [Alt] key while dragging creates a copy of the selection.

▲Dragging the selection to another image window makes a copy in the new window.

The Move Tool Options Bar

Ⓐ Auto Select Layer

When this option is selected, you can drag an image without first selecting its layer. If the option is not selected, the layer that includes the selection must be selected first in the Layers palette. Holding down the [Ctrl] key while clicking an image will automatically select its layer when the Auto Select Layer option is turned off.

▶When the Auto Select Layer option is selected, you can drag without selecting the layer first.

◀If the Auto Select Layer option is not selected, you must first click the layer before using the Move tool.

❸ Show Bounding Box

When this is selected, a bounding box containing eight adjustable points appears around the image. The points can be dragged to transform the image. This is similar to using the [Edit] - [Free Transform] command [Ctrl]-[T]. You will learn about the Free Transform command later in this chapter.

❸ Layer Alignment

The layer alignment option automatically lines up layers. The option is used when there are two or more linked layers within the image.

The Crop tool (▢), which is found in the toolbox, is used to cut out a portion of an image. When you crop an image, you create a smaller image based on your crop selection.

Use the Crop tool to select an area to crop. The Crop border will contain eight adjustment points that you can use to move, resize, or rotate the crop area. To complete the crop, press [Enter]. Pressing [Esc] will undo the crop selection.

<< tip

An Alternate Crop Method

You can also use the Selection tool to create a selection, then select [Image] - [Crop].

▲Select the area to crop.

▲Press [Enter] to crop the image.

The Crop Tool Options Bar

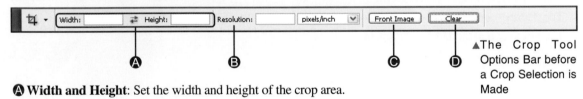

Ⓐ   Ⓑ   Ⓒ   Ⓓ

▲The Crop Tool Options Bar before a Crop Selection is Made

Ⓐ **Width and Height**: Set the width and height of the crop area.

Ⓑ **Resolution**: Set the crop resolution.

Ⓒ **Front Image**: Click to automatically set the size and resolution to that of the front image.

Ⓓ **Clear**: Clears the entered values.

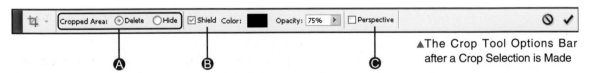

Ⓐ   Ⓑ   Ⓒ

▲The Crop Tool Options Bar after a Crop Selection is Made

Ⓐ **Cropped Area**: Selecting [Delete] removes areas outside of the crop area completely. Choosing [Hide] hides the unwanted areas from view. Hidden areas can be recovered by pressing [Image] - [Reveal All].

Ⓑ **Shield Color**: Indicates which areas are outside of the crop area.

Ⓒ **Perspective**: Check this option to use the adjustment points to give the image perspective.

Changing the Image Size

Each image appears on an image canvas. You can use [Image] - [Image Size] to change the size of the image and canvas at the same time. This command can also be used to change the resolution of the image.

▲Original Image

▲Resizing the Image to a Smaller Size

The Image Size Dialog Box

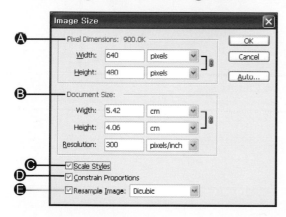

Ⓐ **Pixel Dimensions**: Displays the width and height of the current image.

Ⓑ **Document Size**: Displays the print size and resolution.

Ⓒ **Scale Styles**: When checked, style effects are scaled along with the image.

Ⓓ **Constrain Proportions**: When this option is checked, the ratio of the width to the height is kept constant as you resize the image.

Ⓔ **Resample Image**: If you select the Resample Image option, the dimensions of the image will remain the same regardless of changes made to the resolution. In other words, Photoshop will add or remove pixels so that your image is the same size regardless of its resolution. Without this option selected, the total number of pixels will remain constant, and changes made to the Resolution value will increase or decrease the width and height measurements of your image accordingly. Note that selecting this option and altering your image's resolution will affect the file size of your image.

The size of the canvas can be changed without affecting the size of the image by using the [Image] - [Canvas Size] command. If you reduce the size of the canvas, you will be warned that the image will be cropped. If you increase the canvas size, the additional area will be filled with the background color.

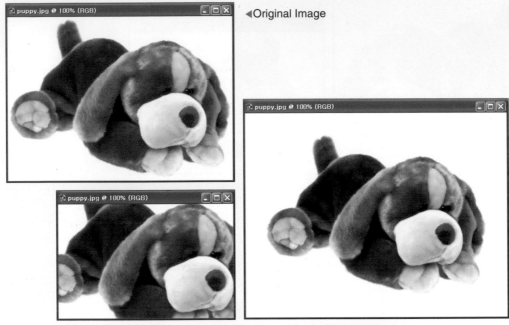

◀Original Image

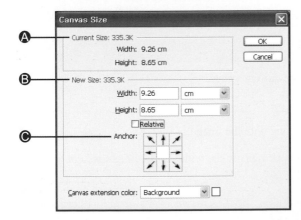

▲Reducing the Canvas Size　　　▲Increasing the Canvas Size

The Canvas Size Dialog Box

Ⓐ **Current Size**: Displays the file size, width, and height values for the current image.

Ⓑ **New Size**: Used to set the new size of the canvas.

Ⓒ **Anchor**: The white square represents the position of the image on the canvas. Click on one of the squares in the grid to anchor the image at that position. This will change how space is added or removed when you change the canvas size. In this case, additional space will be added equally to all sides of the image.

The Slice and Slice Select Tools

Using the Slice tool (🔪) in the toolbox, you can divide images for the Web into smaller sections. Each section or slice is an independent file with its own links, rollovers, or animations. It is common to divide a large Web image into slices to reduce downloading time. After all the slices are downloaded, the slices combine to form the original image. You can create slices by dragging the Slice tool over the image. Slices of an image are saved using the [File] - [Save for Web] command. Each slice is saved with its own format and file name.

The Slice Select tool (🔪), also found in the toolbox, can be used to move or adjust the size of the slices. You can hold down the [Ctrl] key to toggle between the Slice and Slice Select tools.

▲Dragging the Slice Tool to Create Slices ▲Adjusting the Size of the Slice Using the Slice Select Tool

The Slice Tool Options Bar

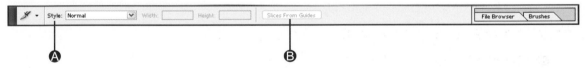

Ⓐ **Style**: Style is used to determine how the slices will be created. The Normal setting sets the slice proportions by dragging the tool. Fixed Aspect Ratio creates fixed width and height ratio slices, and Fixed Size allows the height and width of the slice to be specified.

Ⓑ **Slices From Guides**: Creates slices from the guides within the image.

The Slice Select Tool Options Bar

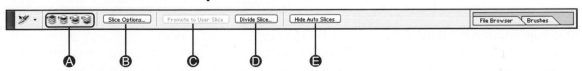

Ⓐ **Slice Order Buttons**: Changes the order of the slices.

Ⓑ **Slice Options**: Used to determine the file name, URL, Target, Message Text, Alt Tag, slice coordinates, and size of the sliced image.

Ⓒ **Promote User Slice**: Converts from Auto Slice mode to the editable User Slice mode.

ⓓ Divide Slice: Divides the slice according to the number of specified horizontal and vertical slices.

ⓔ Hide Auto Slice: Hides the guidelines in Auto Slice mode.

The Transform and Free Transform Commands

The [Edit] - [Transform] and [Edit] - [Free Transform] commands on the menu bar let you apply transformations by creating a bounding box that you can adjust around an image. The Free Transform command can also be accessed with the shortcut keys, [Ctrl]-[T].

Whichever way you create a bounding box, you can use it to apply one or more transformations, such as rotation, scale, skew, distort, and perspective. You can also move the image by dragging inside the box.

After you've adjusted a bounding box, you must press the [Enter] key to apply the changes and transform the image. You can press [Esc] to ignore the changes you have made and revert the image to its original state.

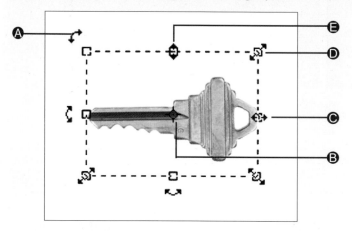

ⓐ Rotation Point: Placing the mouse outside the adjustable points will allow you to rotate the image.

ⓑ Center Point: This is the center point for rotation or size adjustments and can be used to move the image to another location.

ⓒ Width Adjustable Points: You can use the width adjustable points to increase or decrease the width of an image. Dragging the point inside the image beyond the center point will flip the image.

ⓓ Size Adjustable Points: Placing the mouse on the size adjustable points will allow you to adjust the size of the image. Hold down [Shift] as you drag a corner handle to scale the image proportionately.

ⓔ Height Adjustable Points: You can use the height adjustable points to increase or decrease the height of an image. Dragging the point inside the image beyond the center point will flip the image. When the anchor point is dragged to scale or rotate, the center anchor point will change.

The File Browser

The File Browser in Photoshop CS has been improved to increase the speed of previewing images. You can also search for multimedia files and keywords, flag images, and use batch commands. To open the File Browser, select [File] - [Browse] from the menu bar or click on the [Toggle File Browser] icon ( ) at the end of the tool options bar.

The File Browser shows information such as the file name, file properties, and edit history. For images taken with a digital camera, the File Browser also shows the date the picture was taken and the exposure and camera settings.

Files in the File Browser can be listed by file name, file type, file size, or copyright information.

▲ Right-click an image to access image management options.

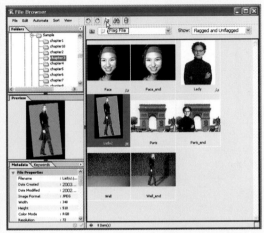

▲ Select the image and click the flag icon ( ) to flag the image.

▲ Select [View] - [Flagged] to see all the images that have been flagged.

<< note

The Sort Menu

Images can be sorted using the options in the Sort menu.

59

1 Blending Pictures

Original Image

Final Image

Project Files
● Lady.jpg, Paris.jpg

Final File
● Paris_end.jpg

Features Used
● Magic Wand Tool, Invert, Move Tool, Free Transform, Auto Levels, Defringe

In this exercise you will blend a picture of a person with a vacation picture so that it seems like the picture was taken on location. The example uses the Magic Wand tool and the Inverse option.

<< note

Resource Files

Remember to copy the resource files on the CD-ROM to your hard drive before you start each exercise in this book.

1 Open \Sample\Chapter3\Lady.jpg and Paris.jpg. Select the Magic Wand tool ( ), set the Tolerance to 32, and check Anti-aliased. Click the background of the Lady.jpg image.

2 Select [Select] - [Inverse] to invert the selection. The image of the woman will now be selected.

3 Use the Move tool (⊕) to drag the selection to the Paris.jpg image.

<< tip

Using the Inverse Selection Command

Where you have a simple background, it is much easier to select the background and invert the selection.

4 The image of the woman is too large compared with the background. Chose [Edit] - [Free Transform] to create a bounding box around the image, then drag the corners to reduce the size of the image. Press [Enter] to apply the transformation.

5 Use the Move tool (⊕) to position the woman on the lower left-hand side of the Paris.jpg image. The composition of the image is complete, but the lighting looks different because the picture of the woman was taken inside whereas the background image was taken outdoors. This problem can be corrected using the Auto Levels command.

<< tip

Using the [Shift] Key

Hold down the [Shift] key while resizing the image to maintain the height and width proportions.

6 Choose [Image] - [Adjustments] - [Auto Levels]. The dark areas will appear darker while the light areas appear lighter. You will learn more about Auto Levels in Chapter 7.

7 There is an obvious white border around the woman. This can be removed by choosing [Layer] - [Matting] - [Defringe] and setting the Width to 1. Click OK to remove the white border.

<< tip

Undoing the Defringe Command

Sometimes a value of 1 pixel doesn't completely remove the border around an image. In this case, press [Ctrl]-[Z] to undo the command, then increase the width in the Defringe dialog box.

8 The white border has been removed. Compare your finished image to the completed image: \Sample\Chapter3\Paris_end.psd.

2 Modifying a Portrait

Original Image

Final Image

Project File
- Face.jpg

Final File
- Face_end.jpg

Features Used
- Lasso Tool, Feather, Move Tool, Free Transform, Liquify

You can use Photoshop to make modifications to a person's appearance. In this example, you will modify the face above by balancing the eyebrows, shaping the left eye, sharpening the bridge of the nose, and shrinking the width of the face.

<< note

Resource Files

Remember to copy the resource files on the CD-ROM to your hard drive before you start each exercise in this book.

1 Open \Sample\Chapter3\Face.jpg from the supplementary CD-ROM. Use the Zoom tool ( ) to magnify the image to 200%.

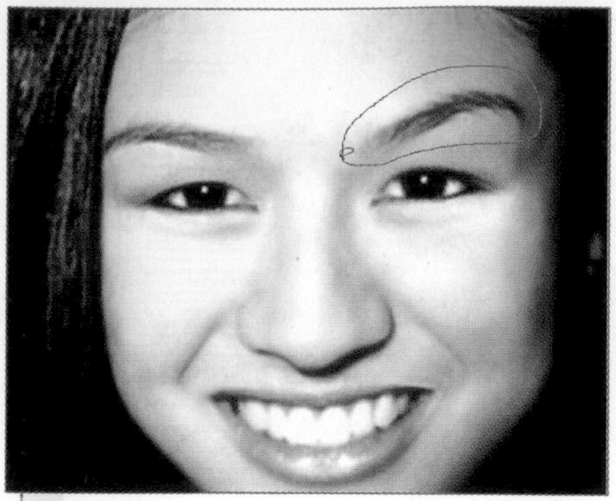

2 Select the Lasso tool ( ) and set the Feather value to 5. Draw a selection around the right eyebrow as shown above. A Feather value of 5 pixels will soften the edges and create a more natural brow shape.

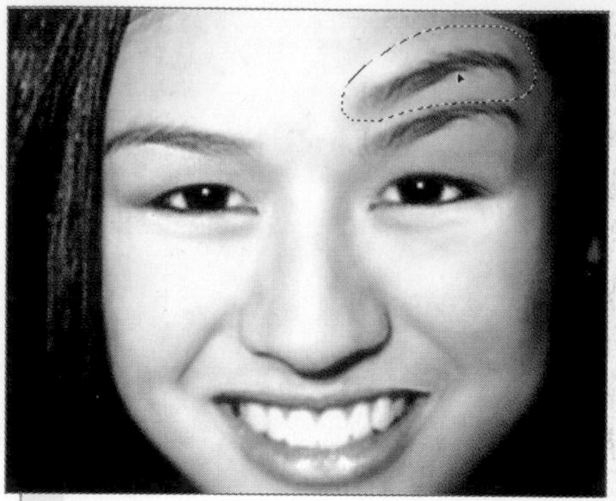

3 Hold down [Alt] and use the Move tool ( ) to drag a copy of the selection.

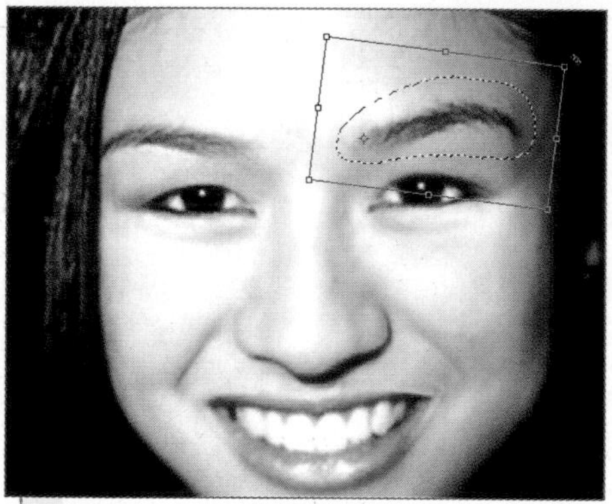

4 Move the duplicate back to its original position and select [Edit] - [Free Transform]. Move the center pointers inwards and rotate the edges clockwise about 6°. Press [Enter] to apply the transformation. Clear the selection with the [Ctrl]-[D] shortcut.

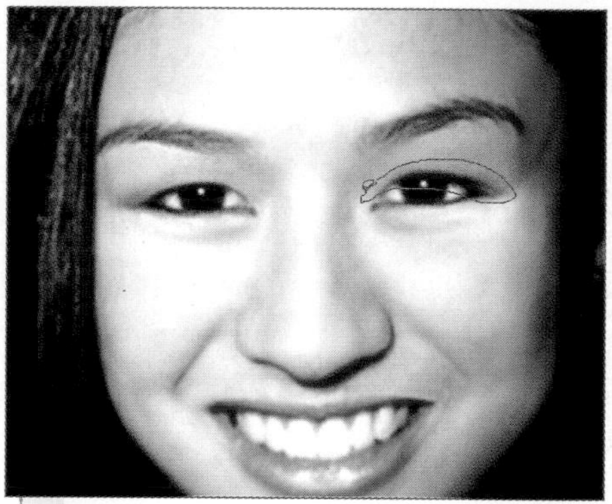

5 Select the Lasso tool ( ) from the toolbox. Set the Feather value to 5 pixels and select the right eyelid.

<< tip

Rotating the Brow

Make sure that you select enough of the brow shape so that you won't reveal the original brow underneath. Rotating the duplicate too much will also reveal the original brow.

6 Use the Move tool (⊞) from the toolbox and hold down the [Alt] key while dragging to make a duplicate.

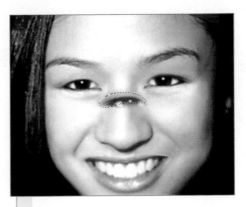

7 The duplicated eyelid will be used on the left eye, so it must be flipped using [Edit] - [Transform] - [Flip Horizontal].

8 Use the Move tool (⊞) to position the eye. Press [Ctrl]-[D] to deselect.

9 To work on the nose, select the Hand tool (✋) and drag the image so that the nose appears in the center.

<< tip

Using the Arrow Keys to Nudge

You can also use the arrow keys on the keyboard to nudge the image into position—one pixel at a time.

10 Select the Lasso tool (⦿) and make sure that the Feather value is set to 5 pixels. Select the right nostril.

11 Hold down the [Alt] key with the Move tool (➕) and press the left arrow key three to four times. This should slim the nose.

12 Select the left nostril and slim the nose in the same way. Clear the selection.

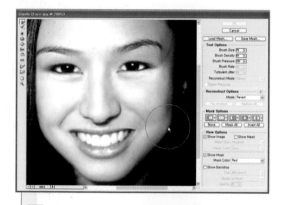

13 You will use the Liquify filter to reduce the width of the face. Choose [Filter] - [Liquify] and make sure that the Warp tool (🖌) is selected. Set the Brush Size to 70 pixels and position the mouse pointer on the left cheek.

14 Drag the mouse inwards slightly to reduce the width of the face.

15 Reduce the size of the right cheek in the same way. Click OK to apply the adjustments.

16 Select [View] - [Actual Pixels] to view the image at its original size. The completed image is saved as \Sample\ Chapter3\Face_end.psd on the supplementary CD-ROM.

Exercise

3 Creating a Shadow

Original Image

Final Image

Project Files
● Lady2.jpg, Well.jpg

Final File
● Well_end.psd

Features Used
● Magic Wand Tool, Move Tool, Inverse, Fill, Merge Linked, Gaussian Blur

In this example, you will add an image of a woman to an image of a wall. You will then create a shadow by making a copy of the woman and coloring it black.

The [Layer] - [Layer Style] - [Drop Shadow] command allows a drop shadow to be created in a single step. Duplicating the image lets you to create a more natural-looking shadow and also allows you to add shadows at different angles.

Select the Woman Image

1 Open \Sample\Chapter3\Lady2.jpg and Well.jpg. Click the Crop tool ( ) and select the area that will be cut out of the image as shown above.

2 Drag outside of the corners of the bounding box to rotate the crop selection. Line up the image with the sides of the bounding box and drag on each anchor point so that the black background is not selected. To apply the crop, double-click inside the bounding box or click the [Commit current crop operation] button (✓) in the options bar.

3 Once cropped, the black background will be removed and the image will be standing straight instead of being on a slant. Select the Magic Wand tool (🪄) and uncheck the Contiguous option. Click the background to select all blue areas within the image. Choose [Select] - [Inverse] (shortcut keys [Shift]-[Ctrl]-[I]) to invert the selection.

<< tip

The Contiguous Option

If the Contiguous option is checked, the small blue patch between the woman's right arm and her body will not be selected.

Making the Shadow

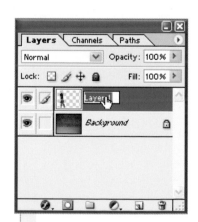

1 Use the Move tool (▶✛) to drag the woman selection onto the Wall.jpg image and position it on the left as shown.

2 Double-click the name Layer 1 and type in the new name, **Lady**. Press [Enter] to change the name.

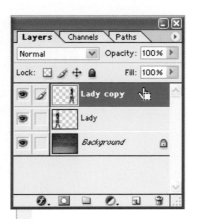

3 Hold down the [Alt] key and drag the Lady image with the Move tool () to make a copy. The Layers palette will include the layer Lady copy. Place the Lady copy image to the right as shown.

4 Hold down the [Ctrl] key and click Lady copy in the Layers palette to select the duplicate image.

<< tip

Making a Copy

If the image is selected, using the Move tool with the [Alt] key creates a copy on the same layer. By deselecting the image first, a duplicate layer is created.

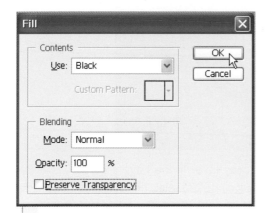

5 Select [Edit] - [Fill]. Set Use to Black and click OK to fill the image.

6 Press [Ctrl]-[D] to deselect. Hold down the [Alt] key and use the Move tool to drag another copy. The Lady copy 2 layer has been created in the Layers palette. Place the duplicate layer over the original image as shown here.

<< tip

Filling the Selection

You could also set the foreground color to black in the Set Foreground Color swatch in the toolbox, then press [Alt]-[Backspace] to fill the selection. Using [Ctrl]-[Backspace] will fill the image with the background color.

Slanting the Shadow

1 Press [Ctrl]-[T] to bring up a Free Transform bounding box. Hold down the [Ctrl] key, click on the top of the box, and drag it to the bottom right-hand corner of the wall to slant the shadow as shown above. Double-click inside the bounding box to apply the transformation.

2 Select the Rectangular Marquee tool (▨) and use it to select the shadow on the wall. Press [Delete] to erase the shadow as shown.

3 Click the Lady copy layer in the Layers palette. Use the Rectangular Marquee tool (▨) to select the image from the middle of the skirt downward to the feet. Press [Delete] to erase this portion of the shadow as shown above. Press [Ctrl]-[D] to deselect.

<< tip
Caution When Deleting Layers

Make sure that the Lady copy 2 layer is selected in the Layers palette before you press the [Delete] key, or you may delete the wrong part of the image. If this happens, press [Ctrl]-[Z] to undo the deletion. You can press [Alt]-[Ctrl]-[Z] to undo even earlier steps.

4 Use the Move tool (⊕) to drag the upper body to the lower half of the body.

5 Select the Lady copy layer and click on the empty space next to the eye icon of the Lady copy 2 layer. A chain icon will appear showing that the two layers have been linked. Select [Layer] - [Merge Linked] to create a single layer from Lady copy and Lady copy 2.

<< tip

Putting the Shadows Together

If the two halves of the body don't fit together properly, you may need to use the Brush tool to fill in the missing areas. You could also use the Eraser tool to erase any excess.

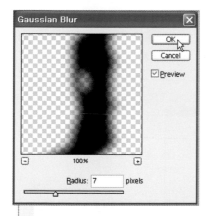

6 Blur the shadow by selecting [Filter] - [Blur] - [Gaussian Blur]. Set the Radius to 7 pixels and click OK. Set the Opacity of the shadow layer to 70% in the Layers palette. Press [Ctrl]-[[] to move the Lady copy layer below the Lady layer. The shadow should now appear behind the image of the woman.

7 Link the Lady and Lady copy layers in the Layers palette so that the layers will move together. Use the Move tool to place the images in the center of the wall.

Making a Transparent Image for a Web Page

Original Image

Final Image

Project File
— bear.jpg

Final File
— bear.gif

Features Used
— Extract, Trim, Save for Web

When an image with a transparent background is placed on a Web page, the background color of the web page shows through. The [File] - [Save for Web] command let's you to create a GIF file with a transparent background. JPEG images cannot have transparent backgrounds.

<< note

Resource Files

Remember to copy the resource files on the CD-ROM to your hard drive before you start each exercise in this book.

1 Open the \Sample\Chapter3\Bear.jpg file from the supplementary CD-ROM. Select [Filter] - [Extract] and select the Edge Highlighter tool ( ). In the tool options bar, set the Brush Size to 15 pixels. Paint the brush around the edge of the image as shown.

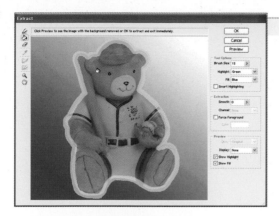

2 Select the Fill tool () and click inside the outline. Press OK to extract the bear from the background.

<< tip

Using the Edge Highlighter Tool

If the edge around the bear image is not closed, the fill will apply to the entire image. To correct this problem, use [Ctrl]-[Z] to undo the command, then trace the image again and apply the Fill tool.

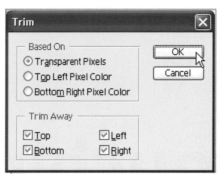

3 The image should appear on a transparent background.

4 Select [Image] - [Trim] to trim the background. In the Trim dialog box, leave the values at their default settings and click OK. Then reduce the size of the bear image.

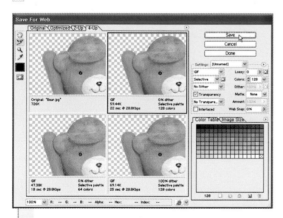

5 Click [File] - [Save for Web]. When the Save For Web dialog box appears, click the 4-Up tab. You will see four image previews. On the top left is a preview of the original image; the other three image previews show the image optimized at various settings. The information on the lower left of each preview shows you the file type, file size, and download time. Select the top-right image preview and select GIF, 128 Colors, and Transparency. Hit the [Save] button.

6 In the Save Optimized As dialog box, enter the file name and click the [Save] button.

<< tip

Preview in Browser

Clicking the [Preview In 'Browser'] button ( ) lets you preview the image in your default browser.

Chapter | 4

Retouching Images

As digital cameras have become better and more affordable, the need for digital image retouching has soared. One of the most-loved features of Photoshop is the program's wide range of powerful tools for touching up images. In this chapter, you will learn to retouch images using the Healing Brush tool, the Patch tool, the Clone Stamp tool, and the History palette. You will also learn to create some interesting effects using the Pattern Stamp tool, the History Brush tool, and the Art History Brush tool.

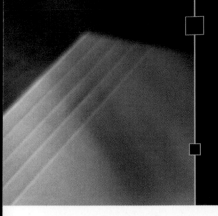

An Overview of Retouching Tools

The Healing Brush and Patch tools retouch areas of an image. The Clone Stamp tool creates an exact copy of part of an image, while the Pattern Stamp tool fills with a pattern. The History Brush tool reverts an image to an earlier state, while the Art History Brush tool adds artistic touches as part of this process. You'll learn about these tools and more in the following sections.

Correction Tools

In earlier versions of Photoshop, image retouching was carried out only with the Clone Stamp tool. Using this tool required great skill because it only created an exact clone of another part of the image. (It was necessary to make other adjustments to try to match the image texture in the retouching area.) Using the Healing Brush and Patch tools for image retouching is easier, as both tools automatically match the underlying image texture. In this section, let's look at the Healing Brush tool, the Patch tool, and the Color Replacement tool.

The Healing Brush Tool ( )

The Healing Brush tool uses a sample area to paint over another area. The sample area is defined by clicking with the [Alt] key held down. Sample areas are normally similar in lighting and texture to the area to be retouched.

1. Open a portrait. Click with the [Alt] key held down to select an unlined or unblemished section of the image.

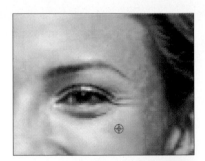

2. Drag the mouse over a lined area or a flaw to cover it with the sample.

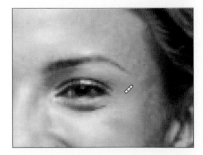

The Healing Brush Tool Options Bar

Ⓐ **Brush**: Select the brush size.

Ⓑ **Mode**: Select the color mode.

Ⓒ **Source**

Sampled: Select the clean source by clicking with the [Alt] key held down. Retouch the damaged area by dragging with the mouse.

Pattern: Dragging the mouse applies the selected pattern while maintaining the original color and texture of the image.

▲Source   ▲Pattern

Ⓓ **Aligned**: This option allows you to sample pixels continuously. If unchecked, the original sample point will be used.

The Patch Tool ( )

The Patch tool works in a similar way to the Healing Brush tool. However, instead of painting with the tool, a selection is used to replace the target area.

1. With the tool options bar set to Source, drag the Patch tool to make a selection.

2. Hold down the mouse and drag the selection to the target area. Release the mouse button.

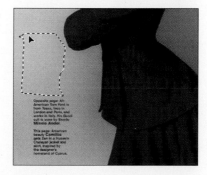

3. The selection frame returns to its original position, filled with the texture from the target area.

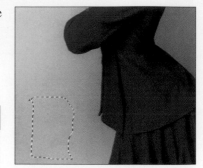

<< tip

Using the Destination Option

If the tool options bar is set to Destination, select the target area first and drag it over to the area to be restored.

The Color Replacement Tool ()

The Color Replacement tool paints with the selected foreground color, while preserving texture.

1. You can remove red eyes from a picture with the Color Replacement tool.

2. Set the foreground color to the desired eye color and set the Mode in the option bar to Color. Drag the Color Replacement tool over the eye to change the color.

The Color Replacement Tool Options Bar

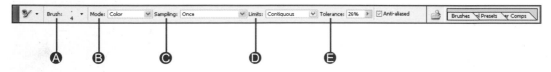

Ⓐ **Brush**: Select the brush size.

Ⓑ **Mode**: Select the color mode.

78

⊙ Sampling

Continuous: Continues to sample as the tool is dragged. This is good for retouching color in adjacent areas.

Once: Only uses a color sample from where the tool was first clicked; selects an area of monotone color.

Background Swatch: Erases areas that contain the current background color.

⊙ Limits

Discontiguous: Changes all colors in the image.

Contiguous: Changes color only in adjacent regions.

Find Edges: Changes color in adjacent regions without affecting the sharpness of edges.

⊙ Tolerance: Enter a value (1-100) or use the slider bar to set up the range. Lower values restrict the range of color values that are changed. Higher values widen the color range and heighten the overall effect on the image.

Clone Tools

Using the Clone Stamp tool, you can stamp out irregularities using a clone (a sample taken from another part of the image) that you specify. The Pattern Stamp tool, on the other hand, lets you create designs with repeated patterns.

The Clone Stamp Tool (🖎)

To use the Clone Stamp tool, hold down the [Alt] key and click to define the source for the clone. Sources defined with the Clone Stamp tool can be used in any file that is opened in Photoshop.

▲Click with the [Alt] key held down to define the source.　▲Drag the tool in an empty area or click to apply the clone.

The Pattern Stamp Tool (🖎)

When using the Pattern Stamp tool, select an existing pattern and drag the tool to apply the pattern.

1. Select the pattern using the Rectangular Marquee tool (▥). Define the pattern by selecting [Edit] - [Define Pattern]. Give the pattern a name and click OK.

2. Select the pattern from the tool options bar and click or drag the pattern over the image.

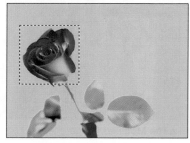 

The History palette contains a record of the previous steps that you've taken. You can revert to an earlier version of your work by going backwards in the list. The History palette is generally useful when using Photoshop, but when you are retouching an image, its utility increases dramatically. This is because you will probably touch up your image using numerous small brush strokes, and will need to go back many steps if you find that you do not like what you've done.

By default, Photoshop saves the last 20 steps, but you can change this by selecting [Edit] - [Preferences] - [General]. Selecting too many steps can overload your computer memory and slow down your work. You can also preserve your work by taking regular snapshots of your work. To create a snapshot, select a previous state in the History palette and click the [Create new snapshot] button at the bottom of the palette. A snapshot of the state you selected will appear at the top of the History palette. Clicking on the snapshot will revert your artwork to the state captured by the shot. A snapshot is useful as a quick way to revert to a previous state and for comparing the effects executed after the snapshot.

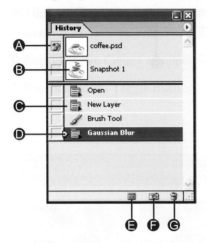

Ⓐ History Brush Icon: You can set the restoration point for the History Brush tool and Art History Brush tool by turning on this icon next to a step.

Ⓑ Snapshot Thumbnail: Shows you a thumbnail of the snapshot. Double-click the snapshot to change the name.

Ⓒ History states: Shows the history of the actions you've taken.

Ⓓ History state slider: The slider indicates the current step. Drag it to move to a previous step. If you make a change to the image after moving to a previous step, the subsequent steps will be reset and you will lose the option to re-apply them. You can prevent this from happening by selecting [History Options] from the History palette pop-up menu and checking Allow Non-Linear History.

Ⓔ New Document: The image in the window is duplicated in a new document. This is the same as the [Image] - [Duplicate] command.

Ⓕ New Snapshot: Saves the image in the window as a snapshot.

Ⓖ Trash: Deletes steps.

The History Palette Pop-Up Menu

Clicking on the arrow (▶) at the top of the History palette will open the palette's pop-up menu.

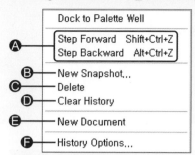

Ⓐ **Step Forward/Backward**: Moves one step backward/forward in the History list.

Ⓑ **New Snapshot**: Takes a snapshot of an image. Snapshots are not saved as separate image files. They can be viewed as thumbnails at the top of the History palette. You can return to a previous image by clicking the relevant snapshot.

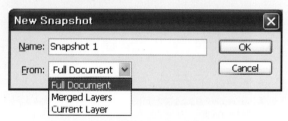

Full Document: Saves the entire layer.

Merged Layers: Combines layers together.

Current Layer: Saves only the current layer.

Ⓒ **Delete**: Deletes the selected History item.

Ⓓ **Clear History**: Clears the steps from the History palette.

Ⓔ **New Document**: Copies the image in the window to a new document.

Ⓕ **History Options**

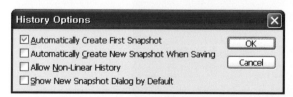

Automatically Create First Snapshot: When an image is first opened, a snapshot is automatically saved in the History palette.

Automatically Create New Snapshot when Saving: A new snapshot is automatically created when you save your work.

Allow Non-Linear History: Normally, when you move a step back in the History palette, all steps after that step will be deleted when you edit your image. Checking this option allows you to keep all steps.

Show New Snapshot Dialog Default: Opens up a dialog box when the Snapshot command is executed.

1

Removing Red Eyes

Original Image

Final Image

Project File
- Beagle.jpg

Final File
- Beagle_end.jpg

Features Used
- Color Replacement Tool

Red eyes can occur when you take pictures using a flash. When the flash goes off, the light reflects off the blood vessels behind the retina and shows up in the photograph as red eyes. You can use Photoshop's Color Replacement tool to fix this problem.

<< note
Resource Files

Remember to copy the resource files on the CD-ROM to your hard drive before you start each exercise in this book.

1 Open \Sample\Chapter4\Beagle.jpg and use the Magnifying Glass tool (🔍) to zoom into the dog's eyes.

2 Select the Color Replacement tool (🖌) from the toolbox and place the mouse pointer on the image. If the mouse cursor is in the shape of a brush, follow steps 3 and 4 to turn it into a round shape. Otherwise, skip these steps and go to step 5.

3 Select [Edit] - [Preferences] - [Display & Cursors]. In Painting Cursors, select Brush Size and click OK.

4 Select the Color Replacement tool and place it on the image. You should see a round brush area on the mouse pointer.

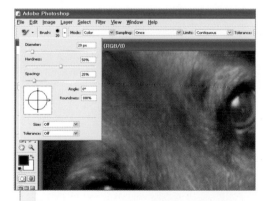

5 Set the foreground color to black in the toolbox. Click the Brush Preset Picker in the tool options bar and set the Diameter to 20, the Mode to Color, the Sampling to Once, and the Tolerance to 30. Select Contiguous in the Limits drop-down box and check the Anti-aliased option.

6 Drag the tool over the eyes to remove the red color.

<< tip
Color Mode

As the Mode was set to Color, the red color is replaced by the black foreground color.

2 Removing Fine Lines and Correcting Skin Tone

Original Image

Final Image

Project File
• Age.jpg

Final File
• Age_end.jpg

Features Used
• Patch Tool, Smudge Tool, Layer via Copy, Gaussian Blur, Blend Mode, Opacity

In this exercise, you will use the Patch tool to remove wrinkles. You will also use the Smudge tool to reshape the face. Finally, you will apply the Gaussian Blur filter and change the blend mode to brighten up the skin tone.

<< note
Resource Files

Remember to copy the resource files on the CD-ROM to your hard drive before you start each exercise in this book.

1 Open \Sample\Chapter4\Age.jpg. Use the Patch tool ( ) to select the lines under the eye.

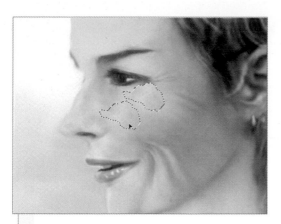

2 Click inside the selection and drag it to an unlined area of the face. Release the mouse.

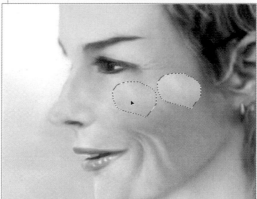

3 The lines under the eye will be replaced by the unlined target area. Use the Patch tool to replace the lines in the cheekbones.

4 Repeat the steps above to remove other lines from the face.

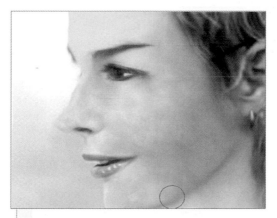

5 Select the Smudge tool and set the Brush Size to 80 pixels in the tool options bar. Use this tool to drag the skin around the jaw line. You could also use [Filter] - [Liquify] to make this adjustment.

6 Use the Smudge tool () to contour the jaw and the nose. Be careful not to overuse the tool as it will create a blurry image that looks unnatural.

7 Correct the skin tone by copying the layer. Select [Layer] - [New] - [Layer via Copy] to create Layer 1 in the Layers palette.

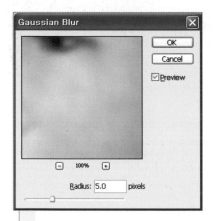

8 Click Layer 1 and choose [Filter] - [Blur] - [Gaussian Blur]. Set the Radius to 5 pixels and click OK. This will blur the overall image and soften the contours of the face.

9 Set the blend mode of Layer 1 to Screen and the Opacity to 30%. The Screen mode will combine Background and Layer 1 to brighten up the skin tone. The opacity setting will ensure that the skin tone isn't too bright.

10 The final image shows a younger looking face.

3 Applying a Pattern to an Uneven Surface

Original Image

Final Image

Project Files
- Scarf.jpg, Flower Pattern.jpg

Final File
- Scarf_end.jpg

Features Used
- Define Pattern, Pattern Stamp Tool, History Brush

It is much easier to apply a pattern to a flat surface than to a lined and folded area. However, there may be times when you need to achieve this. In this exercise, you will register and apply a pattern to a scarf and use the History palette and Opacity to make the pattern appear more natural.

<< note

Resource Files

Remember to copy the resource files on the CD-ROM to your hard drive before you start each exercise in this book.

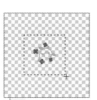

1 Open \Sample\Chapter4\Scarf.jpg and \Sample\Chapter4\Flower Pattern.jpg. Select the Rectangular Marquee tool and set the Feather value to 0 pixels. Drag a selection around the flower in the flower pattern image. Make sure that you use a narrow selection so you can create a pattern of flower images that are close together.

<< note

Defining a Pattern

To define a pattern, the Rectangular Marquee tool must be used with a Feather value of 0 pixels.

2 Select [Edit] - [Define Pattern], enter **Flower** and click OK.

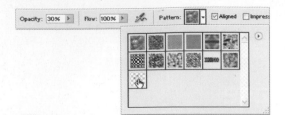

3 Select the Pattern Stamp tool (⬚) from the toolbox. In the tool options bar, set the Opacity to 30% and check Aligned. Click the triangular button (⬚) and select the Flower pattern.

4 Instead of painting the pattern directly onto the Background layer of the scarf image, it will be painted onto a new layer. This will make it easier to modify the pattern. In the scarf image, click the [Create a new layer] button at the bottom of the Layers palette. This will create Layer 1.

5 Use the Pattern Stamp tool (⬚) to paint the pattern onto the scarf. Use sweeping strokes that extend from the edges around the scarf. Don't release the mouse button when dragging as this will increase the opacity of the design.

6 Click the [Create a new layer] button at the bottom of the Layers palette to create Layers 2. Enter a value of 60% for the Opacity and paint the scarf again.

7 Use the Move tool from the toolbox to move Layer 2 so that it does not overlap with Layer 1. Then drag the History Brush tool (⬚) over the patterns outside the scarf to erase them, leaving the pattern inside the scarf.

8 To make the pattern appear more natural, set the Opacity of the History Brush tool (⬚) to 10% and drag the tool over the shadows made by the scarf. The final image is shown above.

90

Using the Art History Brush to Create a Painting Effect

Original Image

Final Image

Project File
— picture.jpg

Final File
— picture_end.jpg

Features Used
— Art History Brush Tool, History Brush Tool, Texturizer

<< note
Resource Files

Remember to copy the resource files on the CD-ROM to your hard drive before you start each exercise in this book.

The History palette contains a record of all the work steps carried out on an image. The original image is preserved, as are any snapshots taken of the image. The Art History Brush can be used to restore images to an earlier point and add artistic touches at the same time. In this section, you will use the Art History Brush to create an image that looks like a painting.

1 Open \Sample\Chapter4\picture.jpg. Select the Art History Brush tool (🖌), click the [Brush Preset Size] button, and select the Hard Round brush. You are using a small brush in order to make an image that looks like a painting. Leave the other values at their default settings and set the Style to Tight Long.

2 Drag the brush on to the image and fill the entire image.

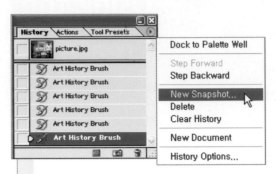

3 Select New Snapshot from the pop-up menu of the History palette.

4 In the New Snapshot dialog box, enter the name **Picture Snapshot** and click OK.

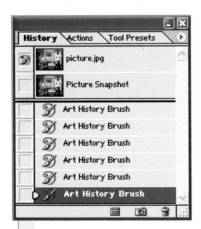

5 The History palette shows picture.jpg and Picture Snapshot in the snapshot list along with their thumbnails.

6 Set the background color to white and press [Ctrl]-[Delete] to fill the image window with the white color. Click the empty box next to the preview icon of Picture Snapshot to add a history brush icon. You can use the brush to return the image to this point.

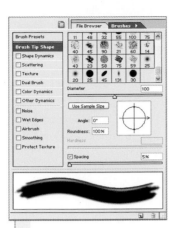

7 Click the Brushes tab in the Well to activate the Brushes palette. Check that all the options on the left of the palette are not selected and click on Brush Tip Shape. Scroll to select brush 14 as shown here. Set the Diameter to 100.

8 Drag the tool over the white image window to display the Picture Snapshot image.

9 Select [Filter] - [Texture] - [Texturizer]. Set the Texture to Canvas, Scaling to 150, Relief to 5, and the Light Direction to Top Right. Click OK to apply the texture.

10 The final image is shown above.

Chapter | 5

Painting and Image Editing

In the last chapter, you learned to retouch images using a number of tools. In this chapter, you will learn to use a few more retouching tools while exploring the tools that can be used to paint in Photoshop. Although Photoshop is popular with photographers and designers for its image-editing aspects, it is also one of the best graphics programs for creating original artwork. Painting in Photoshop is somewhat similar to painting in real life, so it is intuitive, easy to learn, and very rewarding.

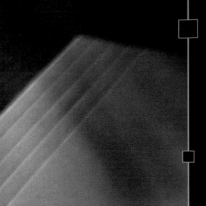

The Essentials of Painting and Image Editing

In this chapter, you will learn to paint with brushes and pencils. You'll also explore how to select and use color. Finally, you will learn to use retouching tools to blur, sharpen, and smudge an image, as well as change image exposure and color saturation.

Painting in Photoshop

Depending on what you are painting, you may need more than just the painting tools to paint in Photoshop. You may need to use the fill tools and the eraser tools, and you will definitely need to know how to work with the Color and Brushes palettes. Let's take a look at each of these tools and palettes.

The Brush ( ) and Pencil ( ) Tools

The Brush tool and Pencil tool are used for painting in Photoshop. The Brush tool is used like a standard paintbrush, while the Pencil tool gives a rough edge to drawings. Images drawn using the Pencil tool can be colored using the Paint Bucket tool or Gradient tool. The Pencil tool is often used for drawing comics and sketches. Zooming in on the image will enlarge the pixels for fine, detailed work.

▲Drawn Using the Brush Tool

▲Drawn Using the Pencil Tool

The Brush Tool Options Bar

Ⓐ Brush: Select the brush size.

Ⓑ Mode: Select the color mode.

Ⓒ Opacity: Set the opacity.

Ⓓ Auto Erase: The brush will paint using the foreground color. When the mouse is used to paint over a previously painted area, it will use the background color.

▲Painting with the Foreground Color

▲Painting on Top of the Foreground Color Using the Background Color

▲Painting on Top of the Background Color Using the Foreground Color

Ⓔ Brushes Palette Toggle Button : Shows/hides the Brushes palette.

Airbrush Tool

Earlier versions of Photoshop included a separate Airbrush tool in the toolbox. Since version 7.0, the Airbrush has been included as an option of the Brush tool. The Airbrush tool works like an aerosol spray. Holding down the mouse button will continuously spray color on the page. You stop painting once you release the mouse button.

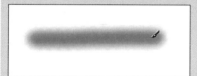
▲Painting Using the Brush Tool

▲Using the Airbrush Tool

Selecting a Color

Painting tools use the foreground color to paint. You can select the foreground color using the Color Picker, the Color palette, the Swatches palette, or the Eyedropper tool.

The Color Picker

The Color Picker dialog box can be opened by double-clicking either the foreground or background color swatch in the toolbox. Drag the spectrum slider to the desired shade and use the mouse to select a color. The Color Picker displays RGB, CMYK, and the Web hexadecimal code at the same time. You can check the Only Web Colors option to use Web-safe colors exclusively.

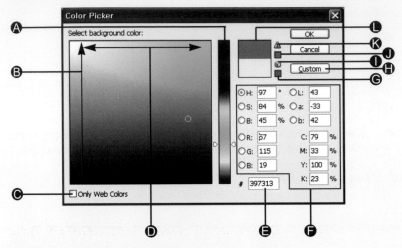

Ⓐ Hue: Use the hue slider to select the desired color.

Ⓑ Brightness: Colors are brighter towards the top of the color preview box.

Ⓒ Only Web Colors: Displays only colors that are Web-safe.

Ⓓ Saturation: Color saturation increases towards the right of the color preview box.

Ⓔ #: Every color has a hexadecimal value that is used for identification.

Ⓕ HSB, RGB, Lab, CMYK: Automatically displays color values. You can type in values to select a specific color.

Ⓖ Web-safe color select: Clicking this box will convert your currently selected color into the closest Web-safe color.

Ⓗ Custom: Displays color charts for picking custom colors.

Ⓘ Web-safe warning icon: This icon appears if your color is not Web-safe.

Ⓙ Print-safe color select: Click this box to convert your currently selected color into the closest print-safe color.

Ⓚ Print-safe warning icon: This icon appears if your color is not print-safe.

Ⓛ Color preview box: This preview box is updated in real-time to display the color you've created.

The Color Palette and Color Palette Pop-Up Menu

The Color palette and its pop-up menu contain options for customizing the palette. To select a color using the Color palette, either type in the specific color values, drag the slider bars, or select the desired color from the spectrum.

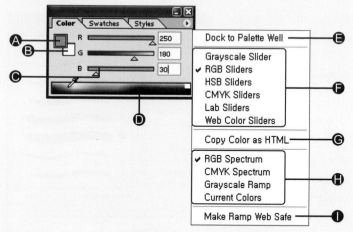

Ⓐ Foreground Color: Click to specify the foreground color. Double-click to display the Color Picker dialog box.

Ⓑ Background Color: Click to specify the background color. Double-click to display the Color Picker dialog box.

Ⓒ Slider: Either move the slider bar to select a color or enter the color value directly.

Ⓓ Color Spectrum Bar: Use the Eyedropper to select the color from the spectrum.

Ⓔ Dock in Palette Well: Displays the Color palette in the well on the right of the tool options bar.

Ⓕ Color Systems: Choose to set the sliders to one of the six color systems.

Ⓖ Copy Color as HTML: Remembers the color as a hexadecimal code for use in Web pages.

Ⓗ Color Spectrums: Choose to set the color spectrum bar to one of the four color systems.

Ⓘ Make Ramp Web Safe: Changes the color spectrum bar to a Web-safe color bar.

The Swatches Palette

In the Swatches palette, click on a color swatch to select a foreground color. Hold down the [Ctrl] key and click to set the background color. Add a foreground color to the Swatches palette by clicking the empty area at the bottom of the palette. The Color Swatch Name dialog box will appear and you will be asked to specify a name. To remove a color from the palette, click while holding down the [Alt] key.

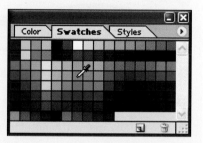

The Brushes palette is found on the right side of the tool options bar. The Brushes palette can be shown and hidden by clicking the toggle button ( ) found at the right corner of the tool options bar.

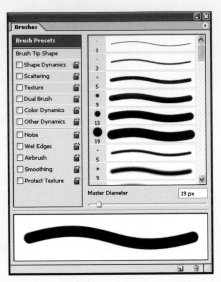

The left window of the Brushes palette contains the options for working with brushes in Photoshop. To select a preset brush shape, click on the Brush Presets option. A list of preset brush shapes will appear in the right window of the Brushes palette. Click on a preset brush shape to select it.

You can modify a preset brush that you have selected. You can change the brush tip by clicking on the Brush Tip Shapes option to reveal the list of available brush tip styles in the right window. You can also edit the brush by checking a brush attribute in the left window and adjusting its options in the right window. For example, you can check the Scattering attribute and set the amount of scatter in the right window. In this section, let's look at the options available when you select Brush Presets, Brush Tip Shapes, or one of the attributes.

Brush Presets Options

Clicking on Brush Presets allows you to select a brush shape from a list of preset brush styles.

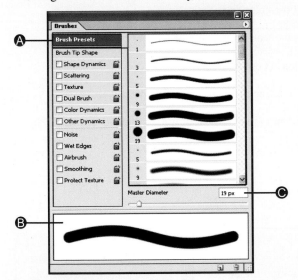

Ⓐ **Brush Presets**: This shows the list of preset brushes, including user-defined brushes.

Ⓑ **Brush Stroke Preview**: Previews the strokes that will be created with the brush shape.

Ⓒ **Master Diameter**: Changes the size of the brush.

Brush Tip Shapes Options

Clicking on Brush Tip Shapes allows you to select a shape to use as a brush tip from a list of preset options.

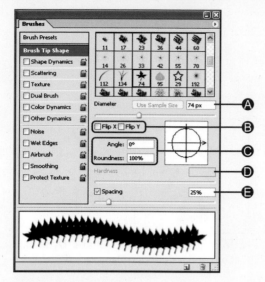

Ⓐ Diameter: Sets the thickness of the line drawn by the brush.

Ⓑ Flip X/Flip Y: Flips the brush along the X-axis and Y-axis.

Ⓒ Angle/Roundness: Sets the angle and roundness of the brush. A setting of 100% will draw a perfect circle while 0% will draw a straight line (similar to a calligraphy pen).

Ⓓ Hardness: Sets the hardness of the brush contours.

Ⓔ Spacing: Sets the spacing between the lines.

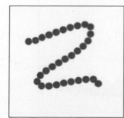

The Shape Dynamics Attribute

Shape Dynamics change the way brush marks vary in a brush stroke.

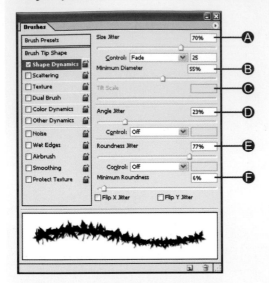

▲Brush Strokes without Shape Dynamics (Left) and with Shape Dynamics (Right)

Ⓐ Size Jitter and Control: Determines how the size of the brush mark will vary.

Ⓑ Minimum Diameter: Sets the percentage of change in the brush line diameter when Size Jitter or Size Control is enabled.

Ⓒ Tilt Scale: When Size Control is set to Pen Tilt, this sets the height of the brush prior to rotation.

Ⓓ Angle Jitter and Control: Determines how the angle of the brush mark will vary.

Ⓔ Roundness Jitter and Control: Determines how the roundness of the brush mark will vary.

Ⓕ Minimum Roundness: When Roundness Jitter is enabled, this determines the minimum roundness for brush marks.

The Scattering Attribute

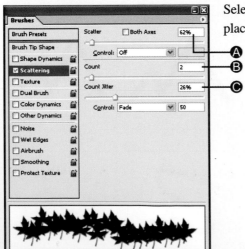

Selecting the Scattering attribute allows you to set the number and placement of marks in a brush stroke.

▲Brush Strokes without Scattering (Left) and with Scattering (Right)

Ⓐ Scatter and Control: Determines how scattered the marks in the brush stroke will be. Checking the Both Axes option will apply the scatter in a radial direction.

Ⓑ Count: Determines the number of brush marks.

Ⓒ Count Jitter and Control: Determines how the number of brush marks varies.

The Texture Attribute

Selecting the Texture attribute allows you to create brush strokes that include a texture.

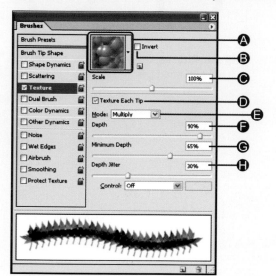

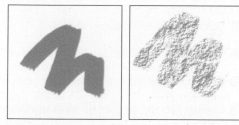

▲Brush Strokes without Texture (Left) and with Texture (Right)

Ⓐ Pattern Picker: Selects the pattern for the brush texture.

Ⓑ Invert: Checking this option will invert the light and dark parts of the pattern.

Ⓒ Scale: Adjust the size of the pattern.

Ⓓ Texture Each Tip: Check to render each tip individually as it is painted.

Ⓔ Mode: Selects the blending mode for the brush and pattern.

Ⓕ Depth: Sets how much paint is used.

Ⓖ Minimum Depth: Determines the minimum amount of paint when the Texture Each Tip option is selected.

Ⓗ Depth Jitter: Adjusts the depth when each texture tip is selected.

The Dual Brush Attribute

Dual brushes refers to brushes with two tips. Checking the Dual Brush attribute sets the option for the second brush tip while the first brush tip takes its values from the Brush Tip Shapes setting.

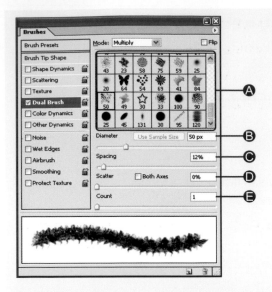

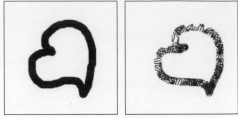

▲Brush Strokes Created with a Single Tip (Left) and with Dual Tips (Right)

Ⓐ **Brush Tip Picker**: Selects the second brush tip.

Ⓑ **Diameter**: Sets the size of the brush tip.

Ⓒ **Spacing**: Adjusts the distance between the brush marks.

Ⓓ **Scatter**: Adjusts the distribution of brush marks.

Ⓔ **Count**: Sets the number of brush marks applied.

The Color Dynamics Attribute

The Color Dynamics attribute determines how color changes in a brush stroke.

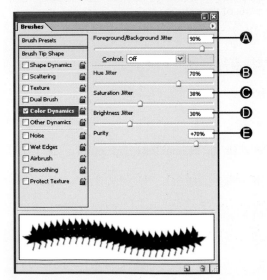

▲Brush Strokes without Color Dynamics (Left) and with Color Dynamics (Right)

Ⓐ Foreground/Background Jitter: Sets the mix between foreground/background colors.

Ⓑ Hue Jitter: Sets the percentage that the hue can vary with each brush stroke.

Ⓒ Saturation Jitter: Sets the percentage that the saturation can vary with each brush stroke.

Ⓓ Brightness Jitter: Sets the percentage that the brightness can vary with each brush stroke.

Ⓔ Purity: Sets the saturation of the color.

Additional Attributes

Below the Other Dynamics attribute are five additional options that are a little different from the attributes you have learned so far. These attributes do not come with their own sets of options, so all you need to do is check the attribute to apply the effect.

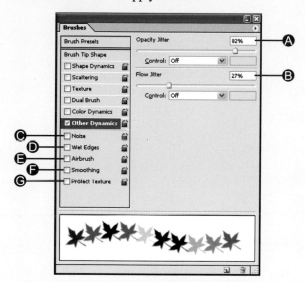

▲Brush Strokes without Paint Dynamics (Left)
and with Paint Dynamics (Right)

Ⓐ Opacity Jitter and Control: Adjusts how the opacity varies with each brush stroke.

Ⓑ Flow Jitter and Control: Sets the flow of paint within a brush stroke.

Ⓒ Noise: When checked, this adds random noise to a brush stroke.

Ⓓ Wet Edges: When checked, this applies a watercolor effect to each brush stroke.

Ⓔ Airbrush: When checked, this applies color continuously as the mouse button is held down.

Ⓕ Smoothing: When checked, this smoothes the curves in the brush strokes.

Ⓖ Protect Texture: When checked, this protects the underlying texture while painting.

The Brushes Palette Pop-Up Menu

The Brushes palette pop-up menu can be accessed in two ways. With the Brushes palette opened, click on the triangle icon on the Brushes tab to open the Brushes pop-up menu. Another way is to select the Brush tool and then click on the Brush drop-down menu on the tool options bar. When the Brush Preset Picker opens, click on the triangle icon at the top-right corner. The screen shot below shows you the Brush Preset Picker.

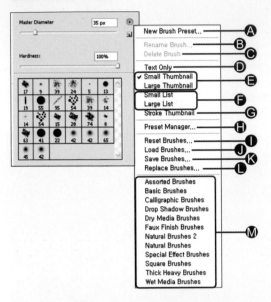

A **New Brush Preset**: Creates a new preset brush shape.

B **Rename Brush**: Renames an existing brush shape.

C **Delete Brush**: Deletes the selected brush.

D **Text Only**: Shows the brush name in text.

E **Small/Large Thumbnail**: Shows the brush stroke as small/large thumbnails.

F **Small/Large List**: Shows the brush shape, size, and name in small/large text.

G **Stroke Thumbnail**: Shows a thumbnail preview of what the brush stroke will look like.

H **Preset Manager**: Used to manage brush sets.

I **Reset Brushes**: Used to reset to the default brushes.

J **Load Brushes**: Used to load brush sets.

K **Save Brushes**: Used to save a modified brush set.

L **Replace Brushes**: Replaces brush sets.

M **Brush Types**: Click on one of the brush types to load the brushes that fall under that category into the Brush Preset Picker or Brushes palette. The following screenshots show you the different brush types.

Brush Types

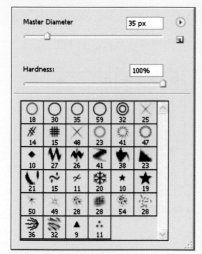

▲Assorted Brushes

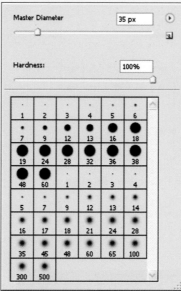

▲Basic Brushes

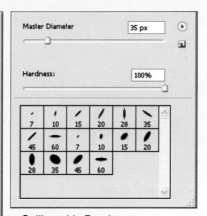

▲Calligraphic Brushes

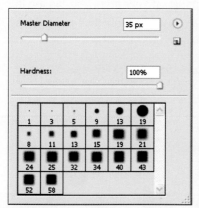

▲Drop Shadow Brushes

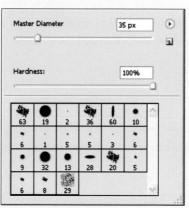

▲Dry Media Brushes

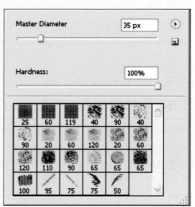

▲Faux Finish

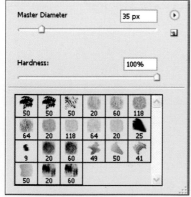

▲Natural Brushes 2

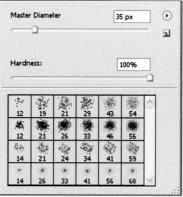

▲Natural Brushes

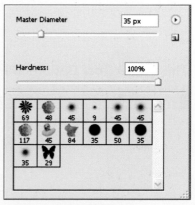

▲Special Effect Brushes

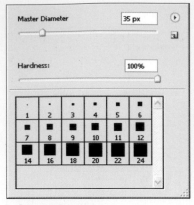

▲Square Brushes

▲Thick Heavy Brushes

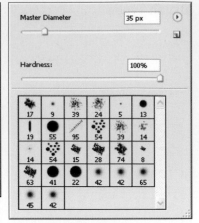

▲Wet Media Brushes

The Eraser Tools

You can correct your painting using the eraser tools in Photoshop. Depending on your need, you can use the Eraser tool, the Background Eraser tool, or the Magic Eraser tool. To use an eraser tool, click and hold the mouse button as you drag the tool over the areas that need to be erased.

The Eraser Tool (🖉)

On the Background layer, the Eraser tool erases the image and reveals the background color. On other layers, the Eraser tool removes the color and replaces it with transparency.

Using the Eraser tool on the Background ▶
layer reveals the background color, which is
white in this case.

The Eraser Tool Options Bar

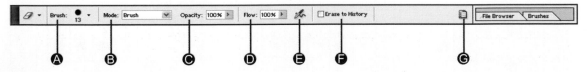

Ⓐ   Ⓑ   Ⓒ   Ⓓ   Ⓔ Ⓕ   Ⓖ

A **Brush**: Selects the eraser size.

B **Mode**: Selects the eraser shape: Brush, Pencil, or Block.

▲Brush   ▲Pencil   ▲Block

C **Opacity**: Selects the opacity of the eraser.

D **Flow**: When using the Airbrush option, Flow adjusts how much color is emitted.

E **Airbrush**: Hold down the mouse for a continuous flow of color.

F **Erase to History**: Erases the image until it is restored to a certain snapshot or point in the History palette.

G **Brushes Palette Toggle Button**: Shows/hides the Brushes palette.

The Background Eraser Tool ()

The Background Eraser tool uses the color in the center of the brush as a guide and erases similar colors.

Click the Background Eraser on an area of ▶ the layer that is to be erased. The pixels in the clicked area, as well as the tolerated area, will be erased.

The Background Eraser Tool Options Bar

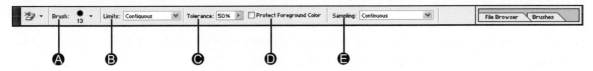

A **Brush**: Selects the eraser size.

B **Limits**

Discontiguous: Clicking a color in the layer will remove the same color from the image, even though the colors are not adjacent.

Contiguous: Removes similar colors from adjacent areas only.

Find Edges: Removes similar colors from adjacent areas, but preserves the object edges between the colors.

C **Tolerance**: Enter a value from 1% to 100% or use the slider bar to select the value. A low value means that only similar colors will be erased.

ⓓ Protect Foreground Color: Prevents colors similar to the foreground color specified in the toolbox from being erased.

ⓔ Sampling

Continuous: While dragging the tool, the sample color to be erased is continuously changed. This option is used to erase colors in an area that contains different colors.

Once: The sample color to erase is selected by the first mouse click and doesn't change. This option is used to erase a single color background.

Background Swatch: Used to erase colors that are the same as the current background color.

The Magic Eraser Tool (⬛)

The Magic Eraser tool is similar to the Magic Wand tool and is used to erase similar colors.

The Magic Eraser tool will erase an area ▶ depending on the Tolerance value.

Fill Tools

The Paint Bucket and Gradient tools are used for filling or changing the color of a large area in an image. To use the fill tools, you must first select the area to be changed using a selection tool.

The Paint Bucket Tool (⬛)

The Paint Bucket tool colors the image with a single color. It is applied by clicking the mouse in the selected area to be colored. Like the Magic Wand tool, the Paint Bucket tool has a Tolerance option and the visibility of the color can be determined by the Opacity setting.

▲Filling a Selection with the Foreground Color

▲Filling a Selection with a Pattern

The Paint Bucket Tool Options Bar

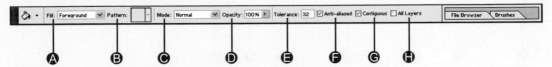

Ⓐ Fill: Fills the image using the foreground color or pattern.

Ⓑ Pattern: Selects the pattern to be used when the Fill option is set to Pattern.

Ⓒ Mode: Determines how the color will be applied to the original image.

Ⓓ Opacity: Sets the opacity.

Ⓔ Tolerance: Determines the tolerance from 0 to 255. A higher tolerance value will paint the color or patterns over a wider area.

Ⓕ Anti-aliased: When checked, a smooth edge will be applied to the image.

Ⓖ Contiguous: When checked, adjacent similar colors will be selected and painted.

Ⓗ All Layers: When checked, all visible areas will be painted regardless of which layer is activated.

The Gradient Tool

The Gradient tool applies a color gradation to a selection. The Gradient tool options bar offers five preset gradient styles and the Gradient Editor can be used to create other gradient effects.

▲Drag the mouse through the desired range to apply a gradient.   ▲The gradient is applied to the selected area.

<< tip

Direction of Gradient

The direction in which the mouse is dragged determines the direction of the gradation.

The Gradient Tool Options Bar

Ⓐ Gradient Preview: Shows a preview of the current gradient. Click on it to open the Gradient Picker and choose from a list of preset gradient styles. Double-clicking on it will open the Gradient Editor dialog box.

Ⓑ Gradient Styles

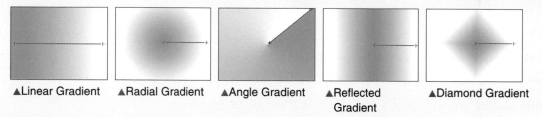

▲Linear Gradient   ▲Radial Gradient   ▲Angle Gradient   ▲Reflected Gradient   ▲Diamond Gradient

Ⓒ Mode: Determines how the gradient color will be blended into the original image.

Ⓓ Opacity: Determines the opacity of the gradient color.

Ⓔ Reverse: Reverses the direction of the gradation.

Ⓕ Dither: Creates a smooth blend mode with few bands in between.

Ⓖ Transparency: Used to determine the use of a transparent mask. If the selected gradient has an Opacity value, check this option to apply the opacity. If this option is not checked, the gradient will appear opaque even though it has an Opacity value.

The Gradient Editor Dialog Box

To open the Gradient Editor dialog box, select the Gradient tool and then go to the tool options bar and click inside the gradient preview that appears at the upper-left.

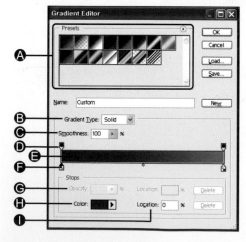

Ⓐ Presets: Contains the preset and saved gradients. Click [New] to create a new gradient.

Ⓑ Gradient Type: Choose Solid for smooth color transitions and Noise for line gradations.

Ⓒ Smoothness: Determines the smoothness of the gradient (i.e., how many colors comprise the transition(s)).

Ⓓ Opacity Stops: Opacity Stops define the transparency value at any chosen point along the gradient. Multiple stops will produce an opacity gradient, where the transparency value transitions smoothly from stop to stop. By clicking above the gradient bar you can add additional stops.

Ⓔ Gradient Bar: Clicking on top of the gradient bar will add an Opacity Stop. Clicking below will add a Color Stop. Dragging a stop away from the bar will remove the stop.

Ⓕ Color Stops: Color Stops define the color value at any chosen point along the gradient. The diamond icon that appears between Color Stops can be dragged to change the Color Midpoint value for those stops. By altering the midpoint you can manipulate how the gradient transitions from one color to the next. By clicking below the gradient bar you can add additional stops.

Ⓖ Opacity: Sets the opacity of the selected Opacity Stop. A value of 100% will appear solid.

Ⓗ Color: Sets the color of the selected Color Stop. Double-clicking on a Color Stop will display the Color Picker.

Ⓘ Location: Sets the position of the selected stop on the Gradient Bar.

Retouching an Image

In this section, let's look at how you can use the sharpness, brightness, and saturation tools to correct and enhance images. You will also be introduced to the filters that create the same effect as these tools. Filters provide an easy way to create a range of artistic and textural effects. Filters can be applied to layers, selections, or entire images, and are applied from the Filters menu.

Sharpness Tools

The Blur tool () is used to blur part of an image. If you want to apply a blur to the whole image, use the Gaussian Blur filter instead. You can apply a Gaussian Blur filter by selecting [Filter] - [Blur] - [Gaussian Blur] from the menu bar.

The Sharpen tool () is used to sharpen edges or contours within an image. Using a high strength setting or applying the tool too much will create a rough texture. If you want to sharpen an entire image, use the Unsharp Mask filter instead. You can apply an Unsharp Mask filter by selecting [Filter] - [Sharpen] - [Unsharp Mask] from the menu bar.

▲Original Image   ▲Dragging the Blur Tool   ▲Dragging the Sharpen Tool

The Smudge tool (📷) extends and transforms pixels to make the image look smoother. This tool can be used to create fire effects or to give the impression of motion. A similar effect is created using the Liquify filter found in the Filter sub-menu in the menu bar.

▲Original Image   ▲Dragging the Smudge Tool

<< tip

The Smudge Tool Options Bar

The Smudge tool options include Strength, which affects the severity of the smudge, and Finger Painting, which applies smudging using the foreground color.

Brightness and Saturation Tools

The Dodge tool () and the Burn tool () are used to correct over or under exposure, or to add light and dark effects to an image. The Dodge tool brightens the original image while the Burn tool darkens or adds shadows to the image.

▲Original Image   ▲Using the Dodge Tool   ▲Using the Burn Tool

The Sponge tool () is used to adjust the saturation of color within an image. When the Saturate option is selected in the tool options bar, the tool adds color. The Desaturate option can be used to remove color.

▲Using the Sponge Tool and the Saturate Option   ▲Using the Sponge Tool and the Desaturate Option

The Range Setting

The Dodge and Burn tools include a Range Setting in the tool options bar. This determines where to apply the change. The settings include: Highlights (changes the light areas in an image), Midtones (changes the middle tones), and Shadows (changes the dark areas of the image). The Exposure value determines how strongly the change will be applied.

Adding Color to Line Drawings

Original Image

Final Image

Project File
• Kitty.jpg

Final File
• Kitty_end.jpg

Features Used
• Magic Wand Tool, Layer via Cut, Brush Tool, Gradient Tool, Pencil Tool

Photoshop can be used to color scanned line drawings. In this exercise, you will use painting tools to color a line drawing of a cat. You will use the Magic Wand tool to make selections and work with layers to wield more control while painting.

Coloring the Image

<< note

Resource Files

Remember to copy the resource files on the CD-ROM to your hard drive before you start each exercise in this book.

1 Open \Sample\Chapter5\Kitty.jpg. Select the Magic Wand tool (🪄) from the toolbox and make sure that the Anti-aliased and Contiguous options are selected. Click the body of the cat to select the image. Hold down the [Shift] key and click the cat's face, ear, and paw.

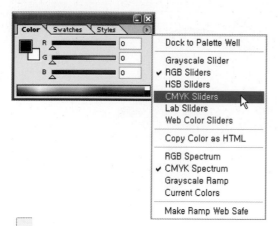

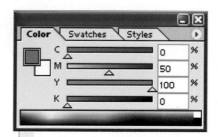

2 In the Color palette pop-up menu, select CMYK Sliders.

3 Move the slider bar or enter the following color values - Magenta: 50, Yellow: 100. This creates an orange color.

4 Press [Alt]-[Delete] to fill the selection with the foreground orange color. Select [Layer] - [New] - [Layer via Cut] or use the shortcut keys [Shift]-[Ctrl]-[J] to move the filled selection into a new layer.

5 The Layers palette will show a new layer - Layer 1. Double-click on the Layer 1 name and type in **body**. Press [Enter] to change the name.

6 Click the Background layer in the Layers palette and use the Magic Wand tool ( ) with the [Shift] key to select the stripes, mouth, and inside of the ears as shown. In the Color palette, enter 50 for Magenta, 100 for Yellow, and 60 for Black. This will create a brown foreground color. Press [Alt]-[Delete] to fill the selection with this color.

7 Use the [Shift]-[Ctrl]-[J] shortcut to copy the selection to a new layer. Rename the layer **pattern**.

8 Click on the Background layer in the Layers palette and use the Magic Wand tool (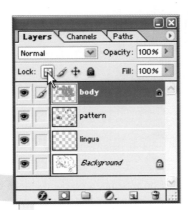) to select the cat's tongue. In the Color palette, enter 70 for Magenta, 0 for Yellow, and 0 for Black. Press [Alt]-[Delete] to fill the selection and use the [Shift]-[Ctrl]-[J] shortcut to copy the selection into a new layer. Name the layer **lingua**.

Adding Textures

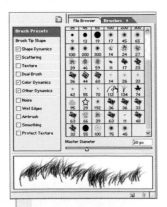

1 Click the body layer in the Layers palette and click the first lock button. This will prevent changes from being made to transparent pixels.

2 Select the Brush tool and click the Brushes tab in the palette well to display the Brushes palette. Click on Dune Grass and set the Master Diameter to 50.

118

3 In the Color palette, enter Magenta 50, Yellow 100, and Black 40 for the foreground color, and Magenta 50 and Yellow 100 for the background color. Drag the Brush tool over the cat's body to add texture.

4 Click the pattern layer and lock the transparent pixels. In the Color palette, set the foreground color to 100% black and paint the pattern. Be careful not to color the cat's ears and mouth, which are located in the same layer.

5 Click the Background layer in the Layers palette. Select the Magic Wand tool (🪄) and make sure that Contiguous and Anti-aliased are checked in the tool options bar. Select the cat's pupils, including the black edges, and press [Shift]-[Ctrl]-[J] to copy this selection into a new layer.

6 Change the name of the new layer to **stroke**. Since you extracted the black lines from the Background, there is currently no image in the Background layer.

Adding the Background

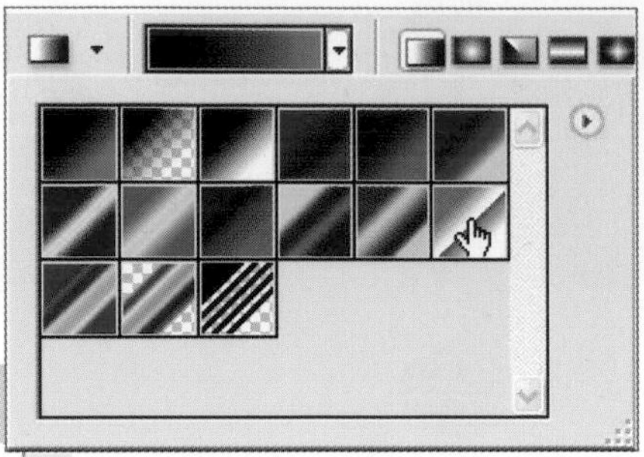

1 Click the Background layer in the Layers palette and select the Gradient tool ( ). Click on the gradient preview to display the Gradient Picker, then double-click on the Chrome gradient.

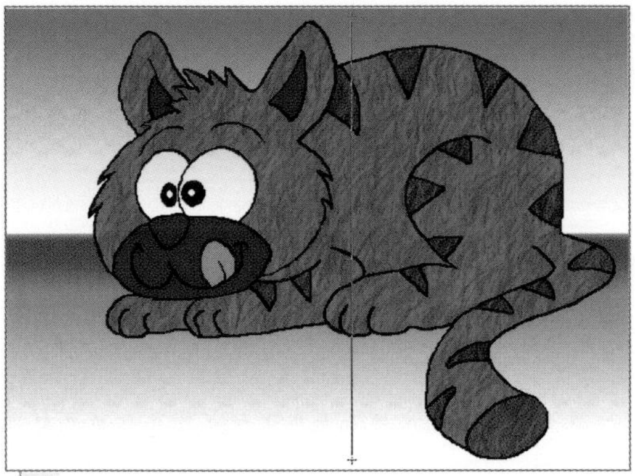

2 As shown here, drag the mouse from top to bottom to apply the gradient.

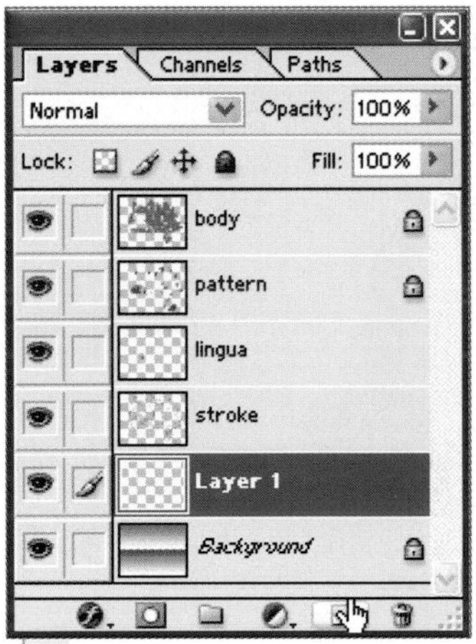

3 Click the [Create a new layer] button at the bottom of the Layers palette to create a new layer. Name it **grass**.

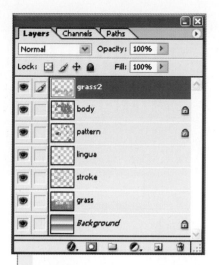

4 Select the Brush tool and click the Brush tab in the palette well to open the Brushes palette. Leave the Dune Grass brush selected and change the Master Diameter to 80. Enter Cyan 100 and Yellow 100 for the foreground color and Cyan 50 and Yellow 100 for the background color. Drag the mouse to apply the color as shown.

5 Click the [Create a new layer] button and name it **grass2**. Drag the grass2 layer above the other layers and add grass so that the cat's paws and tail are hidden.

6 Select the Pencil tool (⬚) from the toolbox and change the foreground color to black. Click the stroke layer. Open the Brush Preset Picker from the tool options bar and set the Master Diameter to 2. Draw the cat's whiskers as shown to complete the image.

Exercise 2 Coloring Black-and-White Images

Original Image

Final Image

Project File
- Pretty.jpg

Final File
- Pretty_end.jpg

Features Used
- Hue/Saturation, Magnetic Lasso Tool, Variations, Color Balance, Actual Pixels, Dodge Tool, Blur Tool

Using Photoshop, you can easily turn color images to black-and-white and vice versa. In this exercise, you will color a black-and-white image. This technique can be used to create color images out of old black-and-white photos.

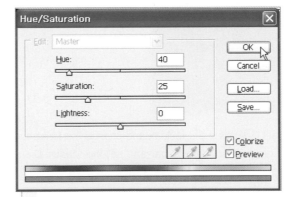

1 Open \Sample\Chapter5\Pretty.jpg. Select [Image] - [Adjustments] - [Hue/Saturation] from the menu bar. Check the Colorize option, set the Hue to 40, and click OK. This will apply a single color to the entire image.

2 Select the Magnetic Lasso tool (![icon]), click the point at which the clothes begin, and drag the mouse along the edges of the clothes to make a selection. You may need to click to add points where the selection is not accurate.

3 Continue along the edge of the clothes until you get back to your starting point. Click on the starting point to close the selection.

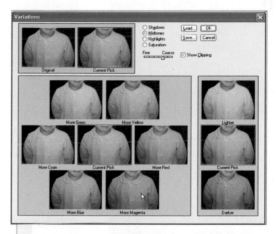

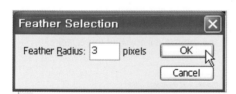

4 Choose [Select] - [Feather] from the menu bar, set the Feather Radius to 3, and click OK. Applying feathering will soften the selection.

5 Select [Image] - [Adjustments] - [Variations] from the menu bar. Move the slider so that it's on the second point of the Fine side. Click More Magenta twice and More Red once to change the color. Click OK and clear the selection.

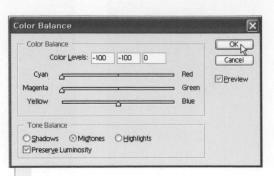

6 Repeat steps 2 and 3 to select the towel with the Magnetic Lasso tool (⬚).

7 Select [Image] - [Adjustments] - [Color Balance] from the menu bar. Set the Color Levels to -100, -100, 0 and click OK. This will color the towel purple.

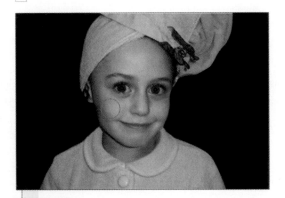

8 Press [Ctrl]-[D] to deselect and use the Zoom tool (🔍) to zoom into the face.

9 Set the foreground color to pink and select the Paint Brush tool (✐). Set the following options: Brush to Soft Round 35, Mode to Color, and Opacity to 10. Use the mouse to paint the cheeks.

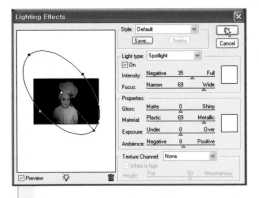

10 Change the color and select a smaller brush to paint the pupils of the eye. Keep the Opacity setting low, at 10% for example, so that the eye color is not too dark. Paint the eyes until the desired color is achieved.

11 You will add lighting effects to the image so that the colors appear more natural. Select [Filter] - [Render] - [Lighting Effects] from the menu bar. Leave the values at their default settings and click OK.

12 Select [View] - [Actual Pixels] from the menu bar to return the image to its original size. You can also double-click the Zoom tool (🔍). The lighting effect makes the image appear more natural.

13 In the Navigator palette, enter 300% for the zoom ratio.

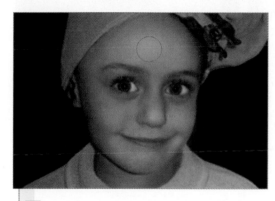

14 Select the Dodge tool (🔍) and choose an appropriate brush size. Drag the tool over the whites of the eyes to make them brighter. Drag the Blur tool (💧) over the skin to make it appear softer, excluding the eyes, nose, and mouth.

<< tip

The Navigator Palette

The red border in the preview window shows how much of the image is currently being displayed. The border can be dragged to show another part of the image.

3 Creating a CD-ROM Cover Insert

Original Image

Final Image

Project File
- Car.jpg

Final File
- Car_end.psd

Features Used
- New, Invert, Gradient, Contract, Layer via Cut, Hue/Saturation, Curves, Paste Into, Lasso Tool, Blend Mode

In this exercise, you will use the Gradient tool and the Circular Marquee tool to create a design for use as an insert for a CD-ROM. You will add an image and apply commands to make the graphic appear more realistic.

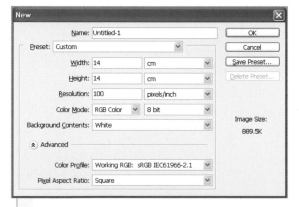

1 Select [File] - [New] to create a new image file. Set both the Width and Height to 14 cm, the Resolution to 100 pixels/inch, the Mode to RGB Color, and the Background Contents to White. Click OK.

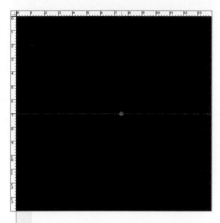

2 Select [Image] - [Adjustments] - [Invert] to invert the white color and create a black background. Select [View] - [Rulers] and point the mouse at the ruler until it changes to an arrow. Click and drag a guide from the ruler to the center of the CD at 7 cm. Release the mouse. Drag a guide from the left ruler to the 7 cm point.

<< tip
Rulers and Guides

Whenever the rulers are displayed, you can drag a guide onto the image regardless of which tool is currently selected. You can use the shortcut keys [Ctrl]-[R] to toggle the display of the ruler. Guides can be moved using the Move tool. To remove a guide, drag it outside of the image window with the Move tool.

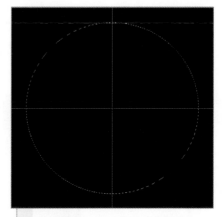

3 Click the [Create a new layer] button in the Layers palette.

4 Select the Circular Marquee tool ( ) and uncheck the Anti-aliased option. Set the Style to Fixed Size and the Width and Height to 12 cm. Hold down the [Alt] key and click the point where the guides intersect to create a circular selection with a diameter of 12 cm.

<< tip
The Anti-Aliased Option

If you leave the Anti-aliased option checked, step 10 will create messy edges.

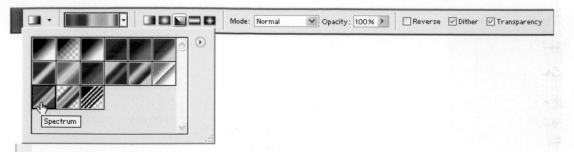

5 Select the Gradient tool (▦). In the Gradient tool options bar, open the Gradient Picker, select Spectrum, and click OK. Click the [Angle Gradient] button. Other options should be kept at their default settings.

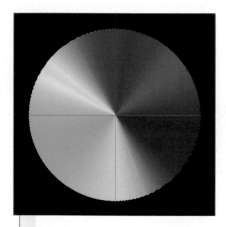

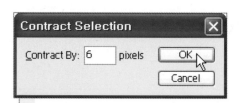

6 Drag from the center upwards to apply the Angle Gradient.

7 To create a semi-transparent CD border, choose [Select] - [Modify] - [Contract], enter 6, and click OK. The selection will be 6 pixels inside the spectrum.

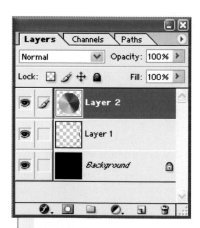

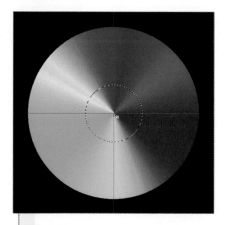

8 Select [Layer] - [New] - [Layer via Cut] to cut out the selected area and place it on Layer 2.

9 Choose the Elliptical Marquee tool (◯) from the toolbox. Change both the Width and Height to 4 cm. Hold down the [Alt] key and click the center point to create a circular selection with a diameter of 4 cm.

128

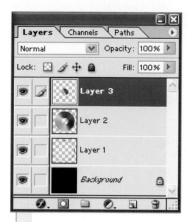

10 Select [Layer] - [New] - [Layer via Cut] to move the selection to Layer 3.

11 Hold down the [Ctrl] key and click the Layer 3 thumbnail to create a selection. Contract the selection by choosing [Select] - [Modify] - [Contract]. Enter 6 and click OK.

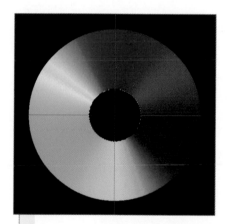

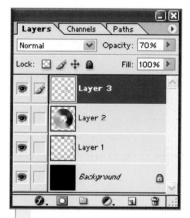

12 Press [Delete] to delete the selected area and clear the selection. Layer 3 will contain an outline.

13 To make a realistic CD image, the opacity and color of each layer must be changed. In the Layers palette, change the Opacity of Layer 3 to 70% to make the image semi-transparent.

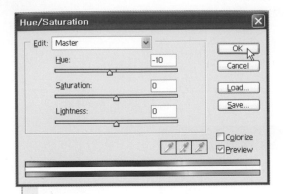

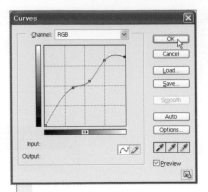

14 Click on the Layer 2 layer and select [Image] - [Adjustments] - [Hue/Saturation]. Set the Hue to -10 and click OK. This will make the color rotate and create a border effect similar to the semi-transparent outline.

15 To create highlights for the CD, select [Image] - [Adjustments] - [Curves]. Adjust the curve in the Curves dialog box as shown. You can click to add points to the curve and drag them to the desired position. Click OK to apply the changes.

<< tip
The Preview Option

Checking the Preview option in the Curves dialog box lets you preview the image while you make changes.

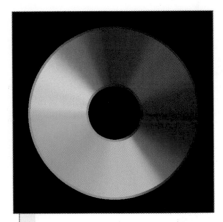

16 Click on Layer 1 and set the Opacity to 70%.

17 Open \Sample\Chapter5\Car.jpg and press [Ctrl]-[A] to select the entire image. Use the shortcut [Ctrl]-[C] to copy the image.

18 Hold down the [Ctrl] key and click on Layer 2 to create a selection based on the contents of Layer 2.

19 Choose [Edit] - [Paste Into] or use the shortcut keys [Shift]-[Ctrl]-[V] to paste the image into the selection. Use the Move tool to place the image as shown.

20 Select the Lasso tool (⌕) and set the Feather value to 20. Make a selection as shown. Press the [Delete] key two to three times to erase the background. Each deletion will appear natural due to the Feather value. Clear the selection.

21 Set the blend mode of Layer 4 to Linear Light to overlay the image on top of the CD.

22 The final image in shown above.

Chapter 6

Paths and Vector Tools

Creating and editing paths is an essential skill that you'll need to know in order to work in Photoshop. Paths are used to make selections as well as for drawing and painting images. A good understanding of the vector tools in Photoshop will also make your work easier. Photoshop provides vector tools that use paths to draw different types of shapes or enter text. As these shapes are vector-based, they are small in file size and can be resized without distortion.

Introduction to Paths and Vectors

Vector images, which are created using paths, are generally simple shapes with clean lines; they are not photo-realistic images. In this chapter, you'll learn about paths and how to use the vector tools found in Photoshop to create type and draw standard and freeform shapes.

What Is a Path?

A path is a line consisting of one or more segments connected by anchor points. An anchor point is a point that indicates where the line starts, passes through, or ends. An anchor point also determines the angle of the line passing through it.

The Elements of a Path

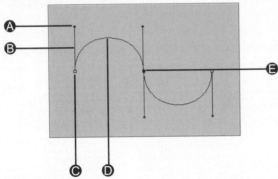

Ⓐ **Direction Point**: An endpoint of the direction line, this point is used to adjust the direction line.

Ⓑ **Direction Line**: A line used to adjust the shape of the curve by defining the angle at which the line passes through the anchor point.

Ⓒ **Unselected Anchor Point**: Unselected anchor points appear with a transparent fill.

Ⓓ **Segment**: A line connecting two anchor points.

Ⓔ **Selected Anchor Point**: Selected points appear with a black fill.

Path Tools

Paths are drawn using a pen tool. They're edited using anchor point tools and path selection tools. Closed paths can be filled with color and paths can be saved and used as selection frames. In this section, let's look at all the tools that are used to draw and edit paths.

The Pen tool () and the Freeform Pen tool (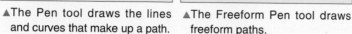) are used for drawing paths. The Pen tool draws a path in a series of curved or straight line segments while the Freeform Pen tool draws a path in one continuous stroke.

▲The Pen tool draws the lines and curves that make up a path.

▲The Freeform Pen tool draws freeform paths.

<< note

The Magnetic Freeform Pen Tool

If you check the Magnetic option of the Freeform Pen tool, you can turn it into a Magnetic Freeform Pen tool. With this option turned on, the tool automatically makes a path based on areas of contrast within the image. This is similar to the Magnetic Lasso tool.

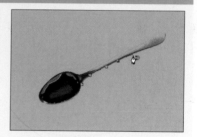

Using the Magnetic ▶ Freeform Pen tool

The Add Anchor Point tool (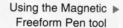), Delete Anchor Point tool, and Convert Point tool are used for editing anchor points on a path.

▲The Add Anchor Point tool adds anchor points to existing paths.

▲The Delete Anchor Point tool deletes anchor points from existing paths.

▲The Convert Point tool changes the properties of anchor points.

The Path Selection tool () and the Direct Selection tool () are used to select and move paths and anchor points, respectively.

▲The Path Selection tool selects a path.

▲The Direct Selection tool selects individual anchor points.

Shortcut Keys

When a path and the Pen tool are selected, you can use the following shortcut keys:

- Place the tool on top of the active path to convert to the Add Anchor Point tool (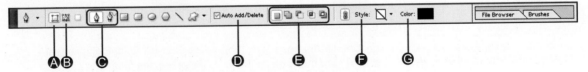).
- Place the tool on top of the active anchor point to convert to the Delete Anchor Point tool ().
- Place the tool on top of the active anchor point and press [Alt] to convert to the Convert Point tool ().
- Place the tool on top of the path and press [Ctrl] to convert to the Direct Selection tool ().

Text on a Path

You can make text align with a path. This technique lets you blend text with images more creatively.

▲Create a path with the Pen tool and click on the path with a type tool. Enter some text. The text will follow the shape of the path.

▲Make a path with the Shape tool and the text will be entered inside the shape.

The Pen Tool Options Bar

Ⓐ **Shape layers**: Creates a layer that contains the path. Styles or effects can be applied to the layer.

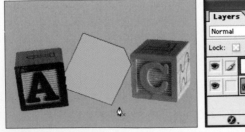

Ⓑ **Paths**: Creates a work path in the Paths palette.

Ⓒ **Pen Tool Selection**: Choose between the Pen tool and the Freeform Pen tool.

Ⓓ **Auto Add/Delete**: Pointing at the path will automatically change the tool to the Add Anchor Point tool. Pointing at an anchor point will change the tool to the Delete Anchor Point tool.

Ⓔ **Path Interaction Options**: Choose from Create new shape layer, Add to shape area (+), Subtract from shape area (-), Intersect shape areas, and Exclude overlapping shape areas.

Ⓕ **Style**: Click on the link button and select a style.

Ⓖ **Color**: Select the color for the shape layer.

Showing and Hiding Paths

Paths can be used as guides for coloring, outlining, and creating selections. When using paths as guides, you may want to show or hide the paths. This can be done in the Paths palette.

◄Clicking the path name will activate and show the path in the image.

◄Clicking below the path name or holding down the [Shift] key and clicking the path name hides the path.

137

The Paths Palette

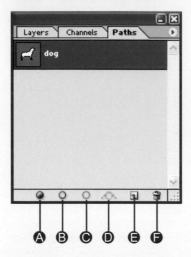

ⓐ Fill path with foregroud color: Fills the selected path with the foreground color.

ⓑ Stroke path with foreground color: Outlines or strokes the selected path with the foreground color.

ⓒ Load path as a selection: Creates a selection based on the path.

ⓓ Make work path from selection: Creates a work path from a selection. This option is only available when there is a selection.

ⓔ Create new path: Makes a new path.

ⓕ Delete current path: Deletes the selected path.

The Paths Palette Pop-Up Menu

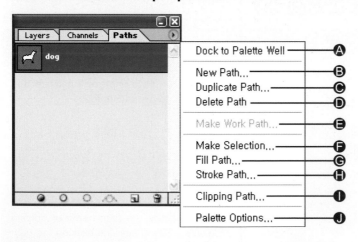

ⓐ Dock to Palette Well: Docks the Paths palette to the Palette well.

ⓑ New Path: Makes a new path.

ⓒ Duplicate Path: Copies the path.

ⓓ Delete Path: Deletes the path.

ⓔ Make Work Path: Makes the selection frame into a path.

ⓕ Make Selection: Makes the path into a selection frame.

ⓖ Fill Path: Fills the path with the foreground color.

ⓗ Stroke Path: Outlines the path with the foreground color.

ⓘ Clipping Path: Makes a clipping path.

ⓙ Palette Options: Used to adjust the size of the palette thumbnail.

Clipping Paths

Some page layout programs do not recognize transparency in an image; these programs will print transparent areas as white. To solve this problem, you have to define the transparent and non-transparent areas of an image using clipping paths. The areas outside the path are considered transparent, and those within are visible. This technique is useful for making a background transparent when printed.

▲In Photoshop, the background is displayed.　▲When a clipping path is used, the background no longer prints when used in a program such as QuarkXpress or PageMaker.

Shape Tools

An easy way to create vector objects is to use shape tools. Photoshop includes a number of preset shapes and you can also save your own shapes. When using the shape tools, you don't need to draw the path by hand. The Direct Selection tool (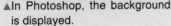) can be used to modify these shapes.

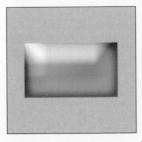  

◀From Left: Drawn Using the Rectangle Tool (▢), Rounded Rectangle Tool (▢), and Ellipse Tool (◯)

139

The Rectangle Tool Options Bar

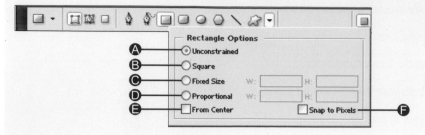

Ⓐ Unconstrained: Draws freeform rectangular shapes.

Ⓑ Square: Draws perfect squares.

Ⓒ Fixed Size: Enter specific dimensions for the shape.

Ⓓ Proportional: Enter dimensions to make rectangular shapes of specific proportions.

Ⓔ From Center: Draws the rectangle from the center.

Ⓕ Snap to Pixels: The corners of the rectangle snap to pixels.

<< tip

Other Tool Options

The tool options bars for the Rectangle, Rounded Rectangle, and Ellipse tools contain similar options, but there are options unique to each tool. In the Rounded Rectangle tool options bar, you will see the Radius option, which determines the roundness of corners. In the Ellipse tool options bar, you will see the Circle option, which lets you draw perfect circles.

The Polygon Tool (⬠)

The Polygon tool draws polygons or star shapes.

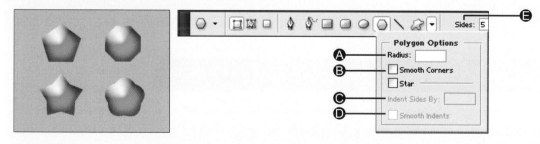

Ⓐ Radius: Sets the radius of the shape.

Ⓑ Smooth Corners: Rounds the corners of the polygon.

Ⓒ Indent Sides By: When Star is checked, specifies the indent for the sides.

Ⓓ Smooth Indents: When Star is checked, this option smooths the indented sides.

Ⓔ Sides: Determines the number of sides in the shape.

The Line Tool (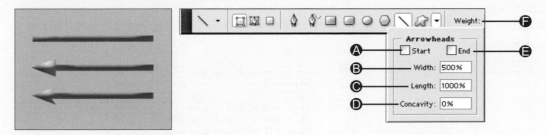)

The Line tool is used to draw lines or arrows.

Ⓐ **Start**: Adds an arrowhead at the start of the line.

Ⓑ **Width**: Sets the width of the arrow.

Ⓒ **Length**: Sets the length of the arrow.

Ⓓ **Concavity**: Determines the arrowhead shape.

Ⓔ **End**: Adds an arrowhead at the finish of the line.

Ⓕ **Weight**: Sets the thickness of the line.

The Custom Shape Tool (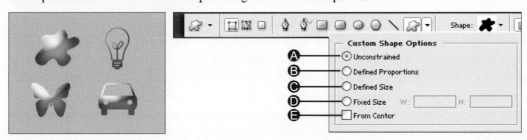)

Draw predefined or user-defined shapes using the Custom Shape tool.

Ⓐ **Unconstrained**: Draws the shape as wished.

Ⓑ **Defined Proportions**: Draws the shape using the default proportions.

Ⓒ **Defined Size**: Draws the shape using the default dimensions.

Ⓓ **Fixed Size**: Draws the shape using the designated size.

Ⓔ **From Center**: Draws the shape from the center.

<< note

The Fill Pixels Option

Selecting the Fill Pixels option (⬜), which is available in the options bar of all the shape tools, lets you create shapes as bitmaps without creating separate paths or layers.

Loading Custom Shapes

The Custom Shape Picker is displayed when the Shape drop-down menu is clicked in the Custom Shape tool options bar. Click the pop-up menu button at the right to reveal more custom shapes. Choose All to load all the preset shapes.

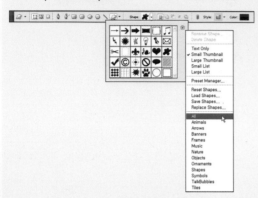 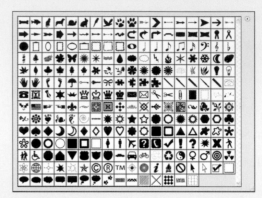

Type Tools

Text is entered as vector objects in Photoshop. There are a total of four type tools in Photoshop. Regardless of the tool that you select, you will need to click the [Commit] button (✓) to apply the changes to your image.

The Horizontal Type tool (T) and the Vertical Type tool (T) let you enter text into an image either horizontally or vertically. The text that is entered will be placed on a separate text layer. A text layer is indicated by a letter T in the Layers palette. Because the text is vector-based, it does not distort when the size of the text is changed. In addition, even after you have entered the text, you can still edit it simply by retyping. But if you change a text layer into a normal layer by rasterizing it, the text cannot be edited, as it is no longer vector-based.

Horizontal Type Tool

Vertical Type Tool

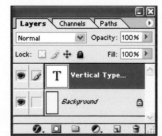

▲Text entered using the Horizontal Type tool and Vertical Type tool.

▲Using the Horizontal and Vertical Type tools creates a new text layer in the Layers palette. A new text layer is created with each text entry.

<< tip

Converting a Vector Shape into a Bitmap

A vector shape can be converted to a bitmap with the Rasterize command. A bitmap is an image that is recorded using pixels.

The Horizontal Type Mask tool (⊞) and the Vertical Type Mask tool (⊞) behave quite differently from the Horizontal/Vertical Type tools. The Horizontal and Vertical Type Mask tools create a text selection in the current layer. These selections can be moved, copied, stroked, and filled.

◀ The Horizontal and Vertical Type Mask tools create a mask to protect areas that will not be edited.

◀ Clicking the [Commit] button in the options bar turns the entered text into a selection.

The Type Tool Options Bar

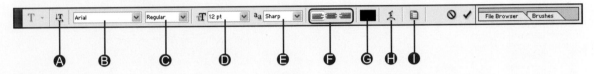

ⒶⒷⒸⒹⒺⒻⒼⒽⒾ

Ⓐ **Change the text orientation**: Changes horizontal text to vertical and vice versa.

Ⓑ **Font family**: Selects the font.

Ⓒ **Font style**: Depending on the selected font, choose Normal, Italic, Bold, or Bold Italic.

Ⓓ **Font size**: Sets the text size.

Ⓔ **Anti-aliasing method**: Used to determine the smoothness of the letter shapes.
  None: No change.
  Sharp: Roughened edges.
  Crisp: Edges are turned inwards.
  Strong: Strong edges.
  Smooth: Smooth edges.

Ⓕ **Text alignment**: Select left, center, or right alignment.

Ⓖ **Text color**: Change the text color.

Ⓗ **Create warped text**: Warp the text in different styles.

Ⓘ **Toggle the Character and Paragraph palettes**: Show/hide the Character and Paragraph palettes.

The Warp Text Dialog Box

Clicking the [Create warped text] button (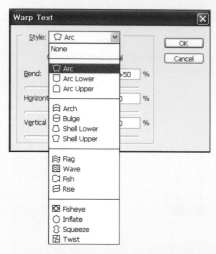) will display the Warp Text dialog box. This can be used to change the shape of the text or paragraph to different styles. This option cannot be used for text that has been rasterized or text that uses a Faux Bold style.

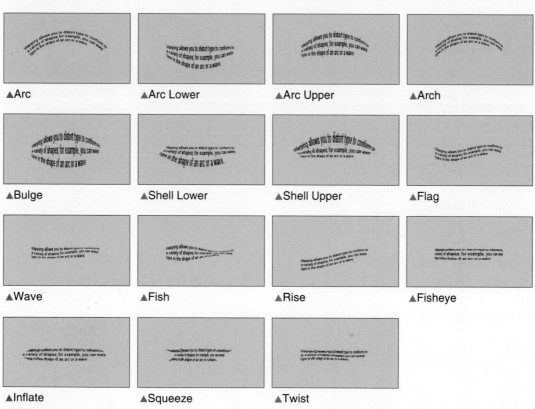

▲Arc   ▲Arc Lower   ▲Arc Upper   ▲Arch

▲Bulge   ▲Shell Lower   ▲Shell Upper   ▲Flag

▲Wave   ▲Fish   ▲Rise   ▲Fisheye

▲Inflate   ▲Squeeze   ▲Twist

The Character Palette

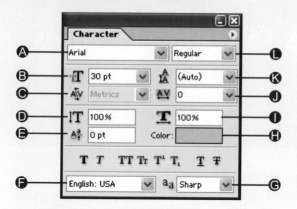

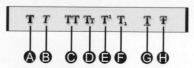

- **Ⓐ Font**
- **Ⓑ Font Size**
- **Ⓒ Kerning**
- **Ⓓ Vertical Scale**
- **Ⓔ Baseline Shift**
- **Ⓕ Select Language**
- **Ⓖ Select Anti-Aliasing**
- **Ⓗ Color**
- **Ⓘ Horizontal Scale**
- **Ⓙ Tracking**
- **Ⓚ Line Height**
- **Ⓛ Style of Font**

- **Ⓐ Faux Bold**: Bold text.
- **Ⓑ Faux Italic**: Italic text.
- **Ⓒ All Caps**: All capital letters.
- **Ⓓ Small Caps**: Small capital letters.
- **Ⓔ Superscript**: Superscript letters.
- **Ⓕ Subscript**: Subscript letters.
- **Ⓖ Underline**: Underlined text.
- **Ⓗ Strikethrough**: Creates a line through the text.

The Paragraph Palette

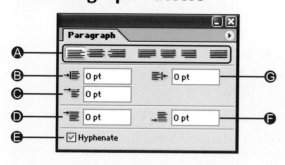

- **Ⓐ Paragraph Alignment and Justification**
- **Ⓑ Left Indent**
- **Ⓒ First Line Indent**
- **Ⓓ Space before Paragraph**
- **Ⓔ Automatic Hyphenation**
- **Ⓕ Space after Paragraph**
- **Ⓖ Right Indent**

Exercise 1

Using Paths to Frame Pictures

Original Image

Final Image

Project Files
frame.jpg, frame2.jpg

Final File
frame_end.psd

Features Used
Pen Tool, Save Path, Paste Into, Inner Shadow

Paths can be used for many different purposes, and it is important to become comfortable with using the Pen tool to draw straight, curved, and freeform lines. In this section, you will learn to create selections with paths. You will also learn how to work with the Pen tool, which can take a little practice to master.

<< note

Resource Files

Remember to copy the resource files on the CD-ROM to your hard drive before you start each exercise in this book.

1 Open \Sample\Chapter6\frame.jpg. Select the Pen tool () from the toolbox and click on the second of the three path style buttons in the options bar. Click the starting point as shown.

146

2 Click on the next point as shown above. A line segment will appear connecting the two points. Continue in this fashion until you have drawn around the star. Continue until you reach the curved section of the moon.

3 In order to draw a curved path, click to add a new anchor point and drag away from the anchor point to create a curve. Two direction lines for the path will appear as you drag.

4 The next path that needs to be drawn is at a sharp angle from your last anchor point. You cannot simply click for your next point because the resulting line will be at the wrong angle. You will first need to convert the anchor point to a corner point in order to draw a path at a sharp angle. Hold down the [Alt] key and click on the anchor point when you see this icon (▶).

5 Click the tool on the bridge of the nose, then click-and-drag the mouse to the tip of the moon. This will create a curved line. Move the mouse until the curve fits the moon's crescent shape, as shown.

Using Paths to Create Neon Lights and Fireworks

Original Image

Final Image

Project File
- festival.jpg

Final File
- festival_end.jpg

Features Used
- Brush Tool, Stroke Path with Brush, Blend Mode, Gaussian Blur

The previous example showed how to create a path and use it for a selection. In this exercise, you'll apply different brush strokes to saved paths to make neon and fireworks effects.

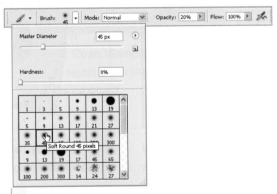

<< note
Resource Files

Remember to copy the resource files on the CD-ROM to your hard drive before you start each exercise in this book.

1 Open \Sample\Chapter6\festival.jpg. Choose the Paint Brush tool (🖌) from the toolbox and select the brush preset Soft Round 45 pixels. Set the Opacity to 20%.

<< tip
Brush Size Shortcut Keys

You can change the brush size using your keyboard: press] to increase the brush size, and press [to reduce the brush size.

2 Click the [Create a new layer] button in the Layers palette. Double-click the layer name and enter **glow**.

3 In the Color palette, set the foreground color to Cyan 50. In the Paths palette, drag-and-drop the festival path onto the [Stroke path with brush] button at the bottom. You could also have clicked the festival path to activate it, then clicked on the button.

4 The brush has now traced a line around the path.

5 Click the triangular button in the Brush Preset Picker and change the Master Diameter to 30. Set the Opacity to 40%. In the Paths palette, drag-and-drop the festival path onto the [Stroke path with brush] button. Another line is created using a smaller brush and a darker color. This creates a smudged effect.

6 Press [three times to reduce the brush size to 10, then change the Opacity to 60%. In the Paths palette, drag-and-drop the festival path onto the [Stroke path with brush] button.

7 Set the foreground color to white and press the [button five times to reduce the brush size to 5. Change the Opacity to 100%. In the Paths palette, drag-and-drop the festival path onto the [Stroke path with brush] button.

8 In the Layers palette, drag-and-drop the glow layer onto the [Create a new layer] button to create the layer glow copy. Drag the glow copy layer below the glow layer and set the blend mode to Overlay.

9 Select [Filter] - [Blur] - [Gaussian Blur]. Set the Radius to 30 and click OK.

10 Select the Ellipse Shape tool (⬭) from the toolbox and, in the options bar, click on the second path type (▣). Hold down the [Shift] key and drag the tool in the image window to make several circles.

11 The Paths palette shows circular paths. Save the paths by double-clicking Work Path and entering **spark**.

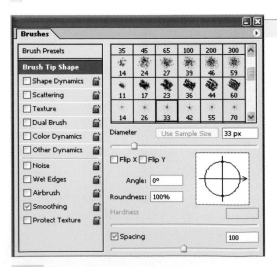

12 Select the Paint Brush tool (✎) and click the Brush tab in the palette well to open the Brushes palette. Click Brush Tip Shape and choose Star 33 Pixels from the list on the right. Set the Diameter to 33 and the Spacing to 100.

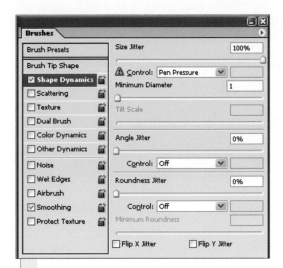

13 Click Shape Dynamics and set the Size Jitter to 100%.

14 Click on Scattering and set the Scatter to 50, the Count to 5, and the Count Jitter to 100%.

15 Set the foreground color to pink and drag-and-drop the spark path onto the [Stroke path with brush] button in the Paths palette. This will create an outline around the circles.

16 Change the foreground color and drag-and-drop the spark path onto the [Stroke path with brush] button in the Paths palette. You may want to repeat this step with different colors to complete the image .

3

Working with Cartoon Characters

Original Image

Final Image

Project File
- Fox&dog.psd

Final File
- Fox&dog_end.psd

Features Used
- Duplicate Layer, Wind, Motion Blur, Layer via Copy, Free Transform, Stroke, Text Tool

In this example, you will add movement to cartoon characters and use the Shape tool to create speech bubbles.

<< note

Resource Files

Remember to copy the resource files on the CD-ROM to your hard drive before you start each exercise in this book.

1 Open \Sample\Chapter6\Fox&dog.psd. You will copy the dog and add a movement effect. In the Layers palette, select the dog layer, choose [Layer] - [Duplicate Layer], and click OK.

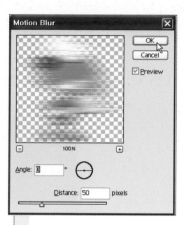

2   The layer dog copy has been created in the Layers palette. Choose [Filter] - [Stylize] - [Wind], select Blast and From the Left, and click OK.

3   Select [Filter] - [Blur] - [Motion Blur], set the Angle to 0 and the Distance to 50, and click OK.

4   In the Layers palette, drag the dog copy layer below the dog layer.

5   Use the Move tool ( ) to move the dog copy layer towards the right, as shown.

6   You will now add movement to the fox's tail. Click the fox layer and select the Lasso tool ( ). In the options bar, set the Feather value to 0 and use the tool to select the fox's tail.

7   Select [Layer] - [New] - [Layer via Copy] or press [Ctrl]-[J]. Use the Move tool to move the fox's tail.

155

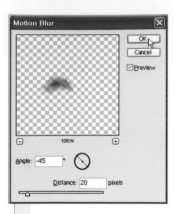

8 Choose [Filter] - [Blur] - [Motion Blur], set the Angle to -45 and the Distance to 20, and click OK.

9 Select [Edit] - [Free Transform] to rotate the fox tail. When the bounding box appears, move the center pointer to the bottom right and use the corner handles to rotate the tail. Click inside the bounding box and drag to move the tail as shown. Press [Enter] to apply the transformation.

10 Press [Ctrl]+[[] to move Layer 1 below the fox layer.

<< tip

Layer Order Shortcut Keys

Press [Ctrl]-[[] to move a layer down and [Ctrl]-[]] to move a layer up in the Layers palette.

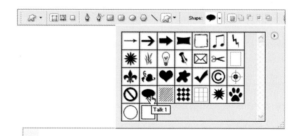

11 Select the Custom Shape tool (📷) from the toolbox and select Shape Layers (🔲) from the options bar. Double-click the Talk 1 shape from the Shape Picker.

12 Set the foreground color to white and drag the mouse on the image to create the shape. Set the Opacity to 70% to make the shape semi-transparent.

156

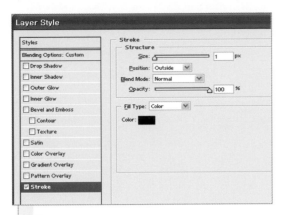

[13] Choose [Layer] - [Layer Style] - [Stroke] to outline the balloon. Set the Size to 1, the Color to black, and click OK.

[14] Select the Type tool ([T]) from the toolbox. Set the Font to Arial, the Font Size to 14, and the Color to black. Deactivate the shape path and drag the Type tool to create an area for the text. Enter **Hey, long time no see! Where have you been?** and click the [Commit] button ([✔]) in the options bar.

[15] Click the balloon layer and use the [Alt] key with the Move tool to drag a copy to the right. Press [Ctrl]-[T] and drag the bounding box corner handles to increase the size. Press [Enter] to apply the transformation.

[16] Selecting the Pen tool ([✎]) from the toolbox and Path ([▦]) from the options bar, draw in the path for the text as shown here.

[17] Selecting the Type tool ([T]) from the toolbox, click it where the path begins and type in, **Hey, Fox! I didn't go anywhere**. Then click Agree in the options bar. The final image is shown to the left.

Chapter 7

Color Correction

Photoshop provides numerous tools for correcting the color and overall look of photographs and graphics. Possible image adjustments include compensating for over- or underexposure, manipulating brightness and contrast values, or changing the range of tones that are present in an image. Menu commands such as Levels, Curves, and Variations provide a visual method for making these alterations. In this chapter, we'll review the various ways in which you can manipulate color in your images.

Color Correction Options

The [Image] - [Adjustments] menu contains a number of sub-menus designed specifically for color correction. These include adjustments for color balance, hue, saturation, brightness, contrast, and tonal range. This chapter covers the Histogram palette and all the commands on the Adjustments menu that are useful for color correction.

The Histogram Palette

The Histogram palette maps the tonal information of an image in a histogram. If the pixels of an image are concentrated in the shadows (on the left of the histogram), this would mean that the image has more dark areas. An image with a full tonal range will have a histogram that is evenly distributed.

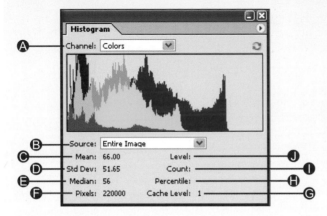

🅐 **Channel**: Select RGB to view the tonal range of the entire image or select one of the color channels to view only a specific color's tonal range.

🅑 **Source**: Select the source for the histogram data—Entire Image, Selected Layer, Adjustment Composite.

🅒 **Mean**: The average image brightness. The larger the mean value, the brighter the image.

🅓 **Std Dev**: The standard deviation—showing how the tonal values are distributed with respect to the mean. The smaller this value, the more evenly distributed the shadows are.

🅔 **Median**: The color at the middle of the image's tonal range.

🅕 **Pixels**: The total number of pixels in the image.

🅖 **Cache Level**: A cache is a memory allotment that enables the computer to execute instructions or retrieve data more quickly than when it uses conventional memory. The Cache Level indicates the image cache used to create the histogram. At Cache Level 1, all the pixels in the image are used to create the histogram. The number of pixels used decreases by four times with every increase to the Cache Level value.

H **Percentile**: When you mouse over a point on the histogram, the Percentile field shows you the percentage of pixels in the image that are of the same shade or darker than the selected point.

I **Count**: The number of pixels at the selected point on the histogram.

J **Level**: The tonal value at the selected point on the histogram, ranging from 0 to 256.

The Levels Command

While the Histogram palette is used to review the image's tonal range, the Levels command ([Ctrl]-[L]) is used for color correction. The command is often used to correct tonal range, brightness, and contrast.

The Levels Dialog Box

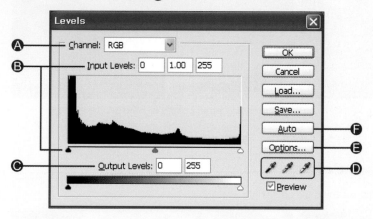

A **Channel**: Select RGB to modify the tonal range of the entire image or select one of the color channels to modify only a specific color's tonal range.

B **Input Levels**: Adjusts brightness and contrast.

C **Output Levels**: Adjusts the tonal range of the entire image.

D **Eyedroppers**: Eyedroppers are used to set the black, white, and gray points in an image.

E **Options**: Options for auto image correction.

F **Auto**: Adjusts the tonal range automatically.

<< **note**

Input Levels and Output Levels

Input Levels: The Input Levels graph or histogram shows 256 shades of gray. The slider on the left is at 0 and represents the darkest pixels in the image, or black. The slider in the middle represents the midtones and the slider on the right represents the brightest pixels, which are white (at 255).

Output Levels: The Output Levels slider is used to adjust the overall tonal range. Output Levels affect the image as a whole, rather than the individual pixels of the image. Moving the white slider to the left will brighten the image, while moving the black slider towards the right makes the image darker.

<< tip

The Cancel Button

When the [Alt] key is held down, the [Cancel] button changes to a [Reset] button that can be used to reset an image to its original state.

Using Input Levels to Sharpen Images

▲Original Image

▲After Using Input Levels to Sharpen the Image

Using Midtones to Correct Color

The midtones slider adjusts the tones between the dark and bright areas.

▲Move the gray slider towards the left to brighten the midtones.

▲Move the white slider towards the left to expand the highlight area.

◄Move the gray slider towards the right to darken the midtones.

Using Channels to Correct Color

Changes can be made to a single color channel to correct a specific color within an image.

▲Brightening the Midtones in the Red Channel

▲Brightening the Midtones in the Green Channel

◄Brightening the Midtones in the Blue Channel

Auto Corrections

Photoshop contains a number of auto correction commands:

Auto Levels ([Shift]-[Ctrl]-[L]): Automatically adjusts image tonal levels.

Auto Contrast ([Alt]-[Shift]-[Ctrl]-[L]): Automatically adjusts image brightness and contrast levels.

Auto Color ([Shift]-[Ctrl]-[B]): Automatically adjusts image color levels.

The Curves Command

The Curves dialog box ([Ctrl]-[V]), as with the Levels command, lets you adjust the entire tonal range of an image. Adjusting the position of the curve, which starts off as a 45° line in the graph, adjusts the image's tonal range. The horizontal axis represents the input levels or original tonal values, while the vertical axis represents the output levels or the new tonal values.

The Curves Dialog Box

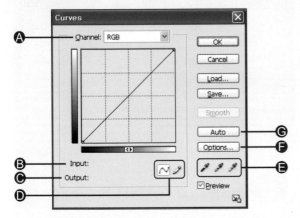

Ⓐ **Channel**: Selects the color channel.

Ⓑ **Input**: Displays the original tonal value of the selected point on the curve.

Ⓒ **Output**: Displays the new tonal value of the selected point on the curve.

Ⓓ **Curves Button/Pencil Button**: The Curves button allows for adjustment of the image by making changes to the curve. The Pencil button allows a curve to be hand drawn.

Ⓔ **Eyedroppers**: Eyedroppers are used set the black, gray, and white points within the image.

Ⓕ **Options**: Opens the Auto Color Correction Options dialog box which lets you decide how color and tones will be corrected.

Ⓖ **Auto**: Applies the settings entered in the Auto Color Correction Options dialog box.

<< tip

Increasing Curve Graph Resolution

Hold down the [Alt] key and click the curve to increases the number of grid lines in the graph.

<< note

Curve Differences in CMYK and RGB Modes

If the image mode is set to CMYK by selecting [Image] - [Mode] - [CMYK Color], the axis for the curve will be reversed from that of an RGB image. The axis for an RGB image starts with shadows at the bottom-left corner, while the axis for a CMYK image starts with the highlights.

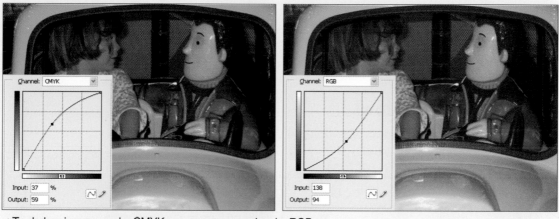

▲To darken images, make CMYK curves convex and make RGB curves concave.

Sharpening Images

Shaping the curve into an S-shape will create a sharp and focused image.

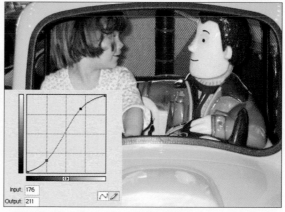

▲Original Image

▲Shaping the Curve to an S-shape

Correcting Brightness

A concave curve will brighten the image, while a convex curve will darken the image.

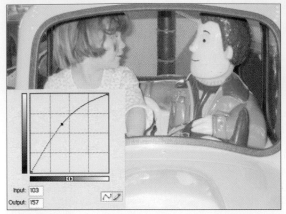

▲Brightened

▲Darkened

Highlights and Shadows

Adjusting highlights and shadows changes the image colors dramatically.

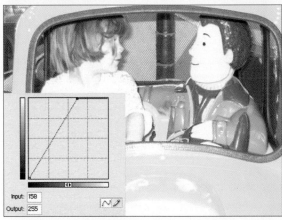

▲Increasing the Highlights

▲Increasing the Shadows

<< tip

Drawing Graph Lines

Click the pencil button ([✎]) and use it to draw directly on the graph. The smooth button ([∿]) can be used to connect disconnected curves and soften the line.

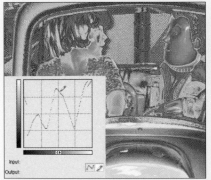

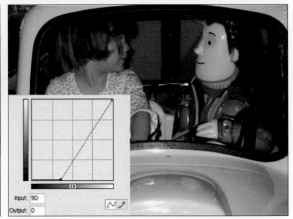

▲Using the Pencil Button

▲Using the Smooth Button

The Color Balance Command

Color Balance ([Ctrl]-[B]) is used to adjust the balance between complementary colors in an image. Adjust the color by selecting Shadow, Midtones, or Highlight and drag the sliders.

▲Original Image

▲Adjusted Image

The Color Balance Dialog Box

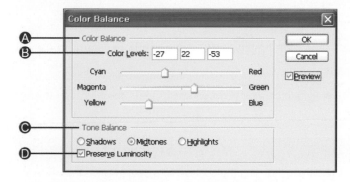

Ⓐ **Color Balance**: Each of the sliders represents two complementary colors. Adjustments to the slider add one color and subtract the other from an image.

Ⓑ **Color Levels**: Another way of adjusting the sliders is to enter the slider values in the Color Levels field.

Ⓒ **Tone Balance**: Choose to make adjustments to the shadows, midtones, or highlights.

Ⓓ **Preserve Luminosity**: The color is adjusted while maintaining luminosity.

<< tip

Using the Color Balance Command

The Color Balance command cannot be used to adjust large areas of white or black. You have to first adjust the image's luminosity to change these areas to gray before adding color.

The Brightness/Contrast Command

The Brightness/Contrast command allows you to adjust the brightness and contrast of an image. Changes made will affect the whole image.

▲Original Image

▲After Adjusting the Brightness

The Brightness/Contrast Dialog Box

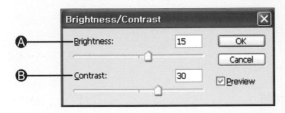

Ⓐ **Brightness**: Moving the Brightness slider to the right brightens the image, while moving it to the left darkens the image.

Ⓑ **Contrast**: Moving the Contrast slider to the right increases pixel contrast, while moving it to the left lessens the contrast.

<< tip

Sharpening an Image

Sharpen an image by adjusting the brightness and then changing the contrast to a setting twice the value of the brightness setting.

The Hue/Saturation Command

The Hue/Saturation command ([Ctrl]-[U]) is used to adjust an image's color, saturation, and brightness. You can also use the colorize option in the Hue/Saturation dialog box to create a monotone effect.

▲Original Image

▲After Changing the Image Color

The Hue/Saturation Dialog Box

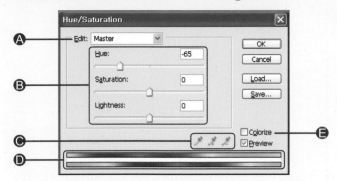

A **Edit**: Choose Master to edit the entire image, or select one of the colors to edit only that color.

B **Hue/Saturation/Lightness**: Hue changes the color. Saturation increases the amount of color as the slider is moved to the right. Lightness increases the lightness of the color as the slider is moved to the right.

C **Eyedroppers**: The Eyedropper ( ) can be used to select the color that will be modified. The +Eyedropper ( ) expands the color area and -Eyedropper ( ) reduces the color area. These cannot be used when using the Master Edit setting.

D **Color Bar**: The top color bar represents the color before adjustment, while the bottom color bar reflects the corresponding new color. For example, in the Hue/Saturation dialog box shown here, the pink hues in the image have been replaced by blue hues.

E **Colorize**: Colors or tones an image.

<< note

Creating Black-and-White Images

There are two ways of creating black-and-white images. You can set the saturation value to -100 in the Hue/Saturation dialog box or use the Desaturate command ([Shift]-[Ctrl]-[U]) to remove color from an image.

The Match Color Command

The Match Color command applies the color from a source image to another image to alter its color, lighting, and tone. This command is often used to create environmental or artistic effects.

▲Original File

▲Source File

▲Applying the Match Color Command

The Match Color Dialog Box

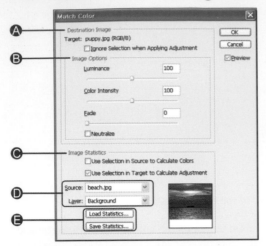

Ⓐ Destination Image: The image to be altered by the Match Color effect is indicated here.

Ignore Selection when Applying Adjustment: When checked, any selections are ignored and the entire target image is modified by the effect.

Ⓑ Image Options

Luminance, Color Intensity, and Fade can be adjusted to alter the final effect. If the target image has a color tint (for example, when the entire image appears reddish), checking the Neutralize box will automatically remove the tint from the image.

Ⓒ Image Statistics

Use selection in Source to Calculate Colors: When checked, the colors are calculated from the source image.

Use selection in Target to Calculate Adjustments: When checked, the colors are calculated from the target image.

Ⓓ Source/Layer: Choose the source image or a layer from the source image on which to base the modification of the target image.

Ⓔ Load Statistics/Save Statistics: Click Save Statistics to save your settings, or click Load Statistics to load a saved settings file.

The Replace Color Command

The Replace Color command allows colors within images to be replaced with other colors.

▲Original Image

▲Replacing the Tree Color

The Replace Color Dialog Box

In the Replace Color dialog box, the color to be changed can be selected by clicking the Eyedropper tool (⌧) on the image or preview window. The Fuzziness setting can be used to expand or reduce the selected colors. In the preview window, white areas represent selected areas and the black areas represent unselected areas. The replacement color can be selected and displayed by adjusting the Hue, Saturation, and Lightness sliders.

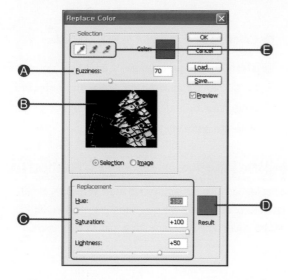

Ⓐ **Fuzziness**: Use the slider bar to increase or decrease the selected colors.

Ⓑ **Preview Window**: Preview the selection. The selection is shown in white if the Selection option is chosen.

Ⓒ **Replacement**: Used to adjust the Hue, Saturation, and Lightness of the selected area.

Ⓓ **Result Window**: Shows the replacement color.

Ⓔ **Eyedropper Tool**: Used to select color from the image. The +Eyedropper (⌧) adds to the selection and the -Eyedropper (⌧) reduces the selection.

The Selective Color Command

The Selective Color command allows a specific color to be changed by altering the cyan, magenta, yellow, and black composition of the color.

▲Original Image

▲Lowering the Amount of Magenta in the Red Channel

The Selective Color Dialog Box

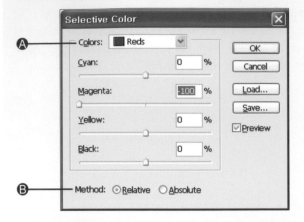

Ⓐ **Colors**: Select the color to be modified.

Ⓑ **Method**: The percentage of a CMYK color to be added or subtracted from the selected color can be calculated relatively or as an absolute percentage.

<< tip

About the Relative and Absolute Methods

For the sake of this explanation, let's assume that a selected color contains 50% cyan and the Cyan slider is set to 10%. When the method is set to Relative, this means that 10% *of 50%* cyan will be added (which is equal to 5% cyan). When the method is set to Absolute, 10% cyan will be added to 50% cyan – for a total of 60% cyan.

The Channel Mixer

The Channel Mixer allows you to adjust the red, green, and blue values in an image.

▲Original Image

▲After Increasing the Amount of Red in the Image

The Channel Mixer Dialog Box

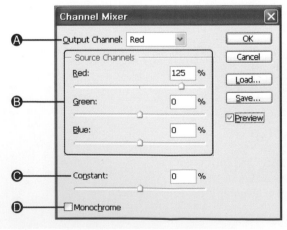

Ⓐ **Output Channel**: Selects the color channel to adjust - red, green, or blue.

Ⓑ **Source Channels**: Adjusts the amount of red, green, and blue in the selected output channel.

Ⓒ **Constant**: Adjusts the contrast for the selected channel.

Ⓓ **Monochrome**: When checked, the image will be changed to grayscale and each channel can be adjusted to create a black-and-white image.

The Gradient Map Command

The Gradient Map command applies a gradient to an image in relation to the image's original tonal range.

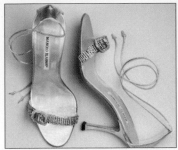

▲Original Image   ▲After Applying a Yellow-to-Blue Gradient

The Gradient Map Dialog Box

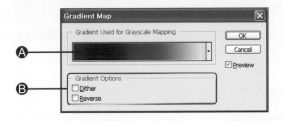

<< tip

Using Gradient Maps

Images with gradient maps applied look natural when the gradient has darker colors on the left and lighter colors on the right.

Ⓐ **Gradient Used for Grayscale Mapping**: The bar shows the gradient color; click the triangular button to show the Gradient Picker. When the bar is clicked, the Gradient Editor dialog box will appear.

Ⓑ **Gradient Options**: Dither smoothes out disconnected color. Reverse will apply the gradient mapping in reverse.

The Photo Filter Command

The Photo Filter command allows you to create effects similar to those achieved by attaching filters to a real-world camera. Many lighting and environmental effects can be achieved with this technique.

▲Original Image   ▲Applying Photo Filter

The Photo Filter Dialog Box

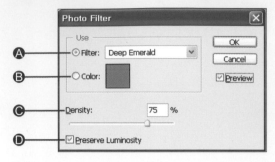

Ⓐ **Filter**: Choose a warming or cooling filter to adjust white balance. To remove a color tint, choose a filter in a complementary color. To create an underwater effect, choose the Underwater filter to add a greenish-blue tint.

Ⓑ **Color**: Lets you specify your own color filter.

Ⓒ **Density**: Adjusts the amount of color applied to the image.

Ⓓ **Preserve Luminosity**: Maintains the image's tonal range. If this option is not selected, applying a photo filter can darken an image.

The Shadow/Highlight Command

The Shadow/Highlight command is used to correct under- or overexposed images while maintaining the overall tonal balance. Click on [Show More Options] to expand the Shadow/Highlight dialog box and adjust the shadows/highlights in greater detail.

▲Original Image

▲After the Shadow/Highlight Adjustment

174

The Shadow/Highlight Dialog Box

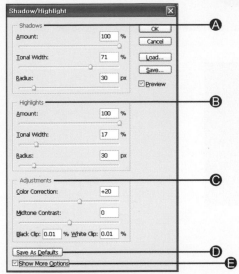

▲Expanded Shadow/Highlight Dialog Box

Ⓐ **Shadows**: Adjusts the dark areas in an image.

Amount: To lighten shadows, set a higher Amount value.

Tonal Width: To apply the adjustments to more shadows, use a higher tonal width.

Radius: The Radius slider determines the number of adjacent pixels that will be used when determining whether a pixel is a shadow. A large radius means that a large group of pixels will be used, applying the adjustments to a larger area.

Ⓑ **Highlights**: Adjusts the bright areas in an image.

Amount: To darken highlights, set a higher Amount value.

Tonal Width: To apply the adjustments to more highlights, use a higher tonal width.

Radius: The Radius slider determines the number of adjacent pixels that will be used when determining whether a pixel is a highlight. A large radius means that a large group of pixels will be used, applying the adjustments to a larger area.

Ⓒ **Adjustments**: Adjusts other settings.

Color Correction: Adjusts the vividness of the colors that have been changed. Increasing the Color Correction value increases vividness.

Midtone Contrast: A higher Midtone Contrast value increases the contrast in the midtones.

Black Clip/White Clip: Sets the amount of shadows or highlights that will be set to pure black or white.

Ⓓ **Save As Defaults**: Saves the current settings as the default for future uses of the Shadow/Highlight command.

Ⓔ **Show More Options**: Check to expand the Shadow/Highlight dialog box. (The dialog box is shown in expanded form above.)

The Invert Command

The Invert command inverts an image's luminosity so that black areas become white and white areas become black. Colors are inverted to their complementary color.

▲Original Image

▲Inverted Image

The Equalize Command

The Equalize command is used to even out image tones. It is particularly useful for correcting overly dark or overly bright scanned images. The darkest areas are recognized as black and the brightest areas are recognized as white. The pixels between (the midtones), are equalized accordingly. This command is used on images with high contrast.

▲Original Image

▲Equalized Image

The Threshold Command

The Threshold command turns images into high contrast black-and-white images. The luminance value of each pixel is displayed in a histogram. Values higher than 128 (the midpoint), are shown as white, and values lower than 128 are shown as black. The slider can be adjusted to change the midpoint.

▲Original Image

▲After Applying a Threshold Level of 128

<< note

Setting the Threshold Level

Setting the Threshold level to 128 is the same as setting the Threshold to 50% in the [Image] - [Mode] - [Bitmap] dialog box. Unlike the Threshold dialog box, it is not possible to adjust the midpoint in the Bitmap dialog box.

Original Image ▶

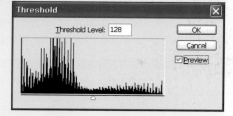

The Posterize Command

The Posterize command simplifies and bands the colors in an image. It can be used to create images with strong colors. Levels set to a value lower than five give the most dramatic poster effect.

▲Original Image

▲After Setting Levels to 2 in the Posterize Dialog Box

▲The Posterize Dialog Box

177

The Variations command allows you to make color adjustments while comparing the effect of the changes on the image.

▲Original Image

▲After Adjusting the Overall Image Color

The Variations Dialog Box

Color is corrected by clicking on one of the six color variation thumbnails. The two thumbnails on the right are used to adjust luminosity. The impact of the correction is altered according to the Fine/Coarse slider.

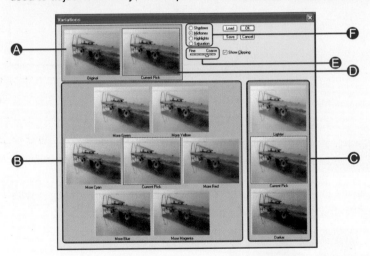

Ⓐ **Original**: Shows the original image. When clicked, all three Current Pick thumbnails will be reset to show the original image.

Ⓑ **Color Adjustment Window**: Color is added every time a thumbnails is clicked.

Ⓒ **Luminosity Adjustment Window**: Luminosity is adjusted when either Lighter or Darker is clicked.

Ⓓ **Current Pick**: Shows the adjusted image.

Ⓔ **Fine/Coarse**: Moving the slider bar towards Fine applies small color adjustments, and moving the slider bar towards Coarse applies larger color adjustments.

Ⓕ **Shadows, Midtones, Highlights, Saturation**: Used to determine where the color adjustments will be made.

Brightening Dark Images

Original Image

Final Image

Project File
- rose.jpg

Final File
- rose_end.psd

Features Used
- Curves, Gaussian Blur, Screen Mode

It is common to adjust dark photographs taken on cloudy days or in poorly lit circumstances. In this example, you will look at brightening underexposed pictures. You could use the Auto Levels command to correct the overall image, but applying the Curves command lets you make more detailed adjustments.

<< **note**

Resource Files

Remember to copy the resource files on the CD-ROM to your hard drive before you start each exercise in this book.

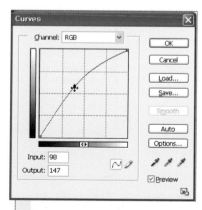

1 Open \Sample\Chapter7\rose.jpg. Choose [Image] - [Adjustments] - [Curves]. Click on the center of the curve and drag it up so that the curve balloons out towards the top left, as shown. As you drag the curve, the Input and Output levels will change. Drag until the Input is set to 98 and the Output to 147. You can also enter these values manually. Click OK.

2 Select [Layer] - [Duplicate Layer] to create the Background copy layer. Choose [Filter] - [Blur] - [Gaussian Blur], set the Radius to 3, and click OK. The image is blurred but appears softer than before.

3 Set the blend mode of the Background copy layer to Screen and change the Opacity to 90%.

4 The Screen mode overlaps the Background copy and Background layers and creates a brighter image.

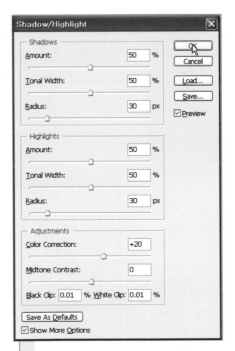

5 Select [Image] - [Adjustments] - [Shadow /Highlight]. Click the [Show More Options] box to reveal additional options.

6 In the Shadow/Highlight dialog box, set the Amount value of both Shadows and Highlights to 50% and click OK. The final image is shown on the previous page.

2 Correcting Overexposed Pictures

Original Image

Final Image

Project File
- Cable.jpg

Final File
- Cable_end.jpg

Features Used
- Healing Brush, Selective Color, Duplicate Layer, Multiply, Merge Down, Auto Color

In this example, you will correct an overexposed image by using the Multiply blend mode and adding color.

1 Open \Sample\Chapter7\Cable.jpg. This image is too bright and includes a person in the foreground. Select the Zoom tool (🔍) from the toolbox and zoom in on this area of the image.

2 Select the Healing Brush tool (![pen]). Hold down the [Alt] key and click the grass to create the source. Drag the tool to remove the person from the picture.

3 Drag the Background layer onto the [Create a new layer] button (![icon]) in the Layers palette to create a Background copy layer. Set the blend mode of the Background copy layer to Multiply and set the Opacity to 70%. This will darken the image.

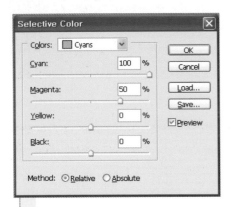

4 Choose [Image] - [Adjustments] - [Selective Color] and, under Colors, select Green. Set both the Cyan and Magenta sliders to 100%. Under Colors, select Cyans and set the Cyan slider to 100% and Magenta to 50%. Click OK.

5 By adding green and cyan to the image, the colors appear more vibrant.

6 Choose [Image] - [Adjustments] - [Auto Color] to automatically adjust the colors in the image. The final image is shown.

3 Changing Image Composition and Correcting a Faded Image

Original Image

Final Image

Project File
• smell.jpg

Final File
• smell_end.jpg

Features Used
• Crop Tool, Levels, Auto Color, Unsharp Mask, Blur Tool

In this example, the original image has too much space on the right, so you will use the Crop tool to change the composition of the picture. You will also sharpen the image.

[1] Open \Sample\Chapter7\smell.jpg and select the Crop tool ( ) from the toolbox. In the options bar, select Front Image to use the size and resolution of the current image. This will preserve the image size and resolution regardless of how the image is cropped.

<< **note**
Resource Files

Remember to copy the resource files on the CD-ROM to your hard drive before you start each exercise in this book.

2 Drag the Crop tool (▢) to select the area to be trimmed as shown here. Double-click inside this area or press [Enter] to crop the image.

3 The person will now appear in the center of the image.

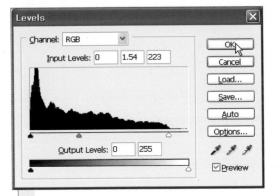

4 The image is too dark and must be adjusted with the Levels command. Choose [Image] - [Adjustments] - [Levels] and enter 0, 1.54, and 223 for the Input Levels. You can also adjust the sliders to these values. Click OK.

<< note

Altering the Image Size

In the Image Size dialog box, the cropped image has the same dimensions as the image in step 1. The Width is 7, the Height 5, and the Resolution 200. You can change the image size or resolution by checking Resample Image and entering new settings.

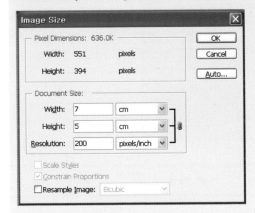

You can open the Image Size dialog box by selecting [Image] - [Image Size] from the main menu.

5 You will emphasize the image border while preserving the image tone. Choose [Filter] - [Sharpen] - [Unsharp Mask], set the Amount to 50, the Radius to 1, the Threshold to 0, and click OK.

6 In the Navigator palette, move the slider to the right to set the image magnification to 200%.

7 Select the Blur tool ( ) from the toolbox and drag it over the skin to equalize the skin tone.

Adding Color to Black-and-White Pictures

Original Image

Final Image

Project File
- Gray.jpg

Final File
- Gray_end.psd

Features Used
- Image Mode, Gradient Map, Color Blend Mode, Copy Merged, Radial Blur, Paste, Overlay Blend Mode

In this example, you will learn how to map color onto a black-and-white image. While it's easy to change color pictures to black-and-white using the [Image] - [Adjustment] - [Desaturate] command, it is more difficult to add color to black-and-white pictures. When adding color, it is important to preserve the luminosity of an image, and a brush should be used with the mode set to Color in the Brush options bar.

<< **note**

Resource Files

Remember to copy the resource files on the CD-ROM to your hard drive before you start each exercise in this book.

Drag

1 Open \Sample\Chapter7\Gray.jpg. In the Layers palette, drag-and-drop the Background layer onto the [Create a new layer] button (⬜) to create the Background copy layer.

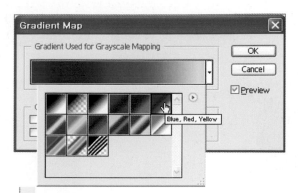

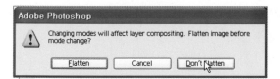

2 In order to add color, you must change the image mode from Grayscale to RGB. Select [Image] - [Mode] - [RGB Color]. When the warning message appears, click Don't Flatten. This will prevent the layers from merging into one.

3 Select [Image] - [Adjustments] - [Gradient Map] and click the right arrow to bring up the Gradient Picker. Double-click the Blue, Red, Yellow gradient and click OK.

4 Set the layer blend mode to Color in the Layers palette so that luminosity disappears, leaving the color behind.

5 Choose [Select] - [All] to select the entire image and select [Edit] - [Copy Merged] to save the image to the clipboard.

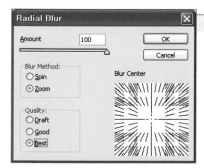

6 Select the Background layer and choose [Filter] - [Blur] - [Radial Blur]. Set the Blur Method to Zoom, the Quality to Best, the Amount to 100, and click OK.

7 The Radial Blur filter has been applied to the Background layer.

8 Apply the same Radial Blur filter to the Background copy layer by selecting the Background copy layer and pressing [Ctrl]-[F].

9 Select [Edit] - [Paste] to paste the image saved on the clipboard. Set the layer blend mode to Overlay and the Opacity to 70%.

10 Color is mapped onto the black and white image and motion has been added. The final image is shown above.

Exercise 5

Adding TV Scan Lines to an Image

Original Image

Final Image

Project File
- Line.jpg

Final File
- Line_end.psd

Features Used
- Gaussian Blur, Blend Mode, Brightness/Contrast, Halftone Pattern

Adding scan lines to an image makes it look modern and edgy. Although you could create a pattern for the scan lines, in this exercise you will use the Halftone Pattern filter.

<< note
Resource Files
Remember to copy the resource files on the CD-ROM to your hard drive before you start each exercise in this book.

<< note
Useful Techniques
You will use the Gaussian Blur filter to clean up the original image. You will also sharpen the image by adjusting the brightness and contrast.

Correcting the Original Image

1 Open \Sample\Chapter7\Line.jpg. In the Layers palette, drag-and-drop the Background layer onto the [Create a new layer] button (⬜) to create the Background copy layer.

2 Choose [Filter] - [Blur] - [Gaussian Blur], set the Radius to 3, and click OK. Applying the blur cleans up the image and creates reflective highlights.

3 In the Layers palette, set the layer blend mode to Screen. Black areas of the layer will be ignored and only the light colors displayed.

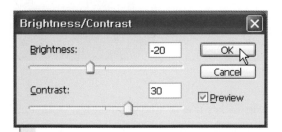

4 Choose [Image] - [Adjustments] - [Brightness/Contrast], set the Brightness to -20 and the Contrast to 30, and click OK. This will reduce the brightness of the image.

5 The image is now brighter and more luminous.

Add Scan Lines

<< note
Scan-Line Techniques

You will use the Halftone Pattern filter to create the scan lines, and adjust the opacity to create clear, horizontal lines on the image.

1 In the Layers palette, click on the [Create a new layer] button (⬜) to create Layer 1. Set the background color to white and press [Ctrl]-[Delete] to fill the layer with the background color.

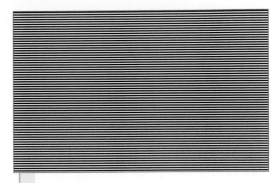

2 Before applying the Halftone Pattern filter, set the foreground color to black. This is necessary because the pattern will be made using the foreground color. Choose [Filter] - [Sketch] - [Halftone Pattern], set the Size to 1, the Contrast to 50, the Pattern Type to Line, and click OK.

3 This will create horizontal lines on the image.

4 In the Layers palette, set the blend mode to Screen and the Opacity to 30% so that the lines are semi-transparent.

5 The completed image is shown above.

Chapter | 8

Working with Layers

Layers allow you to separate an image so that you can work on a section independently without affecting other parts. You can also use layers to apply effects without changing the original image. Because the layers feature is found in most image editing programs, understanding how layers work in Photoshop allows you to pick up other similar software more readily.

What Is a Layer?

A layer is like a piece of transparent film containing an image. By stacking layers, you can create a complex final image while maintaining a separate "work space" for each part of that image. Your options in Photoshop CS will be limited if you don't separate your graphics into individual layers, so it's crucial that you learn to use them effectively.

Layer Basics

Most of the options for working with layers are found in the Layers palette (it is more convenient to work with the Layers palette than the Layer menu). You can select a layer by clicking it in the Layers palette. The modifications that you make will apply only to the selected layer. You can also move a layer to another position among the layers by clicking and dragging the layer in the palette.

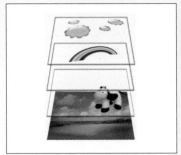 

▲Layers in the Layers palette overlap in the image window to create a single image.

Layers have properties such as opacity and blend mode that can be manipulated when creating or modifying an image. An image can have up to 1,000 layers, each with different blend modes and opacities. (The maximum number of layers may be reduced depending on the memory capacity of your computer.)

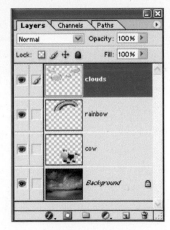

Selecting a Layer in the Layers Palette ▶

The Background Layer

At the bottom of the Layers palette is the Background layer, which works a little differently from other layers. Here are the differences between the Background layer and a regular layer:

• A Background layer cannot be moved to another position among the layers; a Background layer has to remain at the bottom of the Layers palette.

194

- The blend mode and opacity of a Background layer cannot be changed.
- Even when all the images on a Background layer are deleted, the Background layer will appear in white or in the background color—not transparent.

<< tip

Turning a Background Layer into a Normal Layer

You can change a Background layer into a normal layer by double-clicking its preview graphic and changing its name. You are not required to have a Background layer; remove the Background layer if you wish to avoid its limitations.

Flattening Layers

When an image is flattened, all layers are merged into the Background layer. As there are restrictions on the editing that can be done to the Background layer, merging to this layer should be the last step in creating your image. You can select the Flatten command from either the Layer menu or the Layers palette pop-up menu.

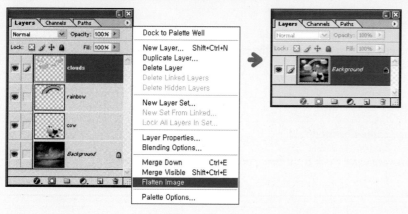

The Layers Palette

Using the Layers palette, you can create fill- or adjustment layers to make corrections to underlying layers without changing the original image. You can also group similar layers together into layer sets. Other advanced layer features include the creation of text layers, applying layer styles, working with clipping groups, and creating layer masks.

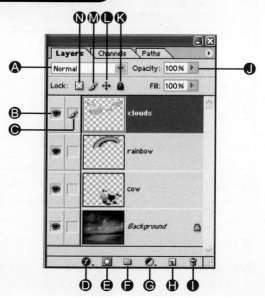

A **Blend Mode**: Determines how the image on this layer will be blended in the regions where layers overlap.

B **Eye Icon**: Indicates layer visibility–click the icon to show/hide the corresponding layer.

C **Status Icon**: The icon that appears in this box indicates the status of the layer. The brush (▨) indicates that the layer is selected and you can edit the layer as normal. A chain (▨) indicates a linked layer and a circle in a square (▨) indicates a layer mask.

D **Add a Layer Style Button**: Adds an effect to the layer.

E **Add Layer Mask Button**: Applies a mask to the layer.

F **Create a New Set Button**: Organizes layers into folders.

G **Create New Fill or Adjustment Layer Button**: Creates an adjustment layer for the image.

H **Create a New Layer Button**: Creates a new layer. You can create a copy of an existing layer by dragging and dropping it onto this button.

I **Delete Layer Button**: Deletes the selected layer.

J **Opacity**: Determines the opacity (i.e., transparency) of the layer.

K **Lock All**: The image cannot be moved or modified.

L **Lock Position**: The image cannot be moved.

M **Lock Image Pixels**: The image cannot be modified.

N **Lock Transparent Pixels**: Prevents any work from being done on transparent regions.

The Layers Palette Pop-Up Menu

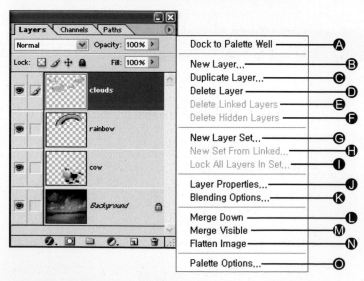

A **Dock to Palette Well**: Places the palette at the top-right corner of the workspace.

B **New Layer**: Creates a new layer.

196

C **Duplicate Layer**: Duplicates the selected layer.

D **Delete Layer**: Deletes the selected layer.

E **Delete Linked Layers**: Deletes linked layers. This option is only available when there are linked layers.

F **Delete Hidden Layers**: Deletes hidden layers. This option is only available when there are hidden layers.

G **New Layer Set**: Creates a new layer set.

H **New Set From Linked**: Places the selected layer and all linked layers inside a layer set. This option is only available when there are linked layers.

I **Lock All Layers in Set**: Locks all layers inside the layer set. This option is only available when there is a layer set.

J **Layer Properties**: Select to set the layer name and color.

K **Blending Options**: Select to set the layer blending options.

L **Merge Down**: Combines the selected layer with the layer beneath it.

M **Merge Visible**: Combines all visible layers into a single layer.

N **Flatten Image**: Combines all layers (hidden layers remain unchanged).

O **Palette Options**: Select to set the options for the Layers palette.

The Layer Menu

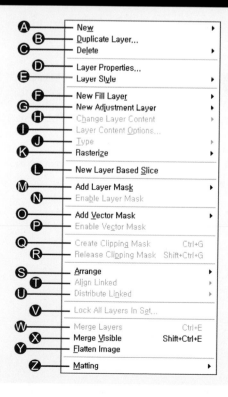

A **New**: Creates a new layer.

B **Duplicate Layer**: Duplicates the layer.

C **Delete**: Deletes the layer.

D **Layer Properties**: Used to edit the layer name and color.

E **Layer Style**: Used to configure and edit the Layer Style effect.

F **New Fill Layer**: Creates a new layer filled with color.

G **New Adjustment Layer**: Creates a new adjustment layer.

H **Change Layer Content**: Changes the layer content to a different adjustment layer.

I **Layer Content Options**: Used to modify an adjustment layer.

J **Type**: Contains options for changing text layers into paths or vector shapes, changing text direction, and distorting text.

K **Rasterize**: Changes vector images into bitmap images.

L **New Layer Based Slice**: The image is sliced according to the selected layer.

M **Add/Remove Layer Mask**: Creates or deletes a layer mask.

N **Enable/Disable Layer Mask**: Select Disable Layer Mask to deactivate a layer mask without deleting it. Select Enable Layer Mask to apply a layer mask that has been disabled.

O **Add/Delete Vector Mask**: Creates or removes a vector mask. A vector mask is drawn using the pen or shape tools.

P **Enable/Disable Vector Mask**: Select Disable Vector Mask to deactivate a vector mask without deleting it. Select Enable Vector Mask to apply a vector mask that has been disabled.

Q **Create Clipping Mask from Linked**: Creates a clipping mask from a linked layer.

R **Release Clipping Mask**: Reverts the clipping mask to a normal layer.

S **Arrange**: Used to determine the layer order.

T **Align Linked**: Aligns linked layers.

U **Distribute Linked**: Used to adjust the spacing between linked layers.

V **Lock All Linked Layers**: Locks all linked layers. Choose to lock Transparency, Image, Position, or All.

W **Merge Linked**: Merges all linked layers.

X **Merge Visible**: Combines all visible layers (hidden layers remain unchanged).

Y **Flatten Image**: Combines all layers into a single background layer.

Z **Matting**: Softens layer image edges to assist blending with other layers.

Layer Sets

Layer sets allow you to group layers into a folder so that you can organize them more efficiently. The steps for using layer sets are as follows.

1. Choose [Layer] - [New] - [Layer Set] or click on the [Create a new set] button (⬜) in the Layers palette to open the New Layer Set dialog box. Enter a name for the layer set and click OK.

2. Drag-and-drop layers into the layer set folder icon (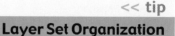) to put the layers into the layer set.

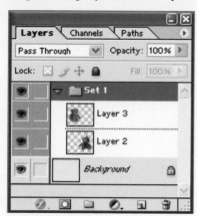

<< tip

Layer Set Organization

In order to manage several layer sets without confusion, it's a good idea to assign a unique color and name to each set.

Adjustment Layers

When you edit an image layer, the image changes permanently (unless you use the Undo command, which may not always be possible). On the other hand, if you use an adjustment layer to apply the same corrections, the changes will be stored on a separate layer without making a permanent change to the underlying image. By using this technique, you can exert far greater control over the adjustments you make, because you can always tweak your adjustment layer without "damaging" the original graphic. You can create a new adjustment layer by using the [Layer] - [New Adjustment Layer] menu selection or holding down the [Create new fill or adjustment layer] button in the Layers palette.

▲Original Image

Adding a Hue/Saturation ▶
Adjustment Layer

▲Image after the Adjustment
Layer is Finished

▲An Adjustment Layer

<< tip

Fill Layers

A fill layer is an adjustment layer that lets you add a solid color, gradient, or pattern on a separate layer.

Shape and Text Layers

Shape and text layers are different from other types of layers in that they are vector-based layers. Shapes and text are made up of paths, allowing the size of the shape or text to be changed without affecting the image quality. The Rasterize command can be used to convert shape and text layers into bitmap layers (i.e., pixel-based).

▲Adding Shape Layers

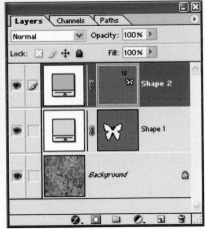

▲Shape Layers in the Layers Palette

Layer Masks

Layer masks are used to cover up part of an image within a layer. The white areas of a mask are transparent and allow that part of the image to be shown. The black parts of the mask are completely opaque and hide that part of the image. Shades of grey in between represent different levels of transparency.

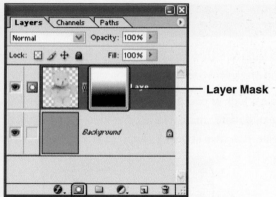

Layer Mask

▲Applying this layer mask hides the lower part of the image.

▲Black masks hide images completely, whereas white masks allow the image to show through.

<< tip

Removing a Layer Mask

You can remove a layer mask by dragging it to the [Delete layer] icon in the Layers palette (the trash can). You will be asked whether you wish to apply, cancel, or discard the mask. You can temporarily hide a layer mask by holding down the [Shift] key and clicking on the mask in the Layers palette. The mask will display a red cross.

Clipping Masks

Clipping masks are used to fill an image on a lower layer with an image on a higher layer. To create a clipping mask, click the space between the layers while holding down the [Alt] key. The mouse pointer will turn into two connected circles. You can apply this to several layers at a time. When a clipping mask has been created, the bottom layer of the mask will appear to the left in the Layers palette, while layers above will be indented.

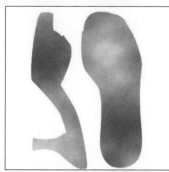

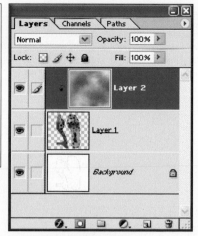

▲Applying a Clipping Mask to the Image

▲A Clipping Mask Layer

Layer styles are used to apply effects such as shadows, strokes, or bevels without changing the original image. You can apply more than one layer style to a layer. You can also create and reuse your own custom layer styles.

In this section, let's have a look at each of the different layer styles–such as bevels, glass, and textures–that can be applied to the text, buttons, images, and other elements of a layer. You can apply preset styles using the Styles palette or create your own styles by using the Layer Styles palette.

▲A text layer with no effects applied (left) and the corresponding Layers palette (right).

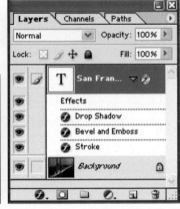

▲After Applying Layer Styles to the Text

▲The Layers palette shows the layer styles or effects that were applied to the text layer. These can be "turned off" to revert to the original text layer. They can also be changed at any time.

The Styles Palette

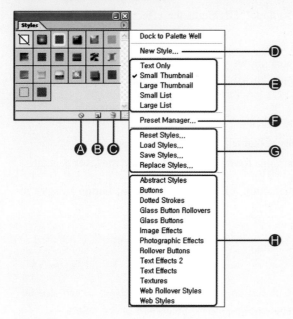

A **Clear Style Button**: This button can be used to remove a layer style.

B **Create New Style Button**: This button creates a new style based on the currently applied style.

C **Delete Style**: Deletes/removes the style.

D **New Style**: Creates a new layer style.

E **Style Display Options**: Shows the styles as thumbnails or as a list.

F **Preset Manager**: A Photoshop feature used to organize preset brushes or palettes.

G **Style Activation Options**: Choose from Reset Styles, Load Styles (from internal library), Save Styles (to internal library), or Replace Styles.

H **Preset Layer Styles**: Choose from different categories of layer styles to load into the Styles palette.

The Layer Style Dialog Box

The Layer Style dialog box looks complex but is easy to use. You can apply preset styles which are found in the Styles palette, or edit styles to create your own. To apply a style, select the layer to which you want to apply an effect and then choose [Layer] - [Layer Style]. Alternatively, you can double-click the preview graphic for the desired layer in the Layers palette. Select a style and, when the preferences for that style appear, adjust the settings. Click OK to apply. To apply a preset style, click on the Styles option at the top-left corner and choose from the style presets that appear.

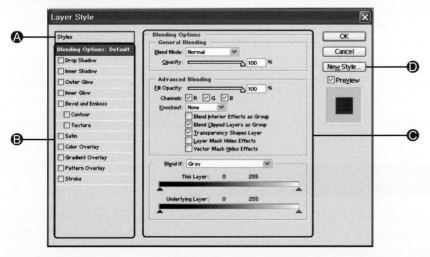

Ⓐ Styles: Click here to bring up the palette of preset styles. Select one to apply it to the layer.

Ⓑ Effects: Check the box of the effect(s) you'd like to apply. Highlight the effect name to bring up the options specific to that effect.

Ⓒ Blending Options: When no style is selected, this area allows you to adjust the blend or opacity of the layer (see below). When a layer style is selected in the left-hand menu, the options specific to that style appear here.

  • General Blending is used to adjust blend modes and opacity.
  • Advanced Blending is used to adjust the Fill Opacity, Channels, or Knockout options.
  • The slider under Blend If is used to adjust the color range for the selected layer and the layer beneath.

Ⓓ New Style: After adjusting the options to your satisfaction, click the [New Style] button to save the current layer style for future use.

Applying a Layer Style to an Object

To apply a layer style to an object, the object should be placed on its own layer. The object should also be placed on a transparent background. If not, the object and the background will be treated as one object.

▲In this example, the Hi! text and orange brush stroke are on the same layer and are treated as a single object in Photoshop. Applying a Drop Shadow layer style to the layer creates a shadow outlining all the objects on the layer.

▲Placing the Hi! text on a separate, transparent layer and then applying the Drop Shadow layer style creates a shadow only for the Hi! text. Notice how the text now appears raised from the brush stroke below.

Note: The Hi! text in the example above was drawn using the Brush tool. For text entered using the Type tool, the text will automatically be placed on a separate, transparent layer.

Setting Up Layer Styles

This section shows you the effect of each of the layer styles on an image, as well as their available options. The first layer style to be found on the left of the Layer Style dialog box is the Drop Shadow layer style. This section starts off by covering the options for the Drop Shadow layer style in detail.

Layer Style Parameter Descriptions

Because many of the layer styles have the same options, options that are already covered in one section will not be repeated in the other sections. There can be minor differences in how a given option will affect different layer styles, but these variations are usually very intuitive.

The Drop Shadow Layer Style

The Drop Shadow style adds a shadow behind the selected image. Adjustments can be made to the shadow color, opacity, angle, and length.

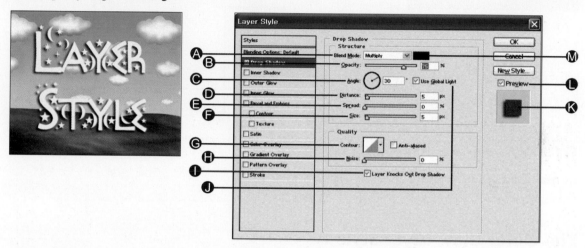

Ⓐ **Blend Mode**: Sets the shadow blending mode. The default mode is Multiply.

Ⓑ **Opacity**: Sets the shadow opacity. The default value is 75%.

Ⓒ **Angle**: Sets the shadow angle. The default value is 30°.

Ⓓ **Distance**: Sets the shadow length. The default value is 5 pixels.

Ⓔ **Spread**: Sets how far the shadow spreads. The default value is 0 pixels. A greater value creates stronger shadows.

Ⓕ **Size**: Sets the size of the shadow spread. The default value is 5 pixels. Greater values create more blurred edges.

Ⓖ **Contour**: Sets the curves for the shadow.

Ⓗ **Noise**: Sets the amount of noise in the shadow.

Ⓘ **Layer Knocks Out Drop Shadow**: Determines the shadow's visibility on a semi-transparent layer.

Ⓙ **Use Global Light**: When checked, the selected angle will apply to all the layer styles in your image (including those on other layers).

Ⓚ **Thumbnail Preview**: Shows you how the selected settings will look using a thumbnail square as an example.

Ⓛ **Preview**: Shows you how the settings will look on the actual image.

Ⓜ **Color**: Sets the color of the shadow.

The Inner Shadow Layer Style

Inner Shadow applies a shadow inside the image and can be used to create a cutout effect.

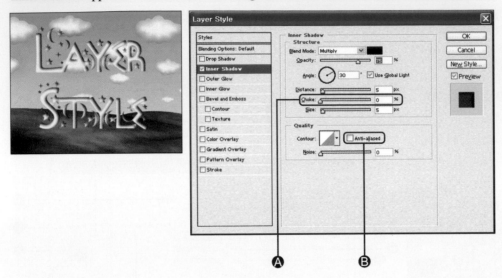

Ⓐ **Choke**: A greater value creates stronger shadows.

Ⓑ **Anti-aliased**: Smooths the edges of the contour.

The Outer Glow Layer Style

Outer Glow is used to add a reflective glow around the image.

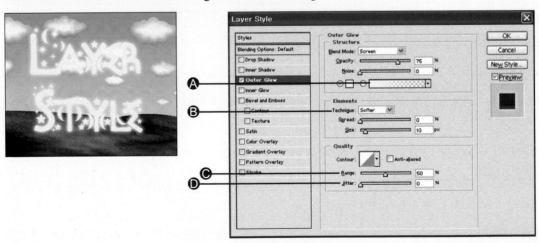

Ⓐ **Gradient**: Click to apply a preset or customized gradient to the glow.

Ⓑ **Technique**: Represents the spread of light. Softer applies soft light and Precise applies distinct light.

Ⓒ **Range**: Sets how the curves contour is applied.

Ⓓ **Jitter**: Sets the degree of jitter.

The Inner Glow Layer Style

This command applies a reflective glow inside the selected image.

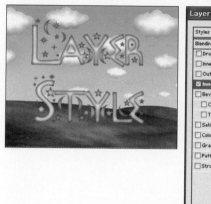
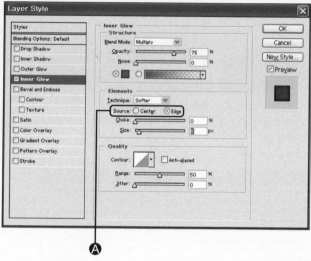

A **Source**: Represents the spread of light. Center sheds the light from the center outwards, and Edge sheds the light from the edges towards the inside.

The Bevel and Emboss Layer Style

The Bevel and Emboss layer style is used to create dimensional effects in the image. There are seven different bevel and emboss styles to choose from in the Bevel and Emboss Layer Style dialog box. Clicking on the Style drop-down menu will reveal the Outer Bevel, Inner Bevel, Emboss, Pillow Emboss, and Stroke Emboss style options. Let's have a look at each of these styles:

▲Outer Bevel: Applies an effect as if the layer is raised above the underlying image.

▲Inner Bevel: Chisels the layer inward to create a 3D effect.

▲Emboss: Creates an effect similar to applying both an outer and inner bevel.

▲Pillow Emboss: Makes the layer appear like it has been embedded in the underlying image.

▲Stroke Emboss: Applies embossing effects to the edges of the layer.

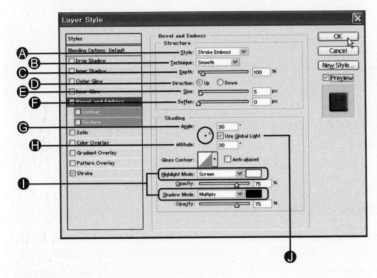

A **Style**: Sets the bevel/emboss style.

B **Technique**: Adjusts the smoothness of the bevel/emboss.

C **Depth**: Adjusts the degree of protrusion.

D **Direction**: Adjusts the direction in which the bevel/emboss protrudes. Setting this to Down reverses the direction of the highlights and shadows.

E **Size**: Sets the size of the bevel/emboss effect.

F **Soften**: Adjusts the softness of the edges.

G **Angle**: Highlights are created in the direction of the indicated angle and shadows are created automatically in the opposite direction.

H **Altitude**: Sets the height of the light.

I **Highlight and Shadow Modes**: Adjusts the blend mode, color, and opacity of the highlights and shadows.

J **Use Global Light**: When checked, the selected angle will apply to all the layer styles in your image (including those on other layers).

208

<< note

Applying the Stroke Emboss Style

To apply the Stroke Emboss effect, the Stroke layer style has to be selected together with the Bevel and Emboss style (in the left column of the Layer Style dialog box).

Additional Settings

There are two other settings for the Bevel and Emboss layer style besides the structural and shading settings which were covered in the preceding section. These two settings are the Contour and Texture settings. To access the options for these two settings, click the Contour or Texture checkbox on the left of the Bevel and Emboss Layer Style dialog box.

Contour

This setting applies additional contouring to the bevel/emboss effect.

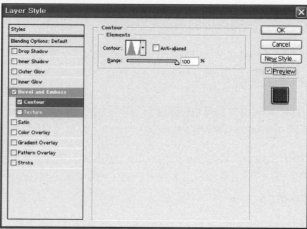

Texture

The Texture setting applies texture mapping inside the embossed image.

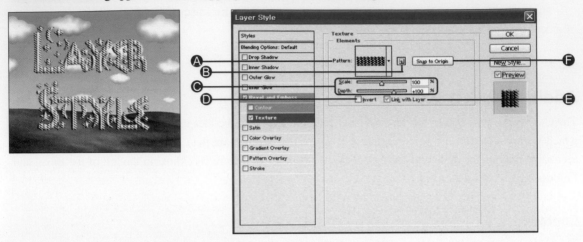

Ⓐ Pattern: Applies a preset or customized pattern to the bevel or emboss.

Ⓑ New Preset: Saves a customized pattern as a new preset pattern .

Ⓒ Scale and Depth: Adjusts the size and depth of the pattern in the texture.

Ⓓ Invert: Flips the texture.

Ⓔ Link with Layer: Specifies that the texture moves with the layer. If this option isn't selected, the texture will shift "inside" the layer when it's moved.

Ⓕ Snap to Origin: Snaps the texture's origin with the image if the Link with Layer option is not selected. If the Link with Layer option is selected, this option snaps the texture's origin with the layer's top-left corner.

The Satin Layer Style

Satin can be used to create shiny metallic effects.

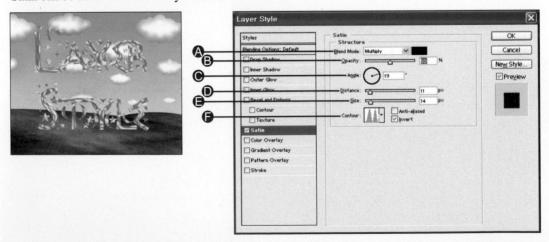

ⓐ **Blend Mode**: Select the blend mode of the shine.

ⓑ **Opacity**: Sets the opacity of the shine.

ⓒ **Angle**: Determines the angle of the shine.

ⓓ **Distance**: Modifies the distance of the shine.

ⓔ **Size**: Adjusts the size of the shine.

ⓕ **Contour**: Chooses the shape of the reflection.

The Color Overlay Layer Style

Color Overlay colors the layer using a single color.

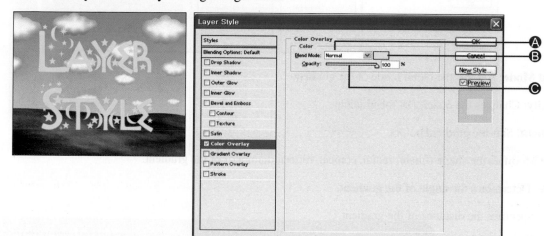

ⓐ **Blend Mode**: Sets the blend mode for the overlay.

ⓑ **Color Select**: Chooses the overlay color.

ⓒ **Opacity**: Adjusts the opacity.

Hard Light: If the color is lighter than 50% gray, this mode will make the image lighter, much like the Screen mode. If the color is darker, the image will appear darker, like applying the Multiply mode. The effect is similar to using a strong spotlight.

Vivid Light: If the color is lighter than 50% gray, the image is lightened by increasing the image brightness. The reverse happens for colors darker than 50% gray.

▲Hard Light   ▲Vivid Light

Linear Light: If the blend color is lighter than 50% gray, the image is lightened by increasing the brightness.

Hard Mix: Simplifies the color.

Pin Light: If the blend color is lighter than 50% gray, darker pixels are replaced and lighter pixels don't change. The reverse is true for colors darker than 50% gray.

▲Linear Light   ▲Hard Mix   ▲Pin Light

Difference: Subtracts either the blend color from the base color or the base from the blend color, depending on which is brighter. Blending with white inverts the color while blending with black produces no change.

Exclusion: This mode is similar to Difference, but creates a softer effect.

▲Difference   ▲Exclusion

Hue: Creates a color using the luminance and saturation of the base color, but with the hue of the blend color.

Saturation: Creates a color with the luminance and hue of the base color, and the saturation of the blend color.

▲Hue   ▲Saturation

Color: Creates a color with the luminance of the base color, and the hue and saturation of the blend color.

Luminosity: Creates a color with the hue and saturation of the base color and luminance of the blend color. This mode is the reverse of the Color mode.

▲Color   ▲Luminosity

216

Using Layer Blend Modes to Create Luminosity

Original Image

Final Image

In this example, you will learn to create a selection border from the contents of a layer. You'll also use layer blend modes to change a dark, silhouette-like image into a more colorful and luminous image.

Project File
- Princes.psd

Final File
- Princes_end.psd

Features Used
- New Layer, Feather

1 Open \Sample\Chapter8\Princes.psd. The image in this example is separated into several layers. In the Layers palette, click the [Create a new layer] button (🔲) to create Layer 1.

2 Select Layer 1. Hold down the [Ctrl] key and click the black layer to create a selection based on the contents of the layer.

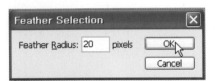

3 Choose [Select] - [Feather] from the menu bar. Set the Feather Radius to 20 pixels and click OK. This will soften the selection.

4 Set the foreground color to dark blue and press [Alt]-[Delete] to fill in the selection on Layer 1. The image should look similar to the one shown here.

5 Hold down the [Ctrl] key and click the black layer to choose the selection border again.

6 Choose [Select] - [Feather]. Set the Feather Radius to 10 pixels and click OK. The selection has been softened but not as much as the last time.

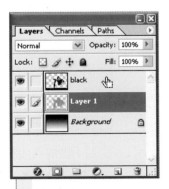

7 Set the foreground color to a lighter blue color and press [Alt]-[Delete] to fill in the selection.

8 Hold down the [Ctrl] key and click on the black layer to load the selection border again.

9 Choose [Select] - [Feather]. Set the Feather Radius to 5 pixels and click OK.

10 Set the foreground color to white and press [Alt]-[Delete] to fill in the selection.

11 Drag-and-drop Layer 1 onto the [Create a new layer] button ( ) to create Layer 1 copy.

12 Set the blend mode for Layer 1 copy to Overlay and the Opacity to 50% to create strong saturation and brightness contrasts.

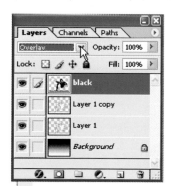

13 Select the black layer and set the layer blend mode to Overlay.

14 Repeat the same steps on the title layer. Since the title is smaller than the picture, a smaller Feather value will have to be applied. The final image is shown above.

2 Using Layer Masks to Blend Images – Example 1

Original Image

Final Image

Project File
- Lake.psd

Final File
- Lake_end.psd

Features Used
- Layer Mask, ZigZag Filter, Ripple Filter, Blend Mode

This example will help you understand how layer masks can be used to blend different parts of an image. You will also learn to use the ZigZag and Ripple filters to create ripples on the water surface.

<< note

Resource Files

Remember to copy the resource files on the CD-ROM to your hard drive before you start each exercise in this book.

1 Open \Sample\Chapter8\Lake.psd. Select the Lasso tool (⌀), set the Feather value to 5 pixels in the options bar, and use the tool to select the bottom of the lake as shown.

2 Choose [Filter] - [Distort] - [Ripple] from the menu bar. In the Ripple dialog box, set the Size to Large, the Amount to 100%, and click OK. Press [Ctrl]-[D] to deselect. This will add a ripple effect to the lake.

3 In the Layers palette, drag-and-drop the ballerina layer onto the [Create a new layer] button (🗖) to make a ballerina copy layer.

4 Choose [Edit] - [Transform] - [Flip Vertical] from the main menu to flip the ballerina copy layer. Using the Move tool (➤⊕), position the flipped image as shown here.

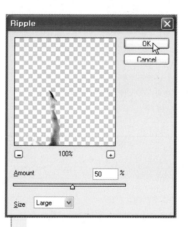

5 Choose [Filter] - [Distort] - [Ripple] from the main menu. Set the Size to Large, the Amount to 50%, and click OK.

<< tip

Reapplying a Filter

If you want to reapply a filter using the same settings as the last time you used the filter, press [Ctrl]-[F]. If you need to change the settings, press [Alt]-[Ctrl]-[F].

6 Set the layer blend mode of the ballerina copy layer to Soft Light and click the [Add a mask] button (🔲) at the bottom of the Layers palette.

7 Set the foreground color to black and the background color to white. Click the Gradient tool (▣) and select the black-to-white gradient. Use the Gradient tool (▣) to drag from top to bottom and create the gradient as shown. You may need to click on the layer mask thumbnail to activate the mask editing mode before applying the gradient. After the gradient is applied, the black areas of the gradient will be used to hide the image.

<< tip

Editing Modes

When you are in the normal editing mode, a brush icon (🖌) will be visible next to the eye icon (👁) in the Layers palette. When you are in the mask editing mode, a mask icon (▣) is visible.

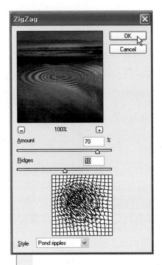

8 Click the Background layer and select the Circular Marquee tool (◯). In the options bar, set the Feather to 15 pixels, the Style to Normal, and use the tool to make a narrow oval near the foot of the image as shown.

9 Choose [Filter] - [Distort] - [ZigZag]. Set the Amount to 70%, the Ridges to 10, the Style to Pond ripples, and click OK. Press [Ctrl]-[D] to deselect the oval.

10 Select the ballerina layer. Use the Move tool (✛) to move the image to the center of the ripples.

11 In the Layers palette, click on the [Add layer mask] button (⬚) to make a layer mask for the ballerina layer.

12 Set the foreground color to black. Select the Brush tool (🖌) and set the Opacity to 50% in the options bar. Paint the toe of the image and move it so that it looks like the feet are submerged in the water. Anything painted black on the layer mask will be hidden in the image.

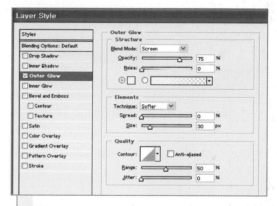

14 Under Elements, set the Size to 30 pixels and click OK.

13 In the Layers palette, click on the [Add a layer style] button (ƒ) and select Outer Glow.

15 The image is now complete.

3

Using Layer Masks to Blend Images - Example 2

Original Image   Final Image

Project File
- Season.psd

Final File
- Season_end.psd

Features Used
- Layer Mask, Layer Styles, Adjustment Layers, Color Halftone Filter, Mosaic Filter, Blend Mode

In this example, you will learn how to blend images of the four seasons using layer masks, layer styles, and adjustment layers. This example also covers the Color Halftone and Mosaic filters.

1. Open \Sample\Chapter8\Season.psd.

<< note

Resource Files

Remember to copy the resource files on the CD-ROM to your hard drive before you start each exercise in this book.

2. Select the fall layer and click the [Add a mask] button ( ) at the bottom of the Layers palette. Set the foreground color to black and the background color to white. Select the Gradient tool ( ) and select the Linear Gradient option in the options bar.

3 Drag the tool from left to right to apply the gradient. As the gradient was applied to the layer mask, the fall image will be hidden by the black areas of the gradient and will appear as the gradient moves from black to white. The image will be fully visible in the white areas of the gradient. The winter image below will appear in the masked (black) areas of the layer mask.

4 Select the summer layer and click the [Add layer mask] button (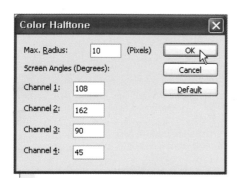) to add a layer mask.

5 Use the Gradient tool (▣) and drag from bottom to top to apply a black-and-white gradient. The summer image becomes more visible as you move from bottom to top.

Color Halftone

Max. Radius:	10	(Pixels)

Screen Angles (Degrees):

Channel 1: 108
Channel 2: 162
Channel 3: 90
Channel 4: 45

OK
Cancel
Default

6 Choose [Filter] - [Pixelate] - [Color Halftone] from the menu bar, set the Max Radius to 10 pixels, and click OK.

7 The Color Halftone filter gives an effect like a magnified shot of a printed image. However, since you applied the filter to the layer mask, the filter is used as part of the mask.

<< tip
The Color Halftone Filter

The Color Halftone filter has no effect on areas of the image that are pure black or white. It will only be applied to the gray colors in between.

8 Select the spring layer and click on the [Add layer mask] button () to add a layer mask.

9 Using the Gradient tool (■), drag from right to left to apply the gradient.

10 In order to apply the gradient to the bottom of the spring image as well, set the blend mode to Darken in the Gradient options bar before applying the gradient again.

11 Applying the gradient with the Darken blend mode will cause the dark colors to accumulate. If the blend mode had been set to Normal, the existing gradient would have been replaced by the newer gradient.

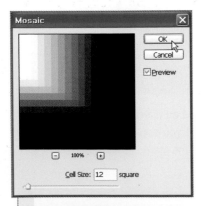

12 Choose [Filter] - [Pixelate] - [Mosaic]. Set the Cell Size to 12 squares and click OK.

13 This will apply a mosaic setting to the spring image layer mask, making a mosaic-like gradation.

14 Select the Type tool (T) from the toolbox. In the options bar, set the font to Monotype Corsiva, the font size to 150 pt, and the font color to yellow. (Select another font if you don't have the Monotype Corsiva font on your computer.) Enter the text **spring** and press [Enter].

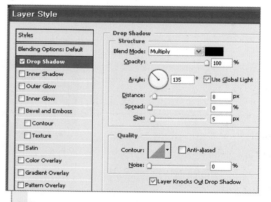

15 In the same way, enter the text **summer**, **fall**, and **winter**. Use the font size 100 and select the colors shown above.

16 Select the spring text layer, click the [Add a layer style] button ( ) and select Drop Shadow. Set the Angle to 135°, the Distance to 8 pixels, and press OK.

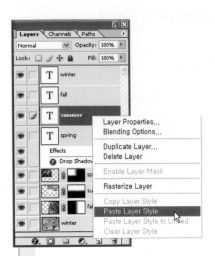

17 The Layers palette will show the (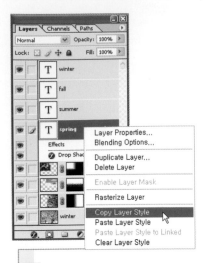) icon next to the spring text layer, indicating that a layer style has been applied. Right-click the active layer and select Copy Layer Style from the shortcut menu.

18 Select the summer text layer. Right-click the layer and choose Paste Layer Style to apply the copied layer style.

19 Check to see that the shadow effect has been applied to the summer text layer.

20 Repeat the steps above to apply a shadow effect to the fall and winter text layers.

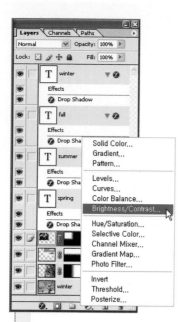

21 Let's use adjustment layers to bring the image into sharper focus. Select the spring layer, click the [Create new fill or adjustment layer] button (●) and select Brightness/Contrast. The adjustment layer will be created above the spring layer and will apply to the entire spring layer. If you need to apply an adjustment layer to a section of an image, select the desired areas before applying the adjustment layer command.

22 Set the Brightness to 10, the Contrast to 20, and click OK.

23 The background image is in sharper focus and the artwork is now complete.

4

Making a Water Droplets Image

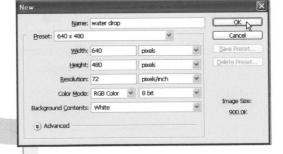

Final Image

The Feather option can be used to create a soft effect for clear images such as water droplets. In this exercise, you will learn to create a shadow by copying layers and applying transformations and filters on the copied layers. You will also learn to merge layers and apply a reverse radial gradient.

Final File
- Waterdrop_end.psd

Features Used
- Magic Wand Tool, Lasso Tool, Color Balance, Merge Layers, Reverse Radial Gradient, Feather, Transform

Making the Water Drop Outline

<< note

Resource Files

Remember to copy the resource files on the CD-ROM to your hard drive before you start each exercise in this book.

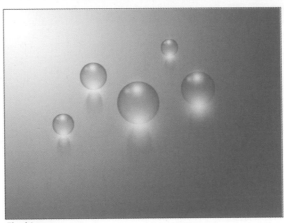

1 From the menu bar, select [File] - [New]. Choose 640 x 480 from the Preset drop-down box and set the Resolution to 72 pixels/inch. Set the Color Mode to RGB Color, the Background Contents to White, and click OK.

2 Click on the foreground color swatch (⬛) in the toolbox and set C to 100%, M to 50%, Y to 0%, and K to 0%. Click OK.

3 Click the Gradient tool (⬛). In the options bar, click [Radial Gradient] (⬛) and check the Reverse option. These options will create a circular gradient in which the gradient colors are applied in reverse. Drag the tool diagonally across the image from top-left to bottom-right to apply the gradient.

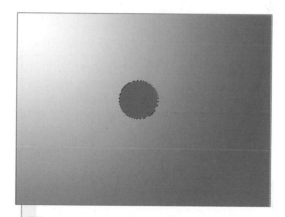

4 In the Layers palette, click the [Create a new layer] button (⬛) to create Layer 1.

5 Select the Ellipse Marquee tool (⬛) and set Feather to 0. Hold down [Alt]-[Shift] and drag from the center of the image to make a circular selection. Press [Alt]-[Delete] to fill the circle with the foreground color.

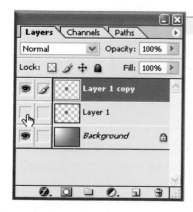

6 Drag-and-drop Layer 1 onto the [Create a new layer] button (⬛) to create Layer 1 copy. Click the eye icon (⬛) of Layer 1 to hide Layer 1. As Layer 1 copy is the same as Layer 1, you will need to hide Layer 1 while you work on Layer 1 copy.

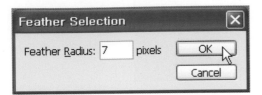

7 Choose [Select] - [Feather]. Set the Feather Radius to 7 pixels and click OK to feather the selection.

8 Press [Delete] twice to remove the color from the image. Press [Ctrl]-[D] to clear the selection. The image color has been removed.

Making the Water Drop

1 In the Layers palette, click the eye icon () of the Layer 1 copy layer to hide the image. Click Layer 1 to activate the layer. Hold down the [Ctrl] key and click Layer 1 to select the circular image.

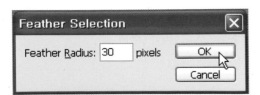

2 Choose [Select] - [Feather]. Set the Feather Radius to 30 pixels and click OK.

3 Hold down the [Shift] key and press the down arrow key twice to move the selection in two 10-pixel intervals. Press [Ctrl]-[D] to deselect.

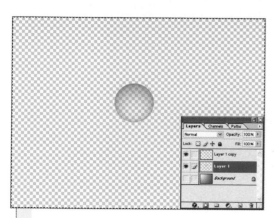

4 Unhide Layer 1 copy and hide the Background layer. You should only be able to see the Layer 1 and Layer 1 copy images. Press [Ctrl]-[A] to select the entire image and choose [Edit] - [Copy Merge] to copy the merged image to the clipboard.

Making Shadows and Highlights

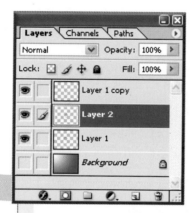

1 Select [Edit] - [Paste] to paste the image on the clipboard. Layer 2 will be created.

2 Choose [Filter] - [Blur] - [Motion Blur]. Set the Angle to 90, the Distance to 50 pixels, and click OK.

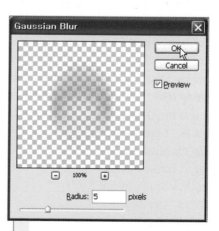

3 Choose [Filter] - [Blur] - [Gaussian Blur]. Set the Radius to 5 pixels and click OK.

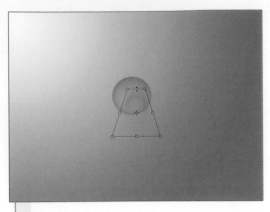

4 Unhide the Background layer. Press [Ctrl]-[T] to create a Transform bounding box. Hold down [Ctrl]-[Alt]-[Shift] and drag the handles in the upper corners to create the shape shown above.

5 Click the mouse inside the bounding box and move the image to position the shadow as shown here. Press [Enter] to apply the transformation. In the Layers palette, drag Layer 2 below Layer 1.

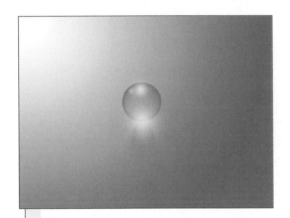

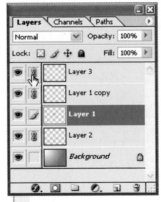

6 Click the [Create a new layer] button (⬚) to create Layer 3. Press [x] to reverse the foreground and background colors. The foreground color should now be white. Select the Brush tool (✎) from the toolbox, then set the brush size to 100 pixels and the Opacity to 70% in the options bar. Click the brush where the two images meet. Reduce the brush size to 50 pixels and click the center of the water drop to color the image. Resize the brush to 20 pixels, reduce the Opacity to 40%, and draw the highlights shown above.

7 Select Layer 1 and click the empty space beside the eye icon of all layers, excluding the Background layer. The layers will be linked. Press [Ctrl]-[E] to merge the linked layers together. As Layer 1 was selected when you merged the layers, the name of the merged layer is Layer 1.

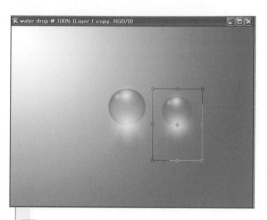

8 Hold down the [Alt] key and use the Move tool (⊹) to copy the water drop image to a new layer.

9 Press [Ctrl]-[T] to create the Transform bounding box. Click the link icon (⧉) in the options bar to set the width and height to the same proportions. Enter 80 for either W or H and press [Enter]. Hold down the [Shift] key and drag the corners of the bounding box inwards.

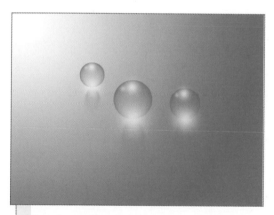

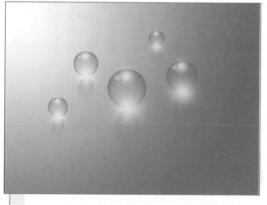

10 In the Layers palette, make another copy of Layer 1 copy called Layer 1 copy 2. Choose [Edit] - [Transform] - [Again] to apply the same Transform values and drag the water drop to a new location.

11 Repeat the step above to copy the layer and press [Shift]-[Ctrl]-[T] to make the image smaller. Repeat this step to create water droplets of different sizes and complete this exercise.

Chapter 9

Channels

The concept of channels can be a little difficult to grasp at first. In Photoshop CS, an image can have up to 56 channels. Some channels contain information about color, while others store information about selections. Channels are often used in advanced image manipulation and it is important to understand them as they can be very effective when creating special lighting and texture effects.

About Channels

Photoshop channels are similar to layers, only they contain information about the colors or selections within an image. There are three types of channels: color channels, which contain the image color information; alpha channels, which store selections; and spot channels, which contain spot colors for printing.

Color Channels

All images can be split into one or more color channels. The number and type of color channels depends on the color mode of the image. If the image is in RGB mode, it will contain a red, green, and blue channel, as well as a channel for the combined colors. Each channel contains 8 bits of information. When combined, the RGB image has 24 bits (8 bits for each of the three channels), and 16,700,000 colors can be displayed on the screen.

Each channel stores color, hue, brightness, and shadow information, and you can see and manage the channels in the Channels palette. A CMYK image will contain a cyan, magenta, yellow, and black channel, as well as a channel for the combined colors.

RGB Channel

The RGB channel is the combination of the Red, Green, and Blue channels. Within the Channels palette, clicking the RGB channel will select all three color channels and the image will be displayed in full color.

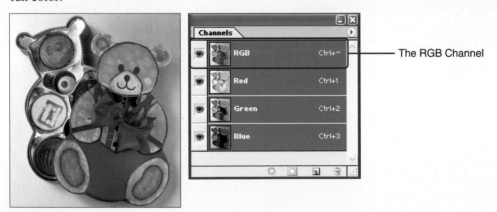

The RGB Channel

▲Selecting the RGB channel in the RGB color mode displays the image in full color.

Red, Green, or Blue Channels

The Red, Green, or Blue channels contain information about their respective colors within an image. By default, selecting any one of these channels in the Channels palette displays the image in grayscale. The white portion represents the areas that contain the selected channel color while the black portion represents the areas that do not. Displaying an image in this manner makes it easy for you to work on a particular color. You can use a painting tool and paint in white to add the selected channel color, or paint in black to do the opposite.

 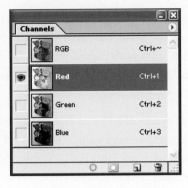

▲Selecting the Red channel displays the image in black and white. The white portion represents the red areas while the black portion represents the areas that contain no red.

<< note

Viewing Colors in the Channels Palette

Although, by default, individual color channels display an image in grayscale, the channels can be set to display in their color by selecting [Edit] - [Preferences] - [Display & Cursors] and checking Color Channels in Color. This affects the display of the channel in the Channels palette but does not affect the image.

 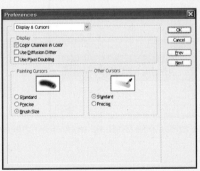 

Spot Channels

Spot channels contain information on spot colors. To understand spot colors, you need to understand the CMYK color mode and how colors print. In Chapter 1, you learned about the RGB and CMYK color modes. You learned that when you edit a color image in Photoshop, it's best to work in RGB mode (your monitor is based on the RGB color scheme, so RGB images are ideally suited for viewing on your screen). You also learned that, if your image is to be sent to a professional printer, the color mode must be changed to CMYK prior to the submission of your files.

Printed colors are created using the four process inks--cyan, magenta, yellow, and black. (Although cyan, magenta, and yellow can theoretically create black, the impurities in the inks will most likely create a deep grayish hue.) Before an image is printed at a professional printer, the cyan, magenta, yellow, and black color plates for the image have to be created. Each of these plates will determine the area each process ink will print to.

A spot color, however, is a matched or exact color that is not printed using the four process inks. A spot color is a color chosen from a color matching system such as PANTONE. To use a PANTONE spot color, for example, you will choose the spot color from PANTONE's color book. Using the book, you can tell exactly how the color will look when printed. To print a spot color, a spot channel has to be created so that a color plate for the spot color can be created at the printer. Spot colors are useful for making sure that a company logo appears in the same color on all printed materials. Spot colors are also used to specify metallic colors that require special inks. For images with fewer than four colors, specifying spot colors will reduce the cost of printing as less ink is used. For example, you will only need a green and a black color plate if the image has only green hues.

▲Spot Color Channel

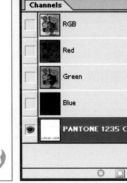

▲A Spot Color Channel within the Channels Palette

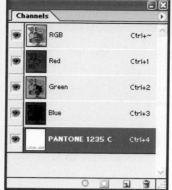

▲Applying the Spot Color Channel   ▲The Channels Palette
 to an Image

Alpha Channels

Alpha channels contain saved selections. You can use almost any of the Photoshop tools to modify the selections within an alpha channel to create special effects.

It is often easier to think of alpha channels as a type of mask. Masks cover up a section within an image and use the black, white, and gray colors to determine what should be shown and hidden. Alpha channels also use black, white, and grays to determine selections.

◄Alpha channels refer to accompanying channels. Alpha channels can be used to make selections in which different effects can be applied.

<< tip

File Size

Photoshop can store up to 56 channels. A file with more channels will be larger in size. A CMYK file will be larger than an RGB file as it contains four channels rather than three.

The Channels Palette

The Channels palette, which is grouped with the Layers and Paths palette, allows you to view and work with channels.

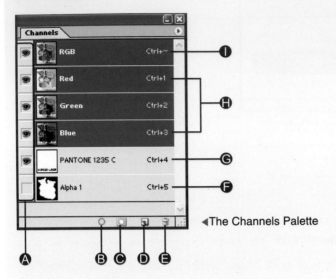

◀ The Channels Palette

Ⓐ **Eye Icon**: Hides/shows the corresponding channel.

Ⓑ **Load Channel as Selection**: Creates a selection based on the selected channel.

Ⓒ **Save Selection as Channel**: Saves the current selection as a channel. This is available only when a selection is made in the image.

Ⓓ **Create New Channel**: Creates a new channel. An existing channel can be dragged and dropped onto this button to create a copy.

Ⓔ **Delete Current Channel**: Deletes the selected channel.

Ⓕ **Alpha Channel**: Alpha channels are used to save selection areas. Once saved, they appear in the Channel palette as shown.

Ⓖ **Spot Channel**: Spot channels show image information for spot colors.

Ⓗ **Red, Green, and Blue Color Channels**: These channels separate the color information in the image according to the color mode (in this case, RGB).

Ⓘ **RGB Channel**: Shows all the colors combined.

The Channels Palette Pop-Up Menu

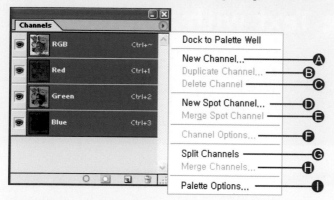

Ⓐ New Channel: Creates a new channel.

Ⓑ Duplicate Channel: Copies the selected channel.

Ⓒ Delete Channel: Deletes the selected channel.

Ⓓ New Spot Channel: Creates a new spot channel.

Ⓔ Merge Spot Channel: Combines the spot channel with the color channel.

Ⓕ Channel Options: Opens the Channel Options dialog box.

Ⓖ Split Channels: Splits the channel into separate images.

Ⓗ Merge Channels: Combines the split channels.

Ⓘ Palette Options: Adjusts the size of the preview image in the Channels palette.

The Channel Options Dialog Box

Clicking on Channel Options in the Channels palette's pop-up menu opens the Channel Options dialog box. This option is only available when the image contains a spot color or alpha channel.

Ⓐ Name: The channel name.

Ⓑ Color Indicates: Shows the area where the selection or mask will be applied.
Masked Areas: Displays the masked area in black and the selected area in white.
Selected Areas: Displays the masked area in white and the selected area in black.
Spot Color: Changes alpha channels to spot channels.

Ⓒ Color: Double-clicking the color window displays the Color Picker, which can be used to change the mask color.

Creating Text with a Stitching Effect

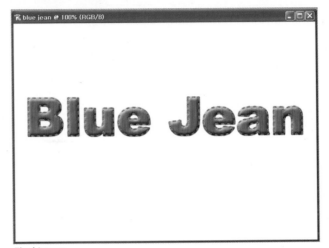

Final Image

Final File
- Jean_end.psd

Features Used
- Add Noise, Motion Blur, New Channel, Expand, Border, Stroke Path, Bevel and Emboss

Photoshop CS provides countless ways in which to stylize text for artistic effect. In this exercise, we'll use several features to create text that looks like stitched denim.

Making the Denim Texture

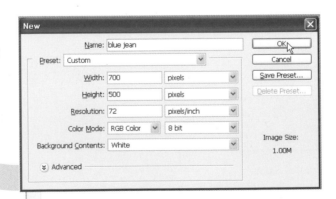

Resource Files

Remember to copy the resource files on the CD-ROM to your hard drive before you start each exercise in this book.

1 Choose [File] - [New] and set the Width to 700, the Height to 500, the Resolution to 72 pixels/inch, the Color Mode to RGB Color, the Background Contents to White, and click OK.

2 Click the foreground color in the toolbox to open the Color Picker dialog box. Set C to 100 and M to 50 to create a blue color and click OK.

3 In the Layers palette, click the [Create a new layer] button to create Layer 1. Press [Alt]-[Delete] to fill the layer with the foreground color.

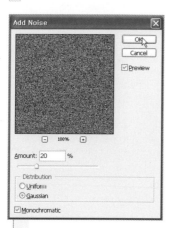

4 Add a rough texture by choose [Filter] - [Noise] - [Add Noise]. Set the Amount to 20, Distribution to Gaussian, check Monochromatic, and click OK.

5 To create lines on the fabric, choose [Filter] - [Blur] - [Motion Blur]. Set the Angle to -90, the Distance to 30, and click OK.

Saving a Text Selection in an Alpha Channel

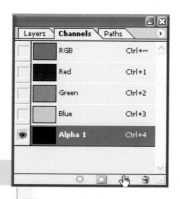

1 In the Channels palette, click the [Create new channel] button to create the Alpha 1 channel.

Blue Jean

2 Select the Type tool (T) from the toolbar. In the options bar, set the font to Arial Black, the font size to 120 pt, and type **Blue Jean**. Click the [Commit] button.

3 Choose [Select] - [Modify] - [Expand], set Expand By to 2, and click OK.

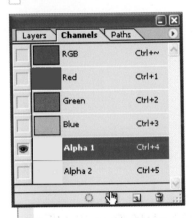

4 Click the [Save selection as channel] button (⬚) in the Channels palette. This will create the Alpha 2 channel. If you select Alpha 2, the selection will appear white on a black background.

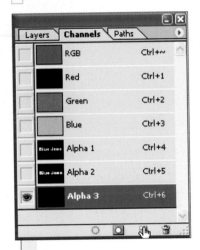

5 Click the [Create new channel] button in the Channels palette to create the Alpha 3 channel.

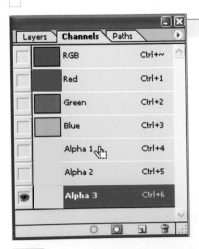

6 Clear any active selection, hold down the [Ctrl] key, and click Alpha 1 to load Alpha 1 as a selection on the Alpha 3 channel.

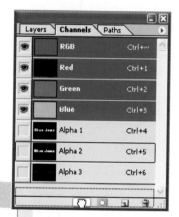

7 Choose [Select] - [Modify] - [Border], set the Width to 1, and click OK. If you zoom in on the selection, you will see that it has changed to two lines.

8 Set the foreground color to white and press [Alt]-[Delete] to fill the selection with white. Press [Ctrl]-[D] to clear the selection.

Applying Layers

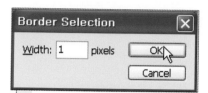

1 In the Channels palette, drag-and-drop the Alpha 2 channel onto the [Load channel as selection] button (⊙) to load the image saved in the Alpha 2 channel as a selection. (Shortcut keys: [Alt]-[Ctrl]-[5].)

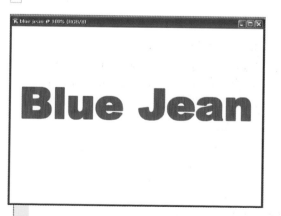

2 Click the [Add a mask] button in the Layers palette. A black mask should have been created for Layer 1.

3 The black areas mask the blue areas of the fabric, while the white areas are the only visible section of Layer 1.

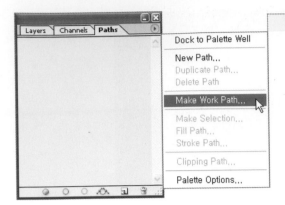

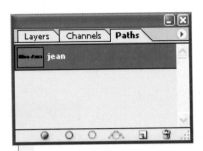

4 Press the shortcut keys [Alt]-[Ctrl]-[4] to load the Alpha 1 image as a selection. Hold down the [Alt] key and click the [Make work path from selection] button in the Paths palette.

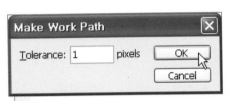

5 Set the Tolerance to 1 and click OK.

6 Double-click Work Path in the Paths palette and rename it **jean**.

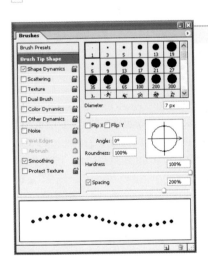

7 In the Layers palette, click the [Create a new layer] button (🗊) to create Layer 2. Set the foreground color to Magenta 50 and Yellow 100. Select the Pencil tool (✏️), then click Brush Tip Shape in the Brushes palette. Set the Diameter to 7 px and the Spacing to 200%.

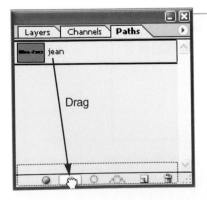

8 In the Paths palette, drag-and-drop the jean path onto the [Stroke path with brush] button (⭕).

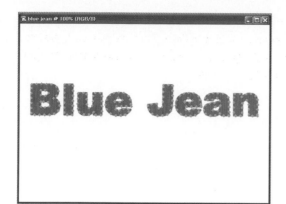

9 This creates an outline along the path.

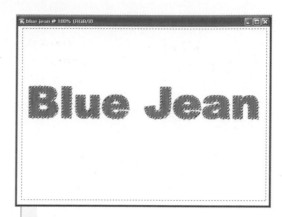

10 Press [Alt]-[Ctrl]-[6] to load Alpha 3 as a selection and choose [Select]-[Inverse] to invert the selection. (Shortcut keys: [Shift]-[Ctrl]-[I].)

11 Press [Delete] to remove the image from the selection, leaving behind only the stitches. Press [Ctrl]-[D] to clear the selection.

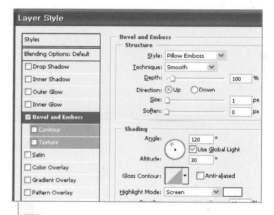

12 Click the [Add a layer style] button () in the Layers palette and select Bevel and Emboss. Set the Style to Pillow Emboss, the Size to 1, and click OK. This causes the fabric to appear sunken and adds dimension to the stitching.

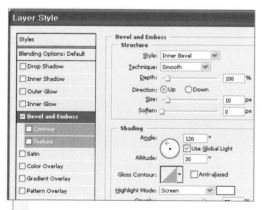

13 Select Layer 1 in the Layers palette, click the [Add a layer style] button (), and select Bevel and Emboss. Set the Style to Inner Bevel, the Size to 10, and click OK.

14 The final image is shown above.

2 Applying Texture to 3D Text

Original Image

Final Image

In this section, we will use a displacement map to apply a source image to 3D text. We will use alpha channels, the displacement map, and lighting effects to create the text.

Saving the Alpha Channel

1 Open \Sample\Chapter9\Back.jpg.

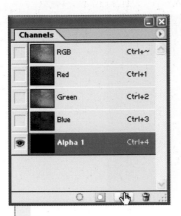

2 Click the [Create new channel] button in the Channels palette to create the Alpha 1 channel.

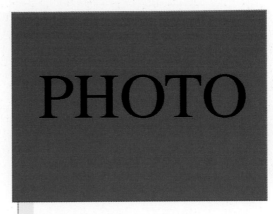

3 Select the Type tool ([T]) from the toolbox. In the options bar, set the font to Times, the font size to 160 pt, and type **PHOTO**. Click the [Commit] button.

<< tip
Temporary Mask

When you insert characters, you will see a change in the background color. This means it is temporarily masked.

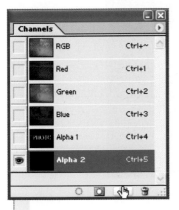

4 In the Channels palette, click the [Create new channel] button to create the Alpha 2 channel.

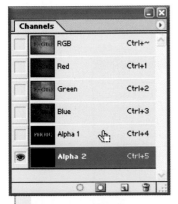

5 If the selection from the Alpha 1 channel is not loaded, select Alpha 2 and [Ctrl]-click Alpha 1.

6 Choose [Select]-[Feather], set the Feather Radius to 7, and click OK to soften the selection.

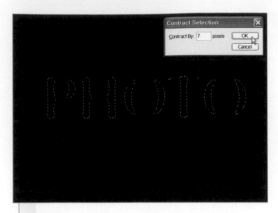

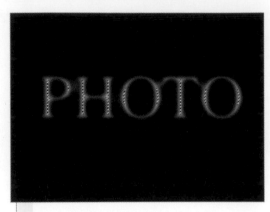

7   Choose [Select] - [Modify] - [Contract], enter 7, and click OK to make the selection smaller.

8   Set the foreground color to white and press [Alt]-[Delete] to fill the selection with white.

9   Select the Alpha 2 channel, hold down the [Ctrl] key, and click Alpha 1 to load Alpha 1 as a selection onto Alpha 2.

10   Choose [Select] - [Inverse] to invert the selection frame. Select black as the foreground color and press [Alt]-[Delete] to fill the selection. Within the Layers palette, use the [Ctrl]-[A] shortcut to select the entire image and press [Ctrl]-[C] to save the image to the clipboard.

Making the Displacement Map Source

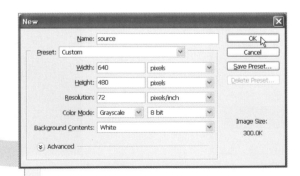

1   Choose [File] - [New], set the Preset Size to 640 x 480, and click OK.

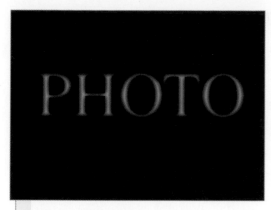

2 Press [Ctrl]-[V] to paste the image into the new Document window.

3 Choose [File] - [Save As], type **Source** for the file name, set the Format to Photoshop (*.PSD, *.PDD), and click OK.

4 Within Back.jpg, make a copy of the Background layer in the Layers palette.

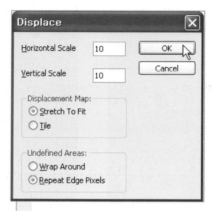

5 On the Background copy layer, choose [Filter] - [Distort] - [Displace]. We'll be using the default values, so click OK to continue.

6 Select Source.psd and click [Open].

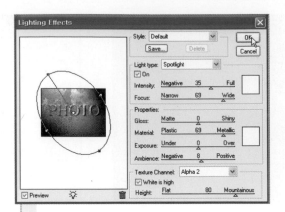

7 In the Source image, the white areas show parts of the image that protrude.

8 Choose [Filter] - [Render] - [Lighting Effects]. Set the Texture Channel to Alpha 2 and move the slider bar towards Mountainous. In the preview window, use the four handles to adjust the direction of the light as shown and click OK.

9 Hold down the [Ctrl] key and click the Alpha 1 channel in the Channels palette to load it as a selection.

10 Choose [Select] - [Inverse] and press [Delete] to delete the background.

Making Shadows

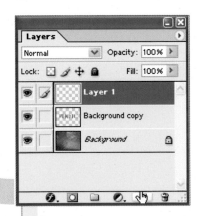

1 In the Layers palette, click the [Create a new layer] button to create Layer 1.

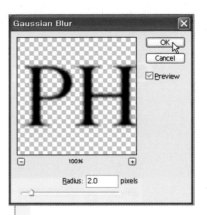

2 Invert the selection again to select the letters. Set the foreground color to black and press [Alt]-[Delete] to fill the selection with black. Press [Ctrl]-[D] to clear the selection.

3 Choose [Filter] - [Blur] - [Gaussian Blur]. Set the Radius to 2 and click OK.

4 In the Layers palette, drag Layer 1 below the Background copy layer and move the shadow to the bottom-right of the letters as shown. The image is now complete.

<< tip
Displacement Map

The displacement map is used to create the effect that the texture is raised across the surface of the letters. Without it, the texture would appear beneath the text.

Chapter | 10

Filters

Of all the tools and commands in Photoshop, the filters feature is the most fun to use. Using filters, exciting special effects can be added to images in a matter of clicks. Filters can be used to add textures, alter lighting, and simulate painting and drawing styles. Between the filters included with Photoshop CS and those that can be purchased from third-party developers as plug-ins (secondary programs that enhance Photoshop), the possibilities are almost limitless!

The Filter Menu

The Filter menu contains a massive number of filters, many of which are grouped into categories such as Artistic and Distort. Filters may be applied to a layer or selection by selecting the desired filter from the Filter menu at the top of the screen. Most filters, once selected, will activate a dialog box that allows you to tailor the filter to your desired effect. If additional filters are added to Photoshop CS through the purchase of third-party plug-ins, these new filters will also appear in the Filter menu.

Applying a Filter

All filters are applied through the Filter menu. Before you learn about the effects created by each of the filters, let's review the general steps for applying filters.

1. First, select the layer containing the artwork that is to be altered by the special effect.

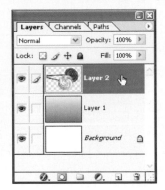

2. If you wish to apply the filter to only a selected area of your layer, use the selection tools to isolate the desired area.

<< tip

Some filters, such as the Artistic filters, can only be used in the RGB color mode. If you are working in CMYK mode, you will need to convert to RGB mode before applying such filters. The image can be converted back to CMYK after the filter has been applied.

3. Select a filter from the Filter menu.

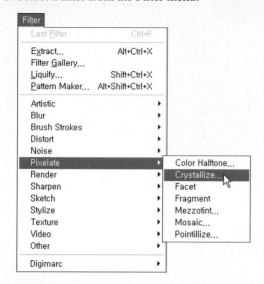

4. When the dialog box for the filter appears, adjust the filter settings and click OK.

5. The filter has been applied to the artwork on the selected layer.

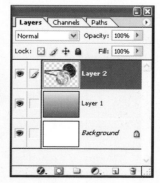

The standard, core filters of Photoshop CS may be found between the Artistic and Other subfolders of the Filter menu. These filters cover an incredible range of special effects, and constitute the "bread and butter" of any Photoshop pro. Let's look at the effect created and the options available for each of the filters in this section.

Artistic Filters

The Artistic group of filters is the largest filter category, with a total of 15 filters. These filters, as the name suggests, apply various artistic effects to the chosen layer or selection. Often, these filters are used to make a digital image look hand-painted.

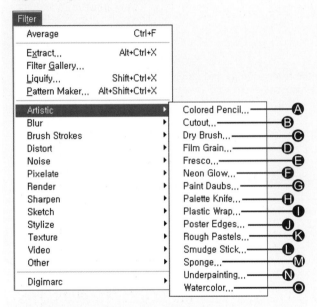

Ⓐ Colored Pencil

The Colored Pencil filter makes the image look as if it was drawn using colored pencils. Edges are given a crosshatch appearance and the background color shows through the pencil strokes.

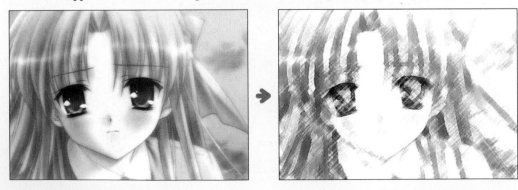

Colored Pencil Options

Pencil Width: Changes the pencil stroke thickness.

Stroke Pressure: Changes the intensity of the pencil strokes.

Paper Brightness: Modifies the brightness of the underlying paper.

⑧ Cutout

The Cutout filter makes the image look as if it were created from pieces of cut out paper.

Cutout Options

Number of Levels: Determines the number of layers of colored paper. The higher the level, the higher the detail in the final image.

Edge Simplicity: Simplifies edges.

Edge Fidelity: Sets the degree of precision at the image's edge.

◉ Dry Brush

The Dry Brush filter paints the edges with a dry brush effect.

Dry Brush Options

Brush Size: The smaller the brush size, the more detailed the image.

Brush Detail: The higher the Brush Detail value, the more detailed the image.

Texture: The higher the Texture value, the rougher the texture of the image.

◉ Film Grain

The Film Grain filter adds small dots or "noise" to the image. A smoother pattern is added to lighter areas of the image.

Film Grain Options

Grain: Sets the dot or noise size.

Highlight Area: The higher the Highlight Area value, the more highlights there will be in the image.

Intensity: A smaller number adds dots to the entire image, while a larger number add dots only to the darker areas of the image.

❺ Fresco

The Fresco filter paints an image with short dabs, creating a dark image with high contrast.

Fresco Options

Brush Size: The smaller the brush size, the more detailed the image.

Brush Detail: The higher the Brush Detail value, the more detailed the image.

Texture: The higher the Texture value, the rougher the texture of the image.

⑤ Neon Glow

The Neon Glow filter is used to add glow effects and soften an image. This effect uses two colors to paint an image. One of the two colors used is the foreground color, the other is user-defined in the Neon Glow dialog box.

Neon Glow Options

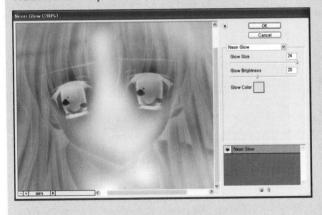

Glow Size: A large Glow Size value will color the highlights with the glow color and the shadows with the foreground color. A small Glow Size value will color the highlights with the foreground color and the shadows with the glow color.

Glow Brightness: When set to 0, the image is filled with the foreground color. At a higher value, highlights appear using the glow color. When set to the maximum Glow Brightness of 50, the glow color is replaced by white.

Glow Color: One of the two colors used to paint the image.

⑥ Paint Daubs

The Paint Daubs filter turns an image into an oil painting.

Paint Daubs Options

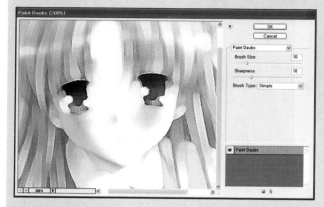

Brush Size: The smaller the brush size, the more detailed the image.

Sharpness: Increasing the Sharpness value makes the edges more defined. At higher Sharpness values, similar colors in the image start banding together.

Brush Type: Choose from Simple, Light Rough, Wide Sharp, Wide Blurry, or Sparkle brushes.

⊕ Palette Knife

The Palette Knife filter creates the effect that a palette knife was used to paint the canvas.

Palette Knife Options

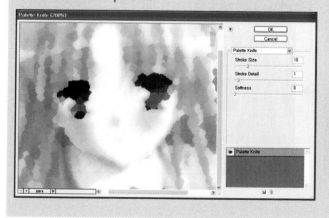

Stroke Size: The higher the value, the more the colors bunch up in the image.

Stroke Detail: The higher the Stroke Detail value, the more detailed the image.

Softness: Alters the degree of smearing in the final image.

ⓓ Gaussian Blur

The Gaussian Blur filter allows you to specify the intensity of the blur. This filter is useful for creating smudged areas, shadows, and fog.

Gaussian Blur Options

Radius: Determines the resolution of the blur effect. At the maximum setting, the entire image will be filled out with a single color.

ⓔ Lens Blur

The Lens Blur filter adds a depth-of-field effect so that some objects stay in focus while others become blurred. Unlike the other blur filters, this filter lets you create a progressive change in depth-of-field without the need to make multiple selections and apply different amounts of blur to each of the selections.

Lens Blur Options

Preview: While an image preview for the other filters is both fast and accurate, you need to choose either a fast preview or a more accurate preview with the Lens Blur filter. This is because the Lens Blur filter is more memory intensive.

Depth Map: The options here determine the depth-of-field in the image.

-*Source*: Choose from None, Transparency, Layer Mask, or an alpha channel to set a source for determining the depth-of-field in the image. Selecting None leaves the image's depth-of-field unchanged. Selecting Transparency sets the entire image to the same depth-of-field. Selecting a layer mask or an alpha channel lets you modulate the depth-of-field in the image. (You need to have applied a layer mask or saved an alpha channel to choose these two options.)

-*Blur Focal Distance*: Sets the point on the image that will be in focus.

-*Invert*: Reverses the specified depth-of-field.

Iris: The options here determine the properties of the camera iris. These properties change the way the blur appears. Because the change is very subtle, you can only see the effect by zooming in on the preview (click on the + icon at the bottom-left corner of the dialog box).

-*Shape*: Determines the shape of the iris.

-*Radius*: Determines the intensity of the blur.

-*Blade Curvature*: Determines the roundness of the iris.

-*Rotation*: Sets the amount of iris rotation.

Specular Highlights: According to Adobe, these options change the highlights in an image. From our own trials, these options had no effect on the image at all. In any case, the effect is subtle, to say the least!

-*Brightness*: Increases the brightness of the highlights.

-*Threshold*: Any pixels brighter than the Threshold value are turned into highlights.

Noise: These options adjust the noise properties (random pixels) in an image.

-*Amount*: Determines the amount of noise that is added to the image.

-*Distribution*: Choose from a Uniform or Gaussian (random) distribution of the noise.

-*Monochromatic*: Sets the noise to gray (by default, noise pixels are multicolored).

ⓕ Motion Blur

The Motion Blur filter blurs an image in a single direction, creating an effect similar to taking a picture of a fast-moving subject.

Motion Blur Options

Angle: Angle of motion. You can also click-and-drag the dial on the right to set the angle.

Distance: Distance of blur effect.

ⓖ Radial Blur

The Radial Blur filter creates a blur with reference to a center point, creating a zoom or spin effect.

Radial Blur Options

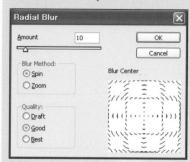

Amount: Area to which the effect will be applied with respect to the Blur Center.

Blur Method
-*Spin*: The blur is created by spinning the image.
-*Zoom*: Creates the effect of a camera zooming in or out of an image.

Quality
-*Draft*: Creates a rough texture.
-*Good*: The created texture has an average degree of detail.
-*Best*: The final image is highly detailed, but the execution of the effect is slow.

Blur Center: Center of the blur. Click or drag to move the blur center.

Smart Blur

The Smart Blur filter applies a blur while maintaining the overall contours of the image.

Smart Blur Options

Radius: Determines the area of the blur.

Threshold: Blur threshold. For pictures of people, use a high Threshold value to create an even skin tone.

Quality: Changes the quality of the effect.

Mode: Choose from three modes: Normal, Edge Only (displays edges in black and white), or Overlay Edge (displays edges in white).

Brush Strokes Filters

The Brush Strokes filters create painted images with brushstroke textures.

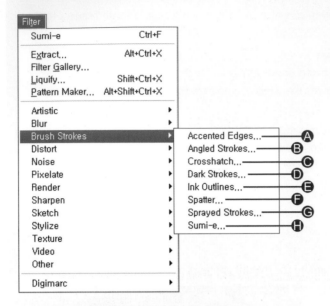

Ⓐ Accented Edges

The Accented Edges filter creates strong edges.

Accented Edges Options

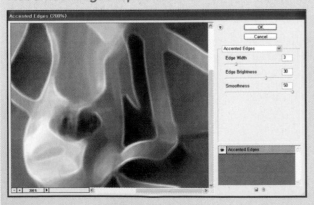

Edge Width: Sets the edge thickness.

Edge Brightness: A low value creates dark edges while a high value creates light-colored edges.

Smoothness: Modifies the smoothness of the brush strokes.

Ⓑ Angled Strokes

The Angled Strokes filter draws an image in diagonal brush strokes, with the light-colored strokes going in one direction and dark-colored strokes going in the opposite.

Angled Strokes Options

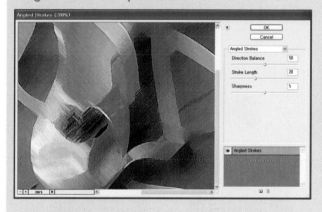

Direction Balance: Alters the number of lines going in the two directions.

Stroke Length: Adjusts the length of the strokes.

Sharpness: Modifies the sharpness of the strokes.

Ⓒ Crosshatch

The Crosshatch filter creates an image that looks like crosshatch pencil lines.

 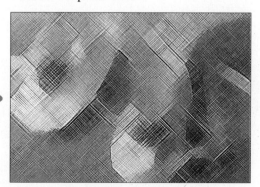

Crosshatch Options

Stroke Length: Adjusts the length of the strokes.

Sharpness: Modifies the sharpness of the strokes.

Strength: A higher Strength value increases the number of strokes.

ⓓ Dark Strokes

The Dark Strokes filter uses short, black strokes in darker areas of the image, and long, white strokes in brighter areas.

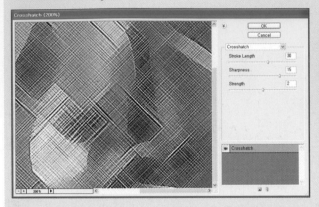 

Dark Strokes Options

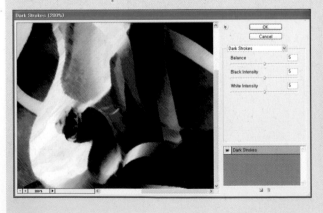

Balance: A smaller value adds strokes to brighter areas, and a larger value adds strokes to the darker areas of the image.

Black Intensity: Darkens the shadows in the image.

White Intensity: Brightens the highlights in the image.

Ⓔ Ink Outlines

The Ink Outlines filter creates image edges that look like they've been drawn with pen and ink.

Ink Outlines Options

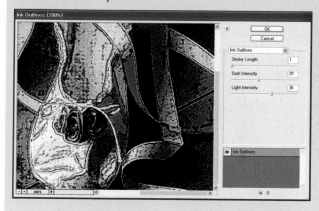

Stroke Length: Adjusts the length of the strokes.

Dark Intensity: Darkens the image.

Light Intensity: Brightens the image.

Ⓕ Spatter

The Spatter filter creates an image that looks like it was sprayed with an airbrush.

Spatter Options

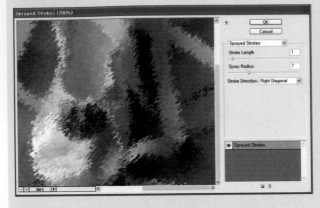

Spray Radius: Determines the resolution of the spray effect.

Smoothness: Changes the smoothness of the image.

ⓖ Sprayed Strokes

The Sprayed Strokes filter uses angled, sprayed strokes of color.

Sprayed Strokes Options

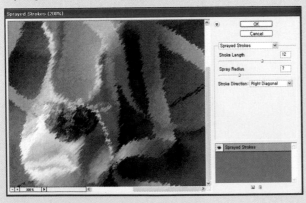

Stroke Length: Sets the length of the strokes.

Spray Radius: Determines the resolution of the spray effect.

Stroke Direction: Selects the direction of the spray.

Ⓗ Sumi-e

The Sumi-e filter creates an image that looks like it was drawn using a wet brush with black ink on rice paper.

Sumi-e Options

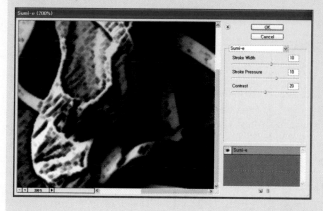

Stroke Width: Sets the stroke thickness.

Stroke Pressure: Changes the stroke pressure.

Contrast: Modifies the image contrast.

Distort Filters

Distort filters are used to change the shape of an image.

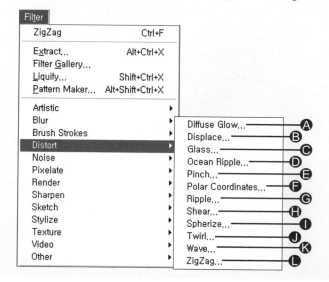

Ⓐ Diffuse Glow

The Diffuse Glow filter adds white noise to the image; lighter areas look luminous. Applying this filter to an image on a white background creates a fog-like effect.

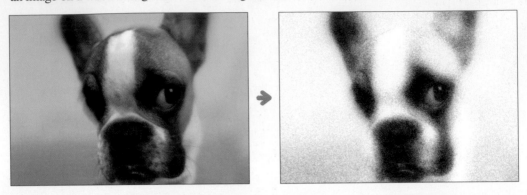

Diffuse Glow Options

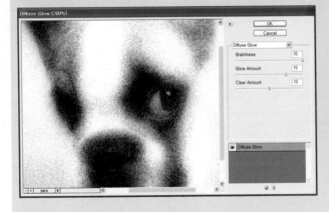

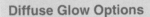

Graininess: Sets the grain size.

Glow Amount: Determines the amount of glow.

Clear Amount: Calculates the area of the fog effect. A larger value adds dots only to brighter areas, and a smaller value adds dots to the overall image.

Ⓑ Displace

The Displace filter uses a displacement map to determine how to distort an image. A displacement map is a PSD image that interacts with the original image to impact the overall effect.

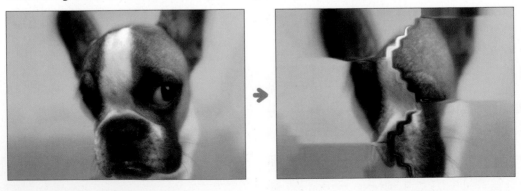

Displace Options

Horizontal Scale: Sets the degree of horizontal distortion.

Vertical Scale: Sets the degree of vertical distortion.

Displacement Map: Determines how the original image will be displayed on the displacement map.

-*Stretch to Fit*: When checked, the map source image is stretched to fit the original image.

-*Tile*: Check this to use the map source image at its original size. The map will be tiled (repeated) to fill the original image.

Undefined Areas: Determines how empty spaces will be treated.

-*Wrap Around*: Select this to fill any empty spaces with a selection from the other side of the image.

-*Repeat Edge Pixels*: Select this to fill any empty spaces with a repeating pattern of edge pixels.

ⓒ Glass

The Glass filter adds a glass pane in front of the image.

Glass Options

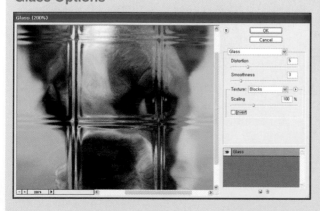

Distortion: Modifies the degree of refraction.

Smoothness: Modifies the smoothness of the refraction.

Texture: Choose from a Blocks, Canvas, Frosted, or Tiny Lens texture. You can also create your own customized textures.
-*Scaling*: Alters the size of the texture details.
-*Invert*: Inverts the applied texture.

ⓓ Ocean Ripple

The Ocean Ripple filter adds small waves or ripples to the image, making it look as if it is underwater.

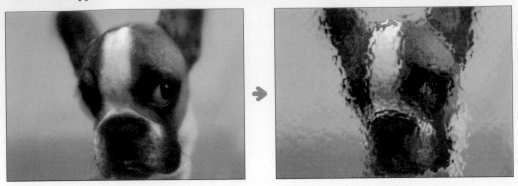

Ocean Ripple Options

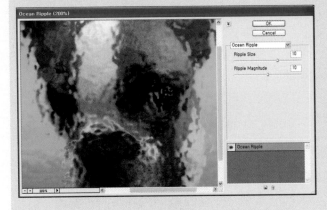

Ripple Size: Alters the size of the ripples.

Ripple Magnitude: Defines the area covered by the ripples.

ⓔ Pinch

The Pinch filter pinches or squeezes an image.

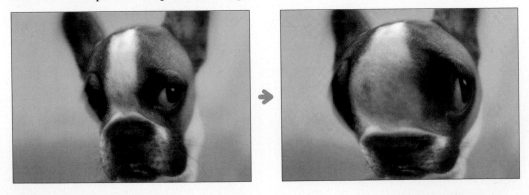

Pinch Options

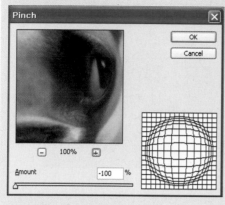

Amount: A positive value creates a concave lens effect and a negative value creates a convex lens effect. A preview of the Pinch filter "map" can be viewed in the box to the right of the Amount slider.

Ⓕ Polar Coordinates

Choosing the Rectangular to Polar option of the Polar Coordinates filter creates an effect similar to holding one side of the image and stretching it one full circle so that both sides of the image meet up. Choosing the Polar to Rectangular option reverses this process.

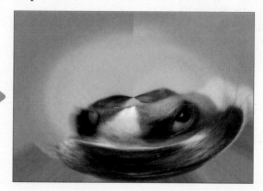

Polar Coordinates Options

Rectangular to Polar: Winds the image around the center.

Polar to Rectangular: Unwinds the image around the center.

Ⓖ Ripple

The Ripple filter adds small waves or ripples to the image.

Ripple Options

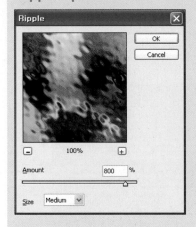

Amount: Changes the number of ripples.

Size: Choose from Small, Medium, or Large ripples.

Ⓗ Shear

The Shear filter distorts the image along a curve.

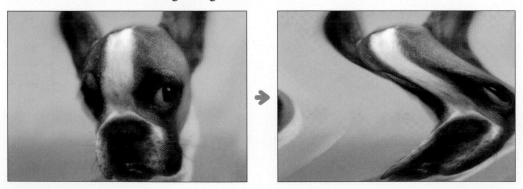

Shear Options

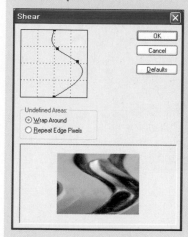

Wrap Around: Select this to fill empty spaces by repeating the image.

Repeat Edge Pixels: Select this to fill empty spaces by repeating only the pixels at the edge.

❶ Spherize

The Spherize filter adds a 3D effect by wrapping the image around a sphere.

Spherize Options

Amount: A positive value creates a concave lens effect and a negative value creates a convex lens effect. A preview of the Spherize filter "map" can be viewed in the box to the right of the Amount slider.

Mode: Choose Normal to create a fish-eye lens effect, Horizontal Only to stretch the image horizontally, or Vertical Only to stretch the image vertically.

ⓙ Twirl

The Twirl filter twirls the image around its center point.

ⓚ Wave

The Wave filter adds waves to the image. This filter is similar to the Ripple filter but it provides more options.

 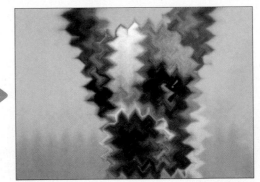

298

Wave Options

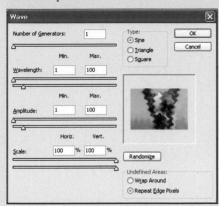

Number of Generators: Determines the number of waves.

Wavelength: Sets the length of the waves. The slider bars beneath the option set the minimum and maximum wave length.

Amplitude: Sets the height of the waves. The slider bars beneath the option set the minimum and maximum wave height.

Scale: Alters the amount of wave distortion.

Type: Determines the wave type. Choose Sine for a normal wave or Triangle for a more pointed wave. The Square option turns the image into small squares arranged in a wave form.

Randomize: Creates random waves.

Wrap Around: Select this to fill empty spaces with the other side of the image.

Repeat Edge Pixels: Select this to fill empty spaces with a repeating pattern of edge pixels.

ⓛ ZigZag

The ZigZag filter creates concentric ripples on the surface of the image.

 ➤

ZigZag Options

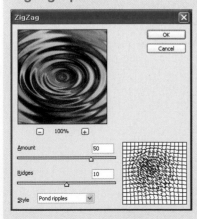

Amount: Determines the direction of the ripples' spin. A preview of the ZigZag filter "map" can be viewed in the box to the right of the Amount slider.

Ridges: Sets the number of concentric circles.

Style: Choose Out from Center or Pond Ripples to create ripples, or choose Around Center to create a whirlpool effect.

Noise Filters

The Noise filters are used to add and remove noise such as specks, dust, and scratches from an image.

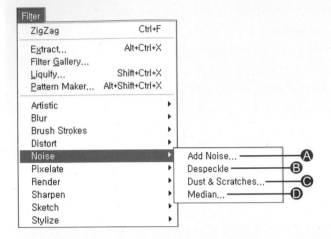

Ⓐ Add Noise

The Add Noise filter adds pixels of varied color and brightness randomly to the image.

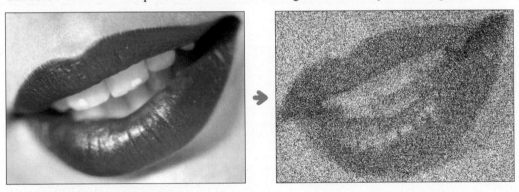

Add Noise Options

Amount: Sets the overall amount of noise.

Distribution: Choose either Uniform or Gaussian (random) to determine the distribution of noise in the image.

Monochromatic: When checked, only black-and-white pixels are added to the image.

Ⓑ Despeckle

The Despeckle filter removes noise from an image without affecting the image details.

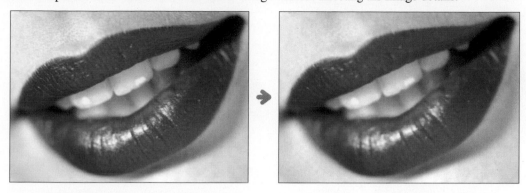

Ⓒ Dust & Scratches

The Dust & Scratches filter removes noise and dust from images by changing dissimilar pixels.

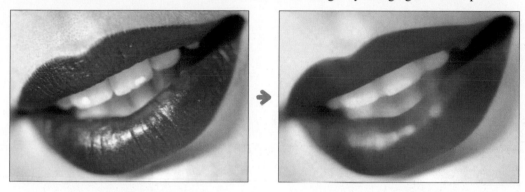

Dust & Scratches Options

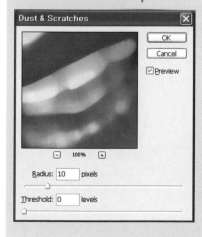

Radius: Sets the amount of pixel averaging. The higher the value, the blurrier the image.

Threshold: Determines the degree to which pixels must be different before they are removed. The lower the threshold, the more pixels are removed.

ⓓ Median

The Median filter blends the brightness of pixels to remove noise, creating a watercolor effect on the image.

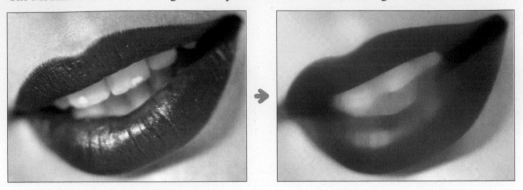

Median Options

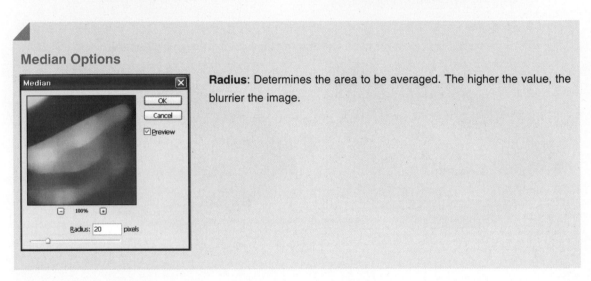

Radius: Determines the area to be averaged. The higher the value, the blurrier the image.

Pixelate Filters

The Pixelate filters alter an image by grouping together pixels to create a pattern.

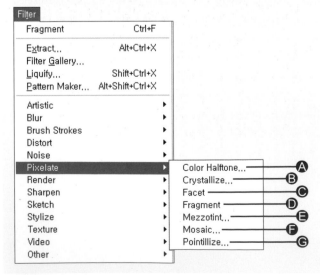

Ⓐ Color Halftone

The Color Halftone filter creates the effect of viewing a printed image at high magnification. The colors in the image will be represented by halftone dots (ink dots). In RGB mode, three colors are used; in CMYK mode, four colors are used.

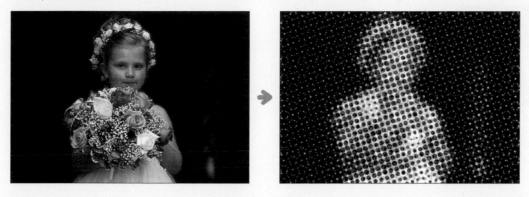

Color Halftone Options

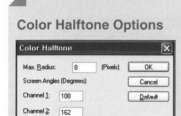

Max. Radius: Sets the size of the halftone dots.

Screen Angles (Degrees): Determines the angle of the halftone dots for each channel (color).

Ⓑ Crystallize

The Crystallize filter creates polygonal pixels of uniform color within the image.

Crystallize Options

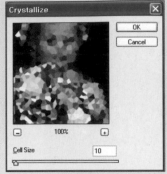

Cell Size: Modifies the size of the polygonal pixels.

ⓒ Facet

The Facet filter clumps similar colors to give the effect of hand painting.

ⓓ Fragment

The Fragment filter creates fluttering or vibrating images by creating four image copies, then averaging and misaligning the images.

🅔 Mezzotint

The Mezzotint filter distorts an image using black dots, lines, or strokes.

Mezzotint Options

Type: Choose from a variety of dot, line, or stroke patterns.

🅕 Mosaic

The Mosaic filter groups adjacent pixels into square blocks.

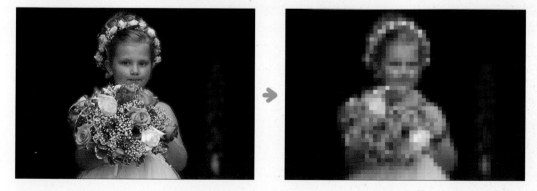

Mosaic Options

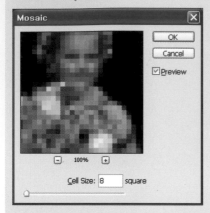

Cell Size: Determines the size of each square.

ⓖ Pointillize

The Pointillize filter breaks up an image into randomly placed dots against the selected background color, as in a pointillist painting. The background color is set using the Background Color swatch in the toolbox.

Pointillize Options

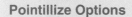

Cell Size: Determines the size of the dots.

Render Filters

Render filters are used to render effects such as 3D shapes, clouds, and lighting effects.

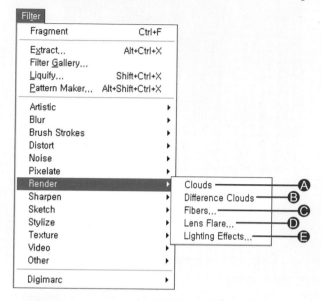

Ⓐ Clouds

The Clouds filter generates a soft cloud pattern using the foreground and background colors set in the toolbox. Hold down the [Alt] key as you choose [Filter] - [Render] - [Clouds] to create clouds with greater contrast.

Ⓑ Difference Clouds

The Difference Clouds filter produces clouds from the foreground and background colors, then blends them into the image using the Difference blend mode. The result is a surreal looking image.

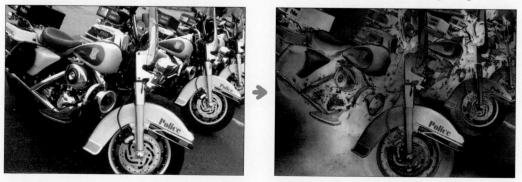

ⓒ Fibers

The Fibers filter creates a fiber texture using the background and foreground colors.

 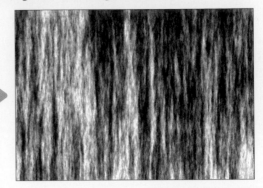

Fibers Options

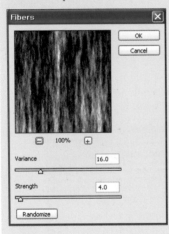

Variance: Creates a smooth image with long fibers at a low value, and a high-contrast image with short fibers at a high value.

Strength: Increasing the Strength value stretches the fibers vertically and makes the fibers more distinct.

Randomize: Clicking this button changes the fiber pattern. You can keep clicking this button until you see a pattern you like.

ⓓ Lens Flare

The Lens Flare filter recreates the lens flare effect of a camera lens.

Lens Flare Options

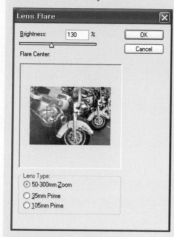

Brightness: Adjusts the brightness of the flare.

Flare Center: Click on the preview image to fix the flare center.

Lens Type: Select a lens type to alter the flare effect accordingly.

Ⓔ Lighting Effects

The Lighting Effects filter lets you add different lighting effects. You can adjust the light type, placement, color, brightness, and intensity.

 →

Lighting Effects Options

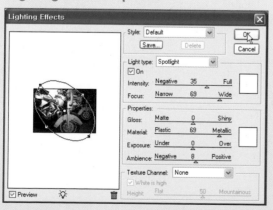

Style: 17 lighting styles are offered.

-*Save*: Click [Save] to store your settings for later use.

-*Delete*: Deletes a lighting style.

Light Type: Determines the position of the light, its intensity, and the coverage area.

-*Directional*: Creates a light that shines from far away in a single direction.

-*Omni*: Creates a light that shines directly above the image.

-*Spotlight*: Creates a light that shines at an angle to the image, creating an elliptical beam of light.

-*Intensity*: Negative values dim or extinguish the light, while moving towards Full brightens the light.

-*Focus*: Sets the spread of the light. This option is only available with the Spotlight selection.

Properties: Sets the properties of other factors that will affect the lighting of the image.

-*Gloss*: This slider determines how much light is reflected by the image. Toward Matte, highlights disappear and the image appears flatter. Shiny surfaces reflect more light.

-*Material*: Choose between Plastic and Metallic. Plastic reflects the color of the light, whereas Metallic reflects the color of the object. The difference between the two effects is very subtle.

-*Exposure*: Increases or decreases the exposure of the light. Values toward Under darken the light, while moving towards Over brightens the image.

-*Ambience*: Determines the amount of light from other sources. As you move towards Negative, ambient light is removed, resulting in a darker image.

Texture Channel: Lets you create texture in the image and adjust how light reflects off the texture.

-*White is High*: By default, the darker the pixels in the image map, the higher the texture relief in the final image. This option reverses this so that lighter areas are higher.

-*Height*: Changes the depth of the texture detail.

Sharpen Filters

The Sharpen filters are used to sharpen blurred images. These filters can only be used to increase image sharpness slightly before they start to distort the image, so concentrate on making sure your source image is as sharp as possible to begin with.

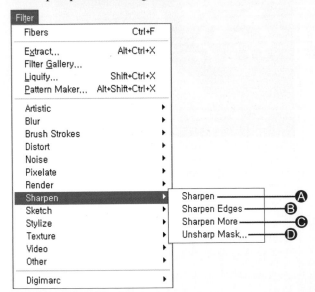

Ⓐ Sharpen

The Sharpen filter increases the color and hue contrast of the pixels to sharpen the image. This is the same as using the Sharpen tool from the toolbox.

Ⓑ Sharpen Edges

The Sharpen Edges filter sharpens edges where they contain significant changes in color.

Ⓒ Sharpen More

The Sharpen More filter acts as if the Sharpen filter was applied twice.

ⓓ Unsharp Mask

The Unsharp Mask filter allows you to adjust sharpness settings.

Unsharp Mask Options

Amount: Sets the degree of the effect.

Radius: Determines the intensity of the edges in the sharpened image. The greater the value, the wider the edge effects and the more obvious the sharpening effect.

Threshold: Sets the degree to which pixels must differ from surrounding pixels before they are treated as edge pixels and sharpened.

Sketch Filters

Sketch filters add texture to images. These filters create a hand-drawn or sketched appearance using the foreground and background colors in the toolbox.

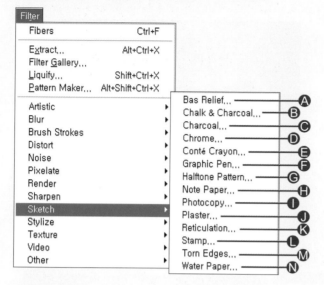

Ⓐ Bas Relief

The Bas Relief filter adds a carved appearance to the image.

Bas Relief Options

Detail: Alters the texture detail.

Smoothness: Modifies the smoothness of protruding areas.

Light Direction: Determines the direction of the light source.

Ⓑ Chalk & Charcoal

The Chalk & Charcoal filter creates an image that looks like it was drawn using chalk and charcoal. The background color is used for highlights and is drawn with chalk. The foreground color is used for the shadows and is drawn with charcoal.

Chalk & Charcoal Options

Charcoal Area: Adjusts the coverage of the charcoal area.

Chalk Area: Adjusts the coverage of the chalk area.

Stroke Pressure: A higher stroke pressure applies more chalk and charcoal to the image.

Ⓒ Charcoal

The Charcoal filter draws an image in charcoal using the foreground color.

Charcoal Options

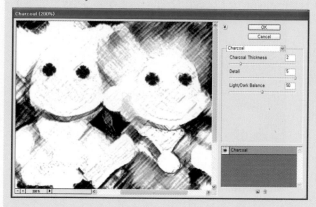

Charcoal Thickness: Sets the stroke thickness.

Detail: Adjusts the detail level of the strokes.

Light/Dark Balance: The smaller the value, the less charcoal is used.

ⓓ Chrome

The Chrome filter changes the image to grayscale and covers it with a metallic surface.

 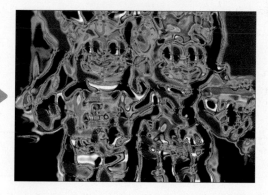

Chrome Options

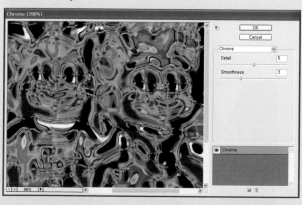

Detail: Adjusts the detail of the chrome effect.

Smoothness: Adjusts the smoothness of the chrome surface.

ⓔ Conte Crayon

The Conte Crayon filter uses the foreground color for dark areas and the background color for light areas. It creates an image that looks like it was drawn using crayon on a rough, textured piece of paper.

Conte Crayon Options

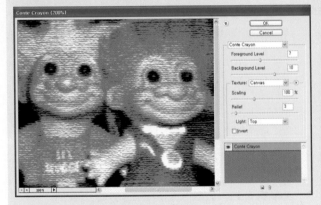

Foreground Levels: Adjusts the amount and coverage area of the foreground color.

Background Levels: Adjusts the amount and coverage area of the background color.

Texture: Choose from Brick, Burlap, Canvas, or Sandstone. You can also click on the triangle icon beside this option to load a PSD file for the texture.

-*Scaling*: Scaling upward makes the pattern in the texture larger and more prominent.

-*Relief*: Adjusts the depth of the texture's surface.

-*Light Direction*: Selects the direction of the light source.

ⓕ Graphic Pen

The Graphic Pen filter uses ink strokes to create an image that looks like it was drawn using a pen with a fine point.

Graphic Pen Options

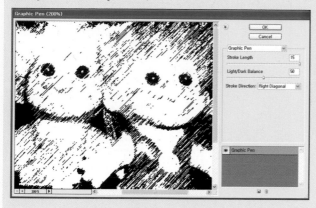

Stroke Length: A low value creates short, dense strokes, while a high value creates long, sparse strokes.

Light/Dark Balance: A low value increases the light areas, while a high value increases the dark areas.

Stroke Direction: Choose from four stroke directions.

ⓖ Halftone Pattern

The Halftone Pattern filter turns an image into halftone shapes such as dots, lines, and concentric circles. The foreground color is used for the halftone shapes and the background color is for the color of the underlying paper.

Halftone Pattern Options

Size: Adjusts the size of the halftone shapes.

Contrast: Alters the degree of contrast in the image.

Pattern Type: Choose from Circle, Dot, and Line.

⒣ Note Paper

The Note Paper filter adds embossing effects to create the effect of an image drawn on textured paper.

Note Paper Options

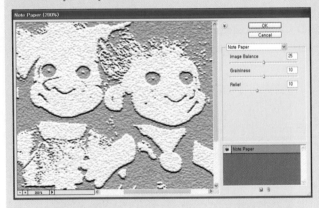

Image Balance: The larger the value, the larger the number of dark areas in the image.

Graininess: Adjusts the grain texture of the underlying paper.

Relief: Modifies the depth of the paper texture.

⒤ Photocopy

The Photocopy filter modifies the image to look like a photocopy.

Photocopy Options

Detail: Fine tunes the image detail.

Darkness: Adjusts the overall image darkness; similar to using a real copy machine.

⑪ Plaster

The Plaster filter creates 3D images that appear to have been molded from plaster then painted over.

Plaster Options

Image Balance: A low value raises the dark areas, while a high value raises the light areas.

Smoothness: Adjusts the smoothness of the raised areas.

Light Position: Sets the position of the light source.

ⓚ Reticulation

The Reticulation filter creates clumps in the image so it looks like it was painted over a net or mesh.

Reticulation Options

Density: Adjusts the detail level of the filter.

Foreground Level: Alters the coverage and intensity of the foreground color area.

Background Level: Alters the coverage and intensity of the background color area.

ⓛ Stamp

The Stamp filter simplifies images, making them appear as if they were stamped on paper.

Stamp Options

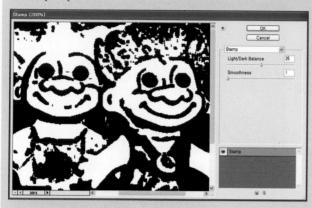

Light/Dark Balance: A high value increases the coverage of the dark areas.

Smoothness: Adjusts the detail of the final image.

Ⓜ Torn Edges

The Torn Edges filter is similar to the Stamp filter, but creates fuzzy edges in the image.

Torn Edges Options

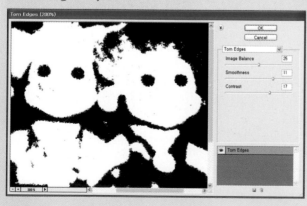

Image Balance: A high value increases the coverage of the dark areas.

Smoothness: Adjusts the detail of the final image.

Contrast: Adjusts the contrast of the final image.

Ⓝ Water Paper

The Water Paper filter creates an image that looks like it was drawn on wet paper.

Water Paper Options

Fiber Length: A high fiber length creates a blurry image, while a lower value increases the level of detail.

Brightness: Adjusts the brightness of the final image.

Contrast: Adjusts the contrast of the final image.

Stylize Filters

Stylize filters create a painted or impressionistic effect.

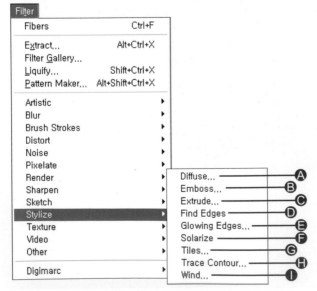

Ⓐ Diffuse

The Diffuse filter shuffles pixels to make the image appear less focused.

Diffuse Options

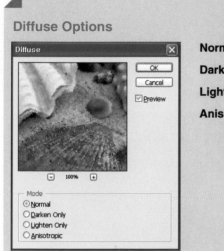

Normal: Diffuses all the pixels in the image.

Darken Only: Diffuses only the dark pixels in the image.

Lighten Only: Diffuses only the light pixels in the image.

Anisotropic: Softens overall image.

Ⓑ Emboss

The Emboss filter fills the image with gray and raises the details of the image to create a textured surface.

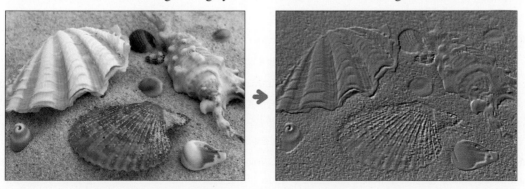

Emboss Options

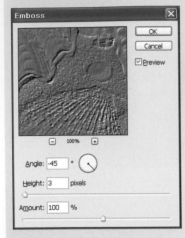

Angle: Determines the angle of the light source.

Height: A low Height value creates edge highlights in the image. A high Height value splits the image into two overlapping, misaligned, and partially transparent images.

Amount: A high Amount value increases the image detail and makes the emboss texture more obvious.

ⓒ Extrude

The Extrude filter paints the image over the top of 3D blocks or pyramids.

Extrude Options

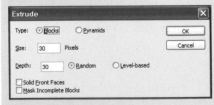

Type: Choose to paint the image over blocks or pyramids.

Size: Sets the size of the blocks or pyramids.

Depth: Determines the degree of extrusion. Select Random to set the depth randomly, or Level-Based so that areas with bright pixels are extruded more than areas with dark pixels.

Solid Front Faces: When using blocks, each block is a solid color (there is no color detail within the blocks).

Mask Incomplete Blocks: When unchecked, the blocks cover the entire image, and the edge of the image is filled with incomplete blocks. When checked, the edge areas that would otherwise be painted over with incomplete blocks are left blank, forming a "clean" border.

ⓓ Find Edges

The Find Edges filter creates outlines around all the edge details in the image. These outlines are drawn against a white background.

ⓔ Glowing Edges

The Glowing Edges filter is similar to the Find Edge filter, but creates neon glow outlines against a black background.

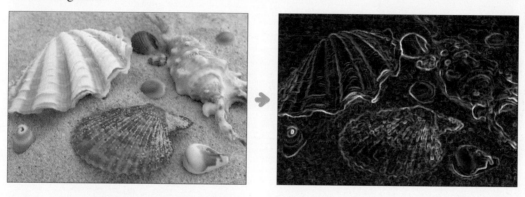

Glowing Edges Options

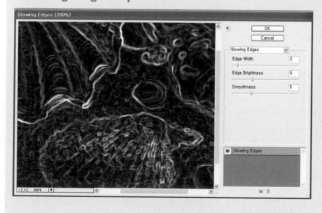

Edge Width: Modifies the thickness of the edge lines.

Edge Brightness: Increasing the edge brightness brings edges that were previously dark and invisible into view, creating more details.

Smoothness: Increasing the smoothness simplifies the image.

F Solarize

The Solarize filter blends a negative of the image with the original image. "Solarize" is also the name of the photography technique of exposing a photographic print to light briefly during development.

G Tiles

The Tiles filter breaks the image into tiles.

Tiles Options

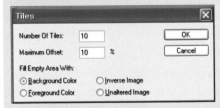

Number of Tiles: Sets the number of tiles along the image's width.

Maximum Offset: Adjusts the spacing between the tiles.

Fill Empty Area With: Fills empty spaces between the tiles with the selected option.

-*Background*: Background color.

-*Foreground*: Foreground color.

-*Inverse Image*: Fills empty spaces with the inverse color of the image.

-*Unaltered Image*: Fills empty spaces with the original image.

Ⓗ Trace Contour

The Trace Contour filter, like the Find Edges filter, creates lines along the edge details in the image. However, the Trace Contour filter makes the edges brighter in color. Remaining areas are filled with white.

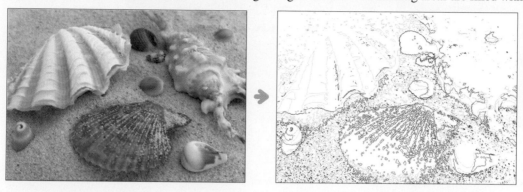

Trace Contour Options

Level: Sets the tonal threshold for determining the areas that will be outlined.

Edge: Determines whether the details of the image must be above or below the Level value to be outlined.

Ⓕ Wind

The Wind filter creates a windswept effect by adding short white lines across the image.

Wind Options

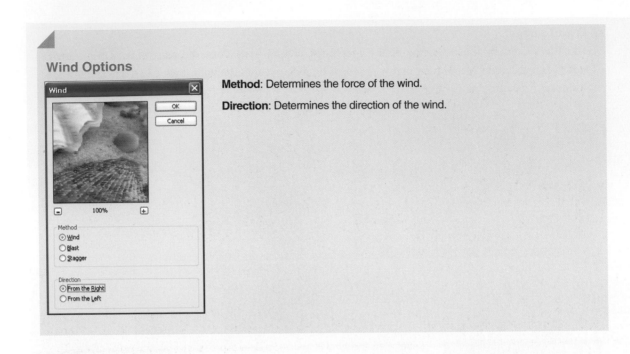

Method: Determines the force of the wind.

Direction: Determines the direction of the wind.

Texture Filters

The Texture filters add texture to images.

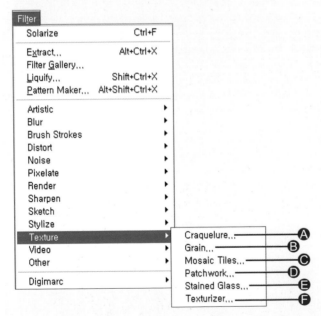

Ⓐ Craquelure

The Craquelure filter adds fine cracks to an image so that it looks like it is painted on a plastered surface.

Craquelure Options

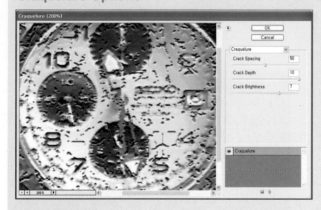

Crack Spacing: Adjusts the spacing of the cracks.

Crack Depth: Adjusts the depth of the cracks.

Crack Brightness: Modifies the brightness of the cracks.

Ⓑ Grain

The Grain filter adds dots, lines, or small particles to the image.

 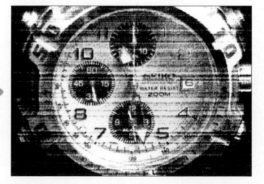

Intensity: Adjusts the number of grains in the image.

Contrast: Determines the image contrast.

Grain Type: Choose from Regular (small dots), Soft (small, soft dots), Sprinkles (small dots using the background color), Clumped (clumped dots), Contrasty (high contrast dots), Enlarged (enlarged dots), Stippled (sprayed dots using the foreground and background colors), Horizontal (black horizontal lines), Vertical (black vertical lines), or Speckle (speckled dots).

ⓒ Mosaic Tiles

The Mosaic Tiles filter creates a texture similar to the Craquelure filter, except the cracks create a mosaic pattern.

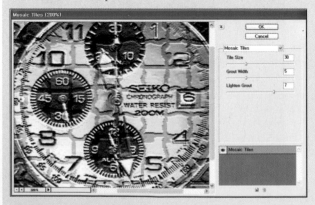

Tile Size: Sets the tile size.

Grout Width: Sets tile spacing between tiles.

Lighten Grout: Adjusts the brightness of the space between the tiles.

330

ⓓ Patchwork

The Patchwork filter breaks the image into a pattern of small squares.

Patchwork Options

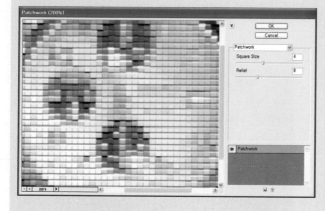

Square Size: Adjusts the size of the squares.

Relief: Adjusts the thickness of the squares.

ⓔ Stained Glass

The Stained Glass filter creates a stained glass effect; the foreground color is used for the edges.

 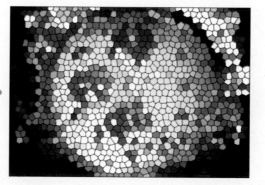

Stained Glass Options

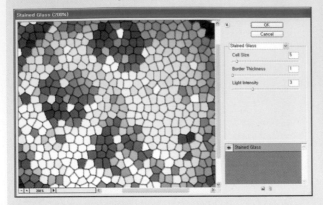

Cell Size: Modifies the size of the cells.

Border Thickness: Sets the thickness of the cell borders.

Light Intensity: Adjusts the brightness of the light shining through the stained glass.

F Texturizer

The Texturizer filter adds a texture to the image.

Texturizer Options

Texture: Choose Brick, Burlap, Canvas, or Sandstone. You can also click on the triangle icon to load a PSD file as a texture.

Scaling: Scaling upwards makes the pattern in the texture larger and more prominent.

Relief: Adjusts the depth of the texture's surface.

Light Direction: Determines the direction of the light source.

Invert: Inverts the surface texture.

Video Filters

The Video filters correct problems in images captured from TV or video. There are two Video filters: the De-Interlace filter and the NTSC Colors filter.

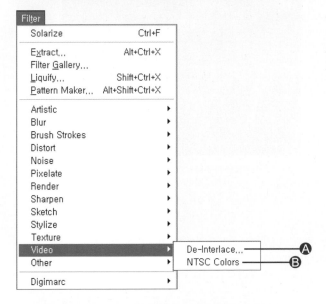

Ⓐ De-Interlace

The De-Interlace filter removes the scan lines that appear in still image captures from TV or video.

De-Interlace Options

Eliminate: Select the scan lines to delete–Odd Fields (remove odd scan lines) or Even Fields (remove even scan lines).

Create New Fields by: Determines how the deleted scan lines will be filled. Choose Duplication to make a copy from the image, or Interpolation to fill the area with midtones.

Ⓑ **NTSC Colors**

The NTSC Colors filter converts the color of the image to the NTSC color system used by TVs.

Other Filters

In spite of the many categories available for classifying filters, there are some effects that just don't fit anywhere. The Other category contains such unusual filters as High Pass, Maximum, and Minimum.

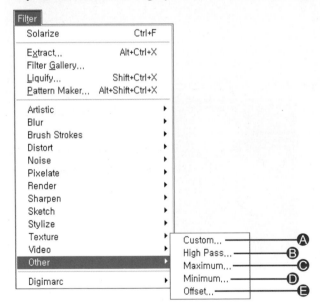

Ⓐ Custom

The Custom filter allows you to create your own filters. To use this filter, you need to enter the brightness values for any given pixel and its surrounding pixels. The filter will then apply your preferences to every pixel in the image.

Custom Options

Center Text Box: This field represents the pixel being evaluated. Enter a value that will be used to multiply the pixel's brightness value.

Other Text Boxes: These fields represent specific pixels adjacent to the center pixel. Enter a value that will be used to multiply the brightness value of the corresponding pixel. You do not need to fill out all these boxes.

Scale: Enter a value to darken the image.

Offset: Enter a value to brighten the image.

Load: Click here to use another custom filter.

Save: Click here to save your settings.

Ⓑ High Pass

The High Pass filter retains edge details with sharp contrasts and fills remaining areas with midtones.

High Pass Options

Radius: The higher the Radius value, the more intense the final effect.

ⓒ Maximum

The Maximum filter spreads out highlights and shrinks the shadows in the image.

Maximum Options

Radius: Increasing the radius expands the highlights.

Ⓓ Minimum

The Minimum filter expands the dark areas in the image and shrinks the white areas.

Minimum Options

Radius: Increasing the radius expands the shadows.

Ⓔ Offset

The Offset filter moves the image horizontally or vertically.

Offset Options

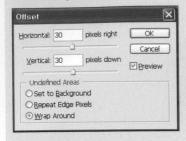

Horizontal: Sets the distance for horizontal movement.

Vertical: Sets the distance for vertical movement.

Undefined Areas: Determines how the empty spaces created at the edges are filled.

-*Set to Background*: Fills the space with the background color.

-*Wrap Around*: Fills edge space with the corresponding section from the other side of the image.

-*Repeat Edge Pixels*: Fills empty spaces with a repeating pattern of edge pixels.

Additional Filter Commands

At the top of the Filter menu are additional commands such as the Extract feature, the Filter Gallery, and the Liquify command. The Extract feature can be used to remove an image from a background. The Filter Gallery shows a preview of some filters, and the Liquify command can be used to distort an image.

Extract ([Alt]-[Ctrl]-[X])

The Extract command is not really a filter in the traditional sense. It is used for extracting selections and not creating special effects. You can use the feature to change an image background, create an image with a transparent background, or create an irregular selection. To use the Extract filter, draw around the edge of an image with the Edge Highlighter tool and fill the area with the Fill tool. Press OK to extract the image, or Preview to clean up the image before clicking OK. The background will be removed and the edges of the image will lose the color components derived from the background. This makes it easy to blend the selection with a new background.

The Extract Dialog Box

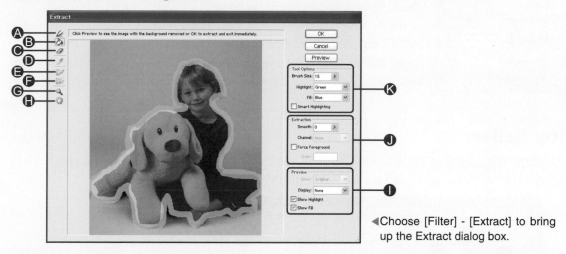

◀Choose [Filter] - [Extract] to bring up the Extract dialog box.

Ⓐ Edge Highlighter Tool (🖊), **[B]**: This tool is used to draw the border defining the area to be retained.

Ⓑ Fill Tool (🪣), **[G]**: This tool is used to select the area to be retained. It cannot be used when the Force Foreground option is checked.

Ⓒ Eraser Tool (🧽), **[E]**: The Eraser tool is used to clean up the border of the preview image. You can also use it to erase part of a filled area.

Ⓓ Eyedropper Tool (💉), **[I]**: The Eyedropper tool is related to the Force Foreground option and is used to determine the color that will be extracted. You can only use this tool on areas to which the Edge Highlighter tool has been applied.

Ⓔ Cleanup (🖌), **[C]**: The Cleanup tool is used to remove artifacts left behind when you preview the extract process.

Ⓕ Edge Touchup Tool (🖌), **[T]**: Drag this tool to make the edges of the preview image more precise.

Ⓖ Zoom Tool (🔍), **[Z]**: This tool zooms in and out from the image.

Ⓗ Hand Tool (✋), **[H]**: The Hand tool moves the image.

Ⓘ Preview

Show: Shows a preview of the extracted area.
Display: Sets up the display of the separated image and background.
Show Highlight: Shows the area selected with the Edge Highlighter tool.
Show Fill: Shows the area filled with the Fill tool.

Ⓙ Extraction

Smooth: Determines the smoothness of the edges of the extracted image.
Channel: Separates the image using channels.
Force Foreground: Choose the Eyedropper tool and select the color to extract.
Color: The Eyedropper tool shows the selected color.

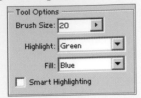

K Tool Options

Brush Size: Choose the size of the brush.

Highlight: Change the color of the Edge Highlighter.

Fill: Change the color of the Fill tool.

Smart Highlighting: When you check this option, the Edge Highlighter tool automatically determines the edges within the brush area.

Filter Gallery

The Filter Gallery contains some of the filters that can be applied to an image. Filters are grouped into categories and the thumbnails show a preview of the filter effects.

Ⓐ Press the Expand/Reduce buttons to show and hide the Filter Gallery menus.

Ⓑ The filter options change according to the selected filter.

Ⓒ Turn a filter on or off using the eye icon. You can also move the stacking order of the filters if you have applied more than one filter to an image. Changing the stacking order changes the final effect on the image.

Liquify [Shift]-[Ctrl]-[X]

The Liquify command distorts the pixels within an image. You can add twirl, pucker, and bloat effects by dragging within the image. Before you start distorting the image, click the Show Mesh option in the Liquify dialog box to display a grid over the image. This allows you to see how the pixels in the image are pushed around.

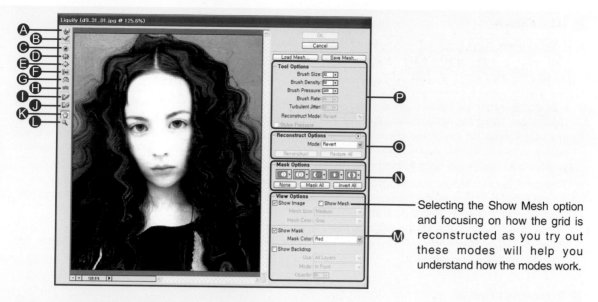

Selecting the Show Mesh option and focusing on how the grid is reconstructed as you try out these modes will help you understand how the modes work.

Ⓐ Forward Warp Tool (🖑), **[W]**: Drag with this tool to warp pixels.

Ⓑ Reconstruct Tool (✎), **[R]**: Restores the image to its original state.

Ⓒ Twirl Clockwise Tool (🌀), **[C]**: Click or drag with this tool to twirl the image clockwise. Hold down the [Alt] key to twirl the image counterclockwise.

Ⓓ Pucker Tool (▦), **[S]**: Click or drag to pucker the pixels toward the brush center.

Ⓔ Bloat Tool (◈), **[B]**: Click or drag to bloat the pixels and expand the image.

Ⓕ Push Left Tool (▥), **[O]**: Use the mouse to shift pixels horizontally.

Ⓖ Mirror Tool (▦), **[M]**: Use the mouse to create an axis on which to reflect the image.

Ⓗ Turbulence Tool (≋), **[T]**: Click or drag to create waves.

Ⓘ Freeze Mask Tool (🖉), **[F]**: Prevent changes from happening in the frozen section. Frozen areas appear in red.

Ⓙ Thaw Mask Tools (🖉), **[D]**: Unfreezes frozen areas.

Ⓚ Hand Tool (✋), **[H]**: Moves the image.

Ⓛ Zoom Tool (🔍), **[Z]**: Zooms in or out from the image.

Ⓜ View Options

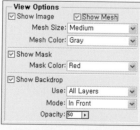

Show Image, Show Mesh: Shows the image and/or mesh.
  -*Mesh Size*: Determines the mesh size.
  -*Mesh Color*: Determines the mesh color.
Show Mask: Shows/hides the mask.
  -*Mask Color*: Sets the mask color. The default is red.
Show Backdrop: Keeps the original image in the background as you edit. You can think of it as using the original image as a guide.
  -*Use*: Choose All Layers or one of the layer names. Selecting All Layers uses the objects on all the layers as the backdrop. Selecting one of the layers shows only the objects on that layer as the backdrop.
  -*Mode*: Determines whether the backdrop is placed in front of, behind, or is blended with the active layer.
  -*Opacity*: Determines the transparency of the backdrop.

ⓃMask Options

None: Removes mask from image.

Mask All: Masks all areas.

Invert All: Inverts masked and unmasked areas.

If an image contains a mask, transparency, or selection, these areas will be shown in the image preview of the Liquify filter. Using the mask options together with the Freeze Mask tool or the Thaw Mask tool, you can create and edit a mask for the image preview. Doing so lets you protect (freeze) or release (thaw) these areas for editing in the Liquify dialog box. Each of the mask option buttons edits the mask in a specific way and clicking on the button lets you choose a channel to edit the preview with.

Replace Selection: Masks according to the masks, transparency, or selected areas in the original image.
Add to Selection: Displays the mask in the original image and lets you add to the selection using the Freeze tool.
Subtract from Selection: Subtracts from the selection.
Intersect with Selection: Adds the selection to the mask selection.
Invert Selection: Converts everything excluding the selection into a mask (currently masked areas are excluded from the new mask).

ⓄReconstruct Options

Click here to restore the original image to the specified degree.

Mode: Choose from Revert (completes reconstruction without smoothing), Rigid (maintains right angles between frozen and unfrozen areas), Stiff (as the distance from the frozen areas increases, the distortions decreases), Smooth (spreads the distortion to unfrozen areas), or Loose (similar to Smooth but with a reduced effect).

Reconstruct: After selecting a reconstruction mode, click this button to apply the effect on the preview image.

Restore All: Undo all the changes that were applied to the image in the Liquify dialog box.

ⓅTool Options

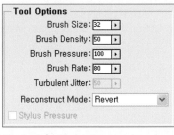

Brush Size: The brush size determines the size of the effect.

Brush Density: Determines how the brush feathers at the edge.

Brush Pressure: The brush pressure determines how quickly effects are added when the tool is dragged. Higher numbers represent faster changes.

Brush Rate: Brush rate determines how quickly the effect is applied when the tool is clicked and held down. Higher numbers represent faster changes.

Turbulent Jitter: Determines how the Turbulence tool changes pixels.

Reconstruct Mode: This mode is only available when the Reconstruct tool ( ) is selected. The options found here include the modes (Revert, Rigid, Stiff, Smooth, Loose) found in the Mode option of the Reconstruct Option category. In addition, three other reconstruct modes (Displace, Amplitwist, Affine) are available for the Reconstruct tool. These three modes work rather differently. When one of these modes is selected, the Reconstruct tool restores the image starting from the point that you first click on the image with the Reconstruct tool.

-Displace: The position of the reconstructed image depends on where you first click the Reconstruct tool.

-Amplitwist: The position, rotation, and scaling of the reconstructed image depend on where you first click the Reconstruct tool.

-Affine: The position, rotation, scaling, and skew of the reconstructed image depend on where you first click the Reconstruct tool.

Stylus Pressure: This option is only available if you are using a stylus tablet. Selecting this option lets you multiply the Brush Pressure value with the pressure you exert on the tablet with the stylus, giving you greater control over the brush pressure.

Pattern Maker [Alt]-[Shift]-[Ctrl]-[X]

The Pattern Maker is used to create patterns from a selection or from the Clipboard. You can use horizontal and vertical offsets to create criss-cross patterns.

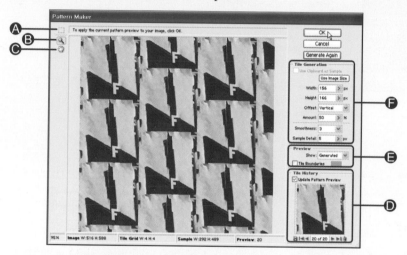

Ⓐ **Rectangular Marquee Tool** (▢), **[M]**: Creates rectangular selections.

Ⓑ **Zoom Tool** (🔍), **[Z]**: Magnifies the selection.

Ⓒ **Hand Tool** (✋), **[H]**: Moves the thumbnail.

Ⓓ **Tile History**

Use Tile History to select a previous pattern state. You can go back up to 20 steps and save or delete the history.

Ⓔ **Preview**

Used to see the original or generated pattern.
Tile Boundaries: Check here to see the tile edges.

Ⓕ **Tile Generation**

Use Clipboard as Sample: Use the selection copied to the Clipboard for the tiling.
Use Image Size: Click to enter the current image size.
Width, Height, Offset, and Amount: These settings determine the pattern size and the direction and amount of overlap in the patterns.
Smoothness: A higher Smoothness setting makes the edges of the tiles less prominent. This can make the image appear to be a single pattern instead of one consisting of many tiles.
Sample Detail: Determines the amount of detail in the original image that will be kept in the tiles.

Digimarc

The Digimarc filters add a digital watermark to an image to store copyright information.
All copyrighted images in Photoshop contain a © in the title.

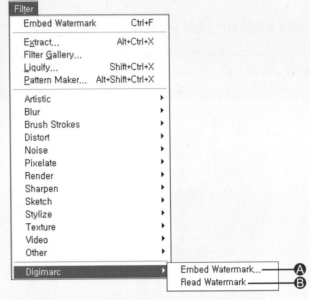

Ⓐ Embed Watermark

Click Personalize to open the Personalize Digimarc ID dialog box. You can enter your user ID to watermark the image. If you don't have an ID, click [Info] and register at the Digimarc homepage. You must pay a fee for this service.

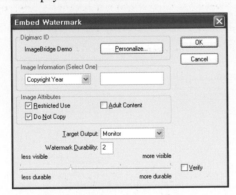

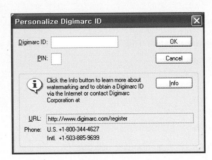

Ⓑ Read Watermark

Allows you to read image copyright information.

Making New Pictures Look Old

Original Image

Final Image

Project File
- olden.jpg

Final File
- olden_end.psd

Features Used
- Grain Filter, Hue/Saturation, Cloud, Wave

In this example, you will artificially age new pictures. You will use the Grain, Cloud, and Wave filters to create noise, uneven brightness, and worn edges to make the image look faded and old. A few image adjustments will also be made to lower the saturation of the image.

<< **note**

Resource Files

Remember to copy the resource files on the CD-ROM to your hard drive before you start each exercise in this book.

1 Open olden.jpg.

2 In the Layers palette, drag the Background layer to the [Create a new layer] button to create the Background copy layer.

3 Choose [Filter] - [Texture] - [Grain]. Set the Intensity to 30, the Contrast to 20, the Grain Type to Vertical, and click OK.

4 Let's lower the saturation and change the image to monotone. Choose [Image] - [Adjustments] - [Hue/Saturation]. Check the Colorize option, set the Hue to 30, the Saturation to 30, the Lightness to 30, and click OK.

5 Let's place the Background layer above the Background copy layer. But first, you must convert it to a normal layer. In the Layers palette, double-click the Background layer. Click OK in the New Layer dialog box.

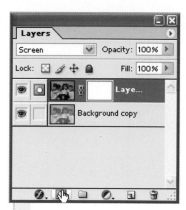

6 Drag Layer 0 above the Background copy layer and change the blend mode to Screen. Click the [Add a mask] button.

7 Choose [Filter] - [Render] - [Cloud] to add black-and-white clouds to the layer mask. The clouds will add irregular tones to the image.

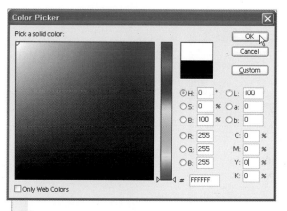

8 Choose [Image] - [Adjustments] - [Brightness/ Contrast] and enter a Brightness setting of 50 and a Contrast setting of 30. Click OK.

9 Click the [Create new fill or adjustment layer] button at the bottom of the Layers palette and select Solid Color. Set the color to white and click OK.

10 Choose the Rectangular Marquee tool and set the Feather value to 30. Create a selection as shown. Set the foreground color to black and fill the layer mask with black.

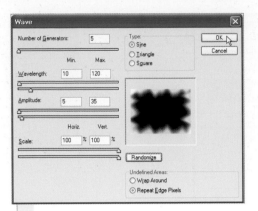

11 Let's distort the edges of the selection. Choose [Filter] - [Distort] - [Wave] and do not change the default settings. Click Randomize several times to randomize the distortion. When you are satisfied with the results, click OK.

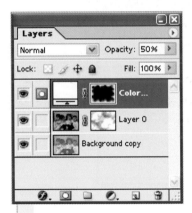

12 In the Layers palette, set the Opacity to 50% and click OK.

13 The final image is shown here.

2 Creating a Pencil Sketch

Original Image

Final Image

Project File
— Art.jpg

Final File
— Art_end.psd

Features Used
— Desaturate, Find Edges, Rough Pastels, Levels

In this example, you will use the Desaturate command to turn a color picture into a black-and-white image. Then you will use the Find Edges and Rough Pastels filters to create a realistic pencil sketch.

<< note
Resource Files

Remember to copy the resource files on the CD-ROM to your hard drive before you start each exercise in this book.

1 Open Art.jpg.

2 Choose [Image] - [Adjustments] - [Desaturate] to remove all color from the image. You now have a black-and-white image.

3 In the Layers palette, drag the Background layer to the [Create a new layer] button to create the Background copy layer.

4 Choose [Filter] - [Stylize] - [Find Edges] to darken the edges of the image. The other areas of the image are filled with white.

5 Choose [Filter] - [Artistic] - [Rough Pastels]. Set the Stroke Length to 6, the Stroke Detail to 4, the Texture to Canvas, the Scaling to 100, the Relief to 30, the Light Direction to Top Right, and click OK.

6 Set the blend mode of Background copy to Screen. This will make the image brighter and will hide any extra lines. The image now looks like a pencil sketch, but the eyes, nose, and mouth are still blurry.

7 Choose the Lasso tool from the toolbox and set Feather to 30 px. Use the tool to select the eyes, nose, and mouth as shown. Add to the selection by holding down the [Shift] key.

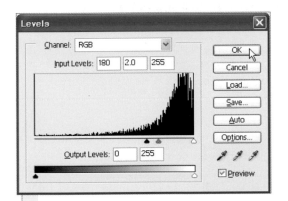

8 Choose [Image] - [Adjustments] - [Levels]. Set the Input Levels to 180, 2.0, and 255, then click OK.

9 Press [Ctrl]-[D] to clear the selection. The final image is shown here.

Configuring the Photoshop Environment

You can change the Photoshop environment by using the [Edit] - [Preferences] menu. In the Preferences dialog box, there are eight sub-menus. In most cases, it is best to use the default preferences, but sometimes you may need to adjust the virtual memory settings or the Image Cache options to suit your own computer. Many of the other options contain advanced settings.

General Preferences

General preferences are options relating to the general Photoshop environment. (Shortcut keys: [Ctrl]-[K].)

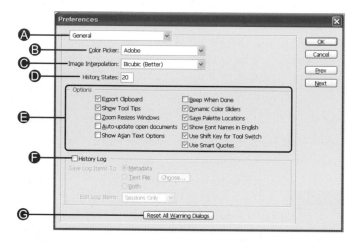

Ⓐ General: Click the drop-down button to reveal the 9 sub-menus.

Ⓑ Color Picker: Adjusts the Color Picker.

Ⓒ Image Interpolation: Photoshop offers three methods of interpolation: Nearest Neighbor (Faster), Bilinear, and Bicubic. Bicubic is the default setting and offers the best image quality.

Ⓓ History States: Sets the number of steps within the History palette, to a maximum value of 1000.

Ⓔ Options

Export Clipboard: The Photoshop clipboard can be used to paste into other applications. Unless you are planning to use the copied Photoshop image in another program, it is best to keep this option turned off.

Show Tool Tips: Pointing at tools or palettes will display tips, shortcut keys, and names.

Keyboard Zoom Resizes Windows: Windows can be resized by clicking the image window and using the arrow keys on the keyboard.

Auto-update open documents: This option provides automatic updates when images are loaded from ImageReady.

Show Asian Text Options: Changes text options for Asian users.

Beep When Done: Sounds a beep after a command has been completed.

Dynamic Color Sliders: Tools that set color with slider bars display the color in a preview window as soon as the color is adjusted. When this option is selected, the colors will be displayed in the slider bar as well as the preview window.

Save Palette Locations: This option saves the palette locations upon exiting from Photoshop. When the program is opened, the palettes will resume their saved positions.

Show Font Names in English: Turn off this option to see font names in another language.

Use Shift Key for Tool Switch: This option is only applicable to tool icons that contain multiple tools. Hold down the [Shift] key and press the shortcut key for the tool to toggle between the embedded tools in order.

Use Smart Quotes: Automatically changes quotes into smart quotes.

❻ History Log: Errors triggered by the [Automate] - [Batch] command should be saved according to the selection—Metadata, Text File, Both.

❼ Reset All Warning Dialogs: If you've selected the Don't Show Again option for warning messages, checking this option will display them again.

File Handling Preferences

File Handling preferences are used to configure save and other file properties.

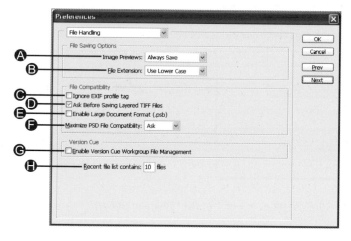

Ⓐ Image Previews: Sets how the icon of the saved file is displayed.

Ⓑ File Extension: Shows file extensions in lowercase or uppercase.

Ⓒ Ignore EXIF profile tag: EXIF, which stands for Exchangeable Image File Format, is a standard for storing image or digital camera information such as camera model, shutter speed, and ISO setting. This information is stored in a tag that accompanies a JPEG file.

D **Ask Before Saving Layered TIFF Files**: Layers can be saved with TIFF files but doing so will increase the file size. In addition, although Photoshop will open all the layer data in TIFF files, many applications will not. Checking this option will instruct Photoshop to ask if you want to save the layers in a TIFF file when saving TIFF files with layers.

E **Enable Large Document Format (.psb)**: Click to use the PSB file format.

F **Maximize PSD Files Compatibility**: This option determines whether the file's compatibility with other Photoshop versions and other applications will be maximized.

G **Enable Version Cue Workgroup File Management**: After a Version Cue workspace has been set up on a network, you need to turn on Version Cue in Photoshop by checking this option. This lets you work in Photoshop with a Version Cue workgroup.

H **Recent file list contains (10) files**: Sets the number of files that will be shown in the [File] - [Open Recent] menu.

Display & Cursors Preferences

This dialog box is used to monitor display and mouse cursor settings.

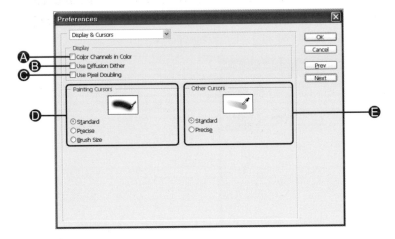

A **Color Channels in Color**: Displays color channels in color in the Channels palette.

B **Use Diffusion Dither**: Dithers images on 8-bit color monitors to make them appear smoother and softer.

C **Use Pixels Doubling**: When images are moved using the Move tool, this option lowers the resolution temporarily so that images can be moved faster.

D **Painting Cursors**: Sets the cursors for painting tools - Standard (painting tool cursor), Precise (cross cursor), Brush Size (round brush cursor).

E **Other Cursors**: Configures cursors for tools other than painting tools.

Transparency & Gamut Preferences

The Transparency & Gamut preferences are used to specify a pattern for layer transparency. They also configure the display of non-printable colors.

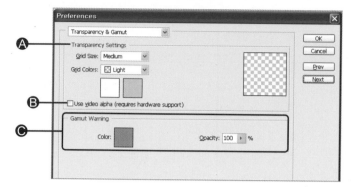

ⓐ Transparency Settings: Sets the look for transparent areas of an image - Grid Size (sets the pattern size), Grid Colors (sets the pattern color).

ⓑ Use video alpha (requires hardware support): This option allows files that contain channels to be recognized by video-editing programs.

ⓒ Gamut Warning: Sets the warning color for areas where colors from an RGB image aren't available in CMYK color mode. Colors can be verified by choosing [View] - [Gamut Warning].

Units & Rulers Preferences

This dialog box sets the units of measurement used in Photoshop.

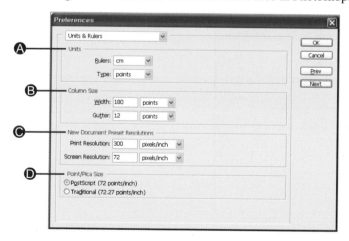

ⓐ Units: Sets the units of measurement - Rulers (measurement units), Type (character units).

ⓑ Column Size: Configures the size of the columns.

ⓒ New Document Preset Resolutions: Determines the preset resolution for new documents - Print Resolution (resolution for printed documents), Screen Resolution (resolution for screen documents).

ⓓ Point/Pica Size: Configures the resolution to fit postscript generators.

Guides, Grid & Slices Preferences

These preferences relate to the colors and styles for guides, grids, and slices.

Ⓐ Guides: Sets the color and style for guides.

Ⓑ Grid: Sets the color, style, and spacing for guides, and the spacing for auxiliary guides.

Ⓒ Slice: Sets the slice line color.

Ⓓ Show Slice Numbers: Displays slice numbers.

Plug-Ins & Scratch Disks Preferences

These preferences determine the plug-in folder and virtual memory.

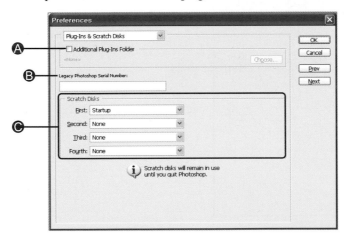

Ⓐ Additional Plug-Ins Folder: Sets the folder for plug-ins. This is used for adding filters to Photoshop.

Ⓑ Legacy Photoshop Serial Number: Enters the serial number for plug-ins that request serial numbers.

Ⓒ Scratch Disk: Designates which drives on your system will serve as virtual memory for Photoshop. Photoshop will prioritize the drives in the specified order. Set the disk with the most space as the first scratch disk.

Memory & Image Cache Preferences

The Memory & Image Cache preferences are used to configure memory for faster speed.

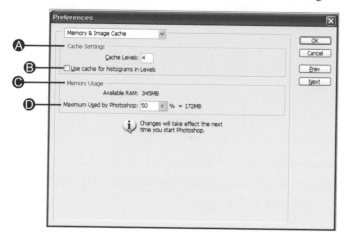

Ⓐ Cache Settings: Cache Levels can take a value from 1 to 8, with 4 being the default setting. The higher this number, the faster the cache speed. This affects the speed at which the image is transformed. Higher cache settings also use more memory.

Ⓑ Use cache for histograms in Levels: Histograms use the cache to display results faster.

Ⓒ Memory Usage: Sets how much memory is allotted to Photoshop. Available RAM refers to the current available memory.

Ⓓ Maximum Used by Photoshop: Displays memory allotted to Photoshop as a percentage of total RAM.

File Browser

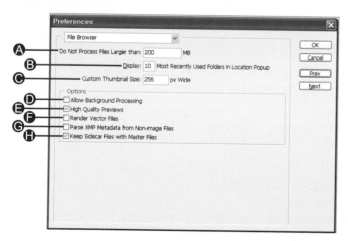

Ⓐ Do Not Process Files Larger than: Because large files can slow down the File Browser, this option instructs the File Browser to skip files larger than a user-determined file size.

Ⓑ Display Most Recently Used Folders in Location Popup: Decides the number of recently used folders to show in the location drop-down menu above the main window.

C Custom Thumbnail Size: Determines the width of the thumbnail that appears in the Preview palette.

D Allow Background Processing: Check this option to use extra processing power to pre-generate cache information such as previews and metadata.

E High Quality Previews: Check this option to see high quality image previews. Checking this option can slow the File Browser down.

F Render Vector Files: Choose this option to display image previews of vector files such as Illustrator files.

G Parse XMP Metadata from Non-Image Files: Displays and lets you edit the metadata of non-image files such as text files. Metadata can be defined as data about other data. For example, the metadata of a text file could include the file name and file type.

H Keep Sidecar Files with Master Files: Lets you keep the sidecar files with the master file. With sidecar files, other applications can process the metadata associated with a file.

Photoshop CS Menus

File Menu

New: Opens a new image file or document. The New dialog box sets the size, resolution, mode, and background color for the new file.
Open: Opens an existing file.
Browse: Opens the File Browser.
Open As: Opens an image using another file format. This command is useful for files that cannot be opened using the Open command.
Open Recent: Shows the most recently opened images.
Edit in ImageReady: Opens the file in ImageReady.
Close: Closes the image.
Close All: Closes all images.
Save: Saves the current file using the existing file name and format, if specified.
Save As: Saves the file using a different file name, file format, or location while maintaining the original file.
Save a Version: Saves a version of the file.
Save for Web: Saves the Photoshop image as a Web image.
Revert: Reverts the image to the last saved state.
Place: Loads Illustrator images (*.ai files, *.eps files) or PDF files as a new layer within the current Photoshop image.
Online Services: Allows images to be sent to remote service providers.
Import: This command is used mostly for scanning images.
Export: Exports images to another program.

Automate: Contains automated commands.

Scripts: Contains common scripts.

File Info: Records and displays file information.

Versions: Lets you work with file versions. Choose to open a previous version of the file, delete a version, or create a new version of the file from an old version.

Page Setup: Sets up paper size, type, printing method, etc. for printed images.

Print with Preview: Shows a preview of how the image will be printed according to the Page Setup options.

Print: Prints the image.

Print One Copy: Prints a single copy of an image.

Jump To: Sends the current file to Adobe ImageReady.

Exit: Exits Photoshop.

[File] - [Automate]

Batch: Batch is used with the Actions palette. It executes actions in the Actions palette and applies them to all files within the same folder.

Conditional Mode Change: This command changes the image mode into one selected by the user. The image must be open in the Photoshop window in order for this command to be used.

Contact Sheet II: Arranges thumbnails of several image files from one folder on a single image window.

Fit Image: After changing either the width or height of an image, the other dimension is automatically adjusted to maintain the original image proportion.

Multi-Page PDF to PSD: Converts PDF files into Photoshop files.

Picture Package: Realigns several images on one page using the setup in the dialog box.

Web Photo Gallery: Creates an image gallery in HTML format using images from one folder.

Edit Menu

Undo/Redo: Undo undoes the last action. Redo is used after Undo and reinstates the action that was undone.

Step Forward: Moves forward one step in the History palette.

Step Backward: Moves back one step in the History palette.

Fade: Fades settings applied to a Filter or Adjustments command.

Cut: Cut out a selection from an image.

Copy: Copies a selection from an image.

Copy Merged: Copies all layers to a single layer.

Paste: Pastes a selection saved using Cut, Copy, or Copy Merged.

Paste Into: Pastes from the clipboard into a selection within an image. The paste occurs on a new layer and a layer mask is applied to the image selection.

Clear: Erases a selection by filling it in with the background color.

Check Spelling: Checks spelling on text layers.

Find and Replace Text: Finds text on text layers and replaces it with different text.

Fill: Fills a selection using colors, patterns, or history and adjusts the opacity and blend mode.

Stroke: Creates stroke lines around a selection.

Free Transform: Creates a bounding box around a selection or layer allowing for free transformation.

Transform: Transforms the image.

Define Brush Preset: Defines a brush needed for painting the image.

Define Pattern: Defines a pattern for use in the [Edit] - [Fill] command, or the Paint Bucket or Pattern Stamp tools.

Define Custom Shape: Defines a user-defined shape made up of paths as a custom shape.

Purge: Clears the clipboard of images that have been saved using the Copy or Cut commands.

Color Settings: Configures the color settings in the palette.

Keyboard Shortcuts: Configures the keyboard shortcuts within Photoshop.

Preset Manager: Manages presets for brushes, swatches, gradients, styles, patterns, contours, custom shapes, and tools.

Preferences: You can change the Photoshop environment using the eight preferences submenus found in this command. In most cases, it is best to use the default preferences, but sometimes you may need to adjust the virtual memory settings or the Image Cache options to suit your own computer. Many of the other options contain advanced settings. All the submenus are covered in detail in the first part of this appendix.

[Edit] - [Transform]

Again: Reapplies the Free Transform or Transform commands.

Scale: Handles are used to adjust the size of a selection.

Rotate: Handles are used to adjust the rotation of an image.

Skew: Handles at the sides are used to skew the image. Handles at the corners are used to skew only one side.

Distort: Handles apply distortion.

Perspective: Handles at the corners add perspective. Handles at the sides skew the image.

Rotate 180°: Rotates the image 180°.

Rotate 90° CW: Rotates the image clockwise 90°.

Rotate 90° CCW: Rotates the image counterclockwise 90°.

Flip Horizontal: Flips the image horizontally.

Flip Vertical: Flips the image vertically.

[Edit] - [Preferences]

General: Configures the general Photoshop environment.

Display & Cursors: Configures monitor display and mouse cursor settings.

Transparency & Gamut: Specifies a pattern for layer transparency and configures the display of non-printable colors.

Units & Rulers: Configures the units of measurement used in Photoshop.

Guides, Grid & Slices: Configures the colors and styles for guides, grids, and slices.

Plug-Ins & Scratch Disks: Configures the placement of the plug-in folder and virtual memory.

Memory & Image Cache: Configures memory for faster speeds.

File Browser: Options for working with the File Browser.

Image Menu

Mode: Refers to the color mode in which the image will be displayed.

Adjustments: Used to make adjustments to images including image color, brightness, and hue.

Duplicate: Copies the current image to a new file.

Apply Image: Combines different images using mathematical formulae to combine the layers and channel color information.

Calculations: Blends channels from one or more images.

Image Size: Changes image size or resolution.

Canvas Size: Changes the canvas size.

Pixel Aspect Ratio: Changes the pixel shape for use in video.

Rotate Canvas: Rotates the canvas.

Crop: Similar to the Crop tool in the toolbox; cuts out an image selection.

Trim: Trims edges from an image.

Reveal All: Expands the canvas size so that the entire image is visible.

Trap: Prevents the fine spaces that appear, due to mismatched color, in images printed in four colors.

[Image] - [Mode]

Bitmap: Displays the image in black or white. Bitmap images do not have brightness information.

Grayscale: Displays the image in up to 256 colors of gray. In this mode, 0 is white and 255 is black. This mode is used before converting to Duotone or Bitmap modes.

Duotone: This mode blends 4 colors to display the image in 256 colors.

Indexed Color: Reduces the number of colors in an image to reduce the size of the image. This mode displays images using up to 256 colors.

RGB Color: This mode uses the three primary colors—red, green, and blue—as well as brightness to represent a variety of colors.

CMYK Color: This mode, used for printing, uses four colors - cyan, magenta, yellow, and black.

Lab Color: This mode uses three color channels. The a-axis represents lightness and colors from green to magenta and the b-axis represents colors from blue to yellow.

Multichannel: Multichannel uses a variety of different channels to display an image. This is used for special circumstances, such as printing images in a different gray tone or in Scitex CT format.

8 Bits/Channel: This means that one channel is composed of 8 bits of information. Most images use 8-bit channels.

16 Bits/Channel: This means that one channel is composed of 16 bits of information.

Color Table: Only used when using the Indexed color mode. The colors in the Color palette can be changed by the user.

Assign Profile: Changes the color profile of a document.

Convert to Profile: Converts colors in a document to a different color profile.

[Image] - [Adjustments]

Levels: Shows the image in 256 levels of brightness. Sliders can be used to adjust image brightness, contrast, and color.

Auto Levels: Automatically adjusts image levels.

Auto Contrast: Automatically adjusts image contrast.

Auto Color: Automatically adjusts the image colors.

Curves: Curves are used to adjust the image brightness, contrast, and color.

Color Balance: Used to add or remove image color to adjust the final image hue.

Brightness/Contrast: Changes image brightness and contrast.

Hue/Saturation: Adjusts image color, brightness, and saturation.

Desaturate: Removes color information from an image.

Match Color: Matches color between multiple images, layers, or color selections.

Replace Color: A section of an image is adjusted for hue, saturation, and lightness.

Selective Color: CMYK colors are adjusted according to the color selection.

Channel Mixer: The slider bars are used to select and mix the colors from each channel.

Gradient Map: The gradient selected in the dialog box is mapped onto the image.

Photo Filter: Creates an effect similar to adding a colored filter to a camera lens.

Shadow/Highlight: Corrects silhouette images in photos.

Invert: Inverts color information (black becomes white and white becomes black) to create an image of complementary colors.

Equalize: Equalizes image brightness.

Threshold: Displays images in pure black or white; a histogram displays from 0 to 255, with 128 being the center. Pixels higher than 128 are displayed as white and pixels lower than 128 are displayed as black.

Posterize: Simplifies image color information. This command is used to create a bold image.

Variations: Adjusts image brightness and color.

Layer Menu

New: Creates a new layer.

Duplicate Layer: Duplicates the layer.

Delete: Deletes the layer.

Layer Properties: Used to edit the layer name and color.

Layer Style: Used to configure and edit the Layer Style effect.

New Fill Layer: Creates a new layer filled with color.

New Adjustment Layer: Creates a new adjustment layer.

Change Layer Content: Changes the layer content to a different adjustment layer.

Layer Content Options: Used to modify an adjustment layer.

Type: Contains options for changing text layers into paths or vector shapes, changing text direction, and distorting text.

Rasterize: Changes vector images into bitmap images.

New Layer Based Slice: The image is sliced according to the selected layer.

Add/Remove Layer Mask: Creates or deletes a layer mask.

Enable/Disable Layer Mask: Select Disable Layer Mask to deactivate a layer mask without deleting it. Select Enable Layer Mask to apply a layer mask that has been disabled.

Add/Remove Vector Mask: Creates or removes a vector mask. A vector mask is drawn using the pen or shape tools.

Enable/Disable Vector Mask: Select Disable Vector Mask to deactivate a vector mask without deleting it. Select Enable Vector Mask to apply a vector mask that has been disabled.

Create Clipping Mask: Creates a clipping mask.

Release Clipping Mask: Reverts the clipping mask to a normal layer.

Arrange: Used to determine the layer order.

Align Linked/Align To Selection: Aligns linked layers.

Distribute Linked: Used to adjust the spacing between linked layers.

Lock All Linked Layers in Set/Lock All Linked Layers: Locks all linked layers. Choose to lock Transparency, Image, Position, or All.

Merge Down/Merge Linked: Merges all linked layers.

Merge Visible: Combines all visible layers (hidden layers remain unchanged).

Flatten Image: Combines all layers into a single background layer.

Matting: Softens layer image edges to assist blending with other layers.

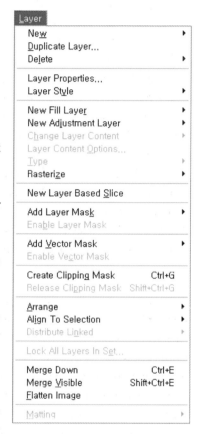

[Layer] - [Layer Style]

Blending Options: Sets blending options for the image.
Drop Shadow: Creates a shadow on the outside of the image.
Inner Shadow: Creates a shadow on the inside of the image.
Outer Glow: Creates a glow effect that shines outwards from the selected image.
Inner Glow: Creates a glow effect that shines inward from the edges of the selected image.
Bevel and Emboss: Adds dimension to the selected image.
Satin: Applies satin/metallic effects to the image.
Color Overlay: Adds color to the image.
Gradient Overlay: Adds a gradient to the image.
Pattern Overlay: Adds a pattern to the image.
Stroke: Strokes the outline of the image using a single color, gradient, or pattern.
Copy Layer Style: Copies the effects applied to the layer.
Paste Layer Style: Pastes the effects copied using the Copy Layer Style command.
Paste Layer Style to Linked: Applies the copied layer style to all linked layers.
Clear Layer Style: Deletes the layer style.
Global Light: Coordinates the angle and height of all layers to which the layer style has been applied.
Create Layer: All layers to which the layer style has been applied are separated into normal layers.
Hide All Effects: Hides the layer style effects of all layers to which the layer style has been applied.
Scale Effects: Used to adjust the size of the layer style in all layers to which the layer style has been applied.

Select Menu

All: Selects all of the current image.
Deselect: Clears a selection.
Reselect: Reactivates the selection.
Inverse: Inverts the selection.
Color Range: Makes a selection based on color range.
Feather: Softens the edges of the selection.
Modify: Used to thicken, round, expand, or contract the selection.
Grow: Expands the selection.
Similar: Selects colors that are similar to the current selection.
Transform Selection: Similar to the [Edit] - [Free Transform] command. Transforms the selection.
Load Selection: Loads a selection that was saved using the Save Selection command.
Save Selection: Saves a selection as an alpha channel.

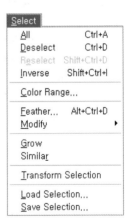

Filter Menu

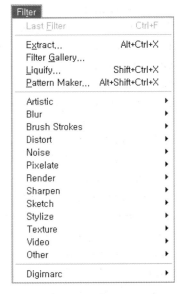

Extract: Used to remove a foreground image from a background.

Filter Gallery: Allows filters to be applied cumulatively.

Liquify: Change an image by pushing, pulling, rotating, reflecting, puckering, or bloating to create a distortion of the original image.

Pattern Maker: Creates patterns based on the contents of the clipboard.

Artistic: Create artistic effects.

Blur: Soften the selection or image. If the Blur filter is applied to layer edges (the edge between transparent and opaque sections), do not check the Preserve Transparency option in the Layers palette.

Brush Strokes: Create brush or ink effects to create artistic images.

Distort: Geometrically distort images.

Noise: Add or remove noise or random color pixels. The Dust & Scratches filter removes noise or scratches from images and the Add Noise filter creates special textures.

Pixelate: Group pixels of similar color value for different effects.

Render: Apply 3D effects, cloud patterns, or light reflection effects.

Sharpen: Raise the contrast of pixels to sharpen images.

Sketch: Add textures to images. This filter is also effective for creating images that appear to have been drawn by hand. Sketch filters are used to redraw images using foreground and background colors.

Stylize: Find and emphasize image contrast to create images in various hand-drawn or -painted styles.

Texture: Add textures to add depth to images.

Video: There are two different kinds of video filters—the NTSC (National Television Standards Committee) color filter, which displays images in colors that can be recreated on television, and the De-Interlace filter, which softens video capture images.

Other: Other filters include Custom filters (i.e., user-defined filters), filters for modifying masks, filters for adding offset effects to image selections, and filters for rapid color adjustment.

Digimarc: A watermark is inserted into the digital format of the image to save or read copyright information.

View Menu

Proof Setup: This command shows the onscreen image using the current channel or mode settings.

Proof Colors: Shows a preview of the Proof Setup image.

Gamut Warning: Replaces gamut warning colors with similar colors.

Zoom In: Magnifies the image.

Zoom Out: Decreases the size of the image.

Fit on Screen: Expands/contracts the image to fit the screen.

Actual Pixels: Shows the image in pixel units at 100%.

Print Size: Shows the actual print size of the image.

Screen Mode: Changes the way the screen appears in Photoshop.

Extras: Checking this option allows you to use the sub-commands under the Show sub-menu.

Show: If the image contains a selection border (Selection Edges), a path (Target Path), notes (Annotation), slices, or displays the grid and guides in the image area, you can use the Show sub-menu to show or hide these elements.

Rulers: Shows/hides the rulers at the edge of the document window.

Snap: Checking this option allows you to use the sub-commands under the Snap To sub-menu.

Snap To: Snaps the image to guides, grid marks, slices, or document bounds.

Lock Guides: Fixes guides in place.

Clear Guides: Removes guides.

New Guide: Creates a new guide.

Lock Slices: Fixes slices in place.

Clear Slices: Removes slices.

Window Menu

Arrange: Arranges windows on the Photoshop screen.

Workspace: Used to create and save palette positions onscreen.

Palette Windows: Select the palettes you would like to appear on your workspace. Currently displayed palettes are marked with a check mark.

Status Bar: Hides the status bar, which displays the current status of the image, located at the bottom of the Photoshop window.

Document Windows: Select from the currently open image files.

Index › › ›

A

Add Noise 323
Adding Textures 118
Adobe Online 18
Accented Edges 286
Actions Palette 19
Adjustments 197
Alpha Channels 241
Angled Strokes 287
Applying Filters 268-269
Artistic Filters 270-280
  Colored Pencil 270
  Cutout 271
  Dry Brush 272
  Film Grain 272
  Fresco 273
  Neon Glow 274
  Paint Daubs 274
  Palette Knife 275
  Plastic Wrap 276
  Poster Edges 276
  Rough Pastels 277
  Smudge Stick 278
  Sponge 278
  Under Painting 279
  Watercolor 280
Average 307

B

Basic Tools 52-57
Bas Relief 313
Bevel 208
  Contour 209
  Texture 210
Blend 213-216
Blur Filters 280-285
  Average 281
  Blur 281
  Blur More 281
  Guassian Blur 282
  Lens Blur 282
  Motion Blur 284
  Radial Blur 284
  Smart Blur 285
Brightness 16, 115, 166, 168
Brush 96, 97
Brush Attributes 100-106

Brushes Palette 21, 100
Brush Stroke Filters 286-291
  Accented Edges 286
  Angled Strokes 287
  Cross Hatch 287
  Dark Strokes 288
  Ink Outlines 289
  Spatter 289
  Sprayed Strokes 290
  Sumi-e 291
Brush Types 107-108

C

Canvas 56
Chalk and Charcoal 314
Channels 163, 238
Channel Mixer 172
Channels Palette 20, 241-243
Character Palette 20, 145
Charcoal 314
Choosing the Right File Format 29
Chrome 315
Clipping Masks 200
Clone Stamp 13, 79
Clouds 307
CMYK 165
Color Balance 167
Color Correction 160-166
Colored Pencil 270
Color Halftone 303
Coloring 116, 122
Color Mode 24-26
  CMYK Color 25
  Grayscale 25
  HSB Color 26
  Lab Color 26
  RGB Color 25
Color Overlay 211
Color Picker 98
Color Palette 18, 98, 99
Color Range 40
Color Replacement 78
Color Swatches 14
Conte Crayon 316
Contour 209
Contrast 168
Correction Tools 12

Craquelure 347
Create New Image 22
Crop 12, 54
Crosshatch 287
Crystallize 303
Curves 164
Custom Filters 335
Cutout 299

D

Dark Strokes 288
De-Interlace 333
Despeckle 301
Difference Clouds 307
Diffuse 323
Diffuse Glow 292
Digimarc 344
    Embed Watermark 344
    Read Watermark 344
Displace 292
Distort Filters 291-299
    Diffuse Glow 292
    Displace 292
    Glass 293
    Ocean Ripple 294
    Pinch 294
    Polar Coordinates 295
    Ripple 296
    Shear 296
    Spherize 297
    Twirl 297
    Wave 298
    ZigZag 299
Drop Shadow 205
Dry Brush 272
Dust & Scratches 301

E

Editing Modes 15
Edit in ImageReady 15
Embed Watermark
Emboss 208
    Contour 209
    Texture 210
Equalize 176
Eraser 13, 108-110
Extract 338
Extrude 324

F

Facet 304
Fibers 308
File Browser 59
File Formats 27-29
    Bitmap (*.BMP, *.RLE, *.DIB) 27
    CompuServe GIF (*.GIF) 27
    JPEG (*.JPG, *.JPEG, *.JPE) 27
    PCX (*.PCX) 27
    PICT (*.PCT, *.PICT) 28
    Pixar (*.PXR) 28
    PNG (*.PNG) 28
    Photoshop (*.PSD, *.PDD) 27
    Photoshop EPS (*.EPS) 27
    Photoshop DCS1.0 (*.EPS) 27
    Photoshop DCS2.0 (*.EPS) 27
    Photoshop PDF (*.PDF, *.PDP) 28
    Raw (*.RAW) 28
    Scitex CT (*.SCT) 28
    TGA (*.TGA, *.VDA, *.ICB, *.VST) 28
    TIFF (*.TIF, *.TIFF) 28
Fill Tools 16
Film Grain 272
Filter Gallery 340
Filters 270
Find Edges 325
Fragment 304
Free Transform 58
Fresco 273

G

Gaussian Blur 113, 114, 282
Glass 293
Glowing Edges 325
Gradient 111-113
Gradient Map 173
Gradient Overlay 211, 212
Grain 329
Graphic Pen 316

H

Halftone Pattern 317
Healing Brush 76-77
Highlights 166, 174-175
High Pass 335
Histogram Palette 18, 160
History Brush 16, 80-81
History Palette 19, 82-83
Hue 168-169

I

Image Mode 24-26
Image Size 55
Info Palette 18
Ink Outlines 289
Inner Glow 207
Inner Shadow 206
Invert 176

L

Lasso 12, 34-37
Layer Menu 200-202
Layers 194-197
   Adjustment 197
   Mask 199
   Shape 199
   Text 199
Layers Palette 19
Layer Styles 198
Lens Blur 282
Lens Flare 308
Levels 161-162
Lighting Effects 309
Liquify 340-342

M

Magic Wand 17, 37-38
Marquee 32-34
Masks 199
Match Color 169, 170
Maximum 336
Median 302
Mezzotint 305
Minimum 337
Mosaic 305
Mosaic Tiles 330
Motion Blur 284
Move Tool 17, 52-53

N

Navigator Palette 18
Neon Glow 274
New Dialog Box 21
   Background Contents 22
   Color Modes 22
   Preset 21
   Resolution 21
   Width and Height 21

Noise Filters 300-302
   Add Noise 300
   Despeckle 301
   Dust & Scratches 302
   Median 302
Note Paper 318
Notes Tools 14
NTSC colors 334

O

Ocean Ripple 294
Offset 337
Other Filters 334-338
   Custom 335
   High Pass 335
   Maximum 336
   Minimum 337
   Offset 337
Outer Glow 206

P

Paint Bucket 110
Paint Daubs 274
Painting Tools 17, 96-97
Palette Knife 275
Palettes 18-21
   Actions Palette 19
   Brushes Palette 21
   Channels Palette 20
   Character Palette 20
   Color Palette 18
   Histogram Palette 18
   History Palette 19
   Info Palette 18
   Layers Palette 19
   Navigator Palette 18
   Paragraph Palette 20
   Paths Palette 20
   Styles Palette 19
   Swatches Palette 19
   Tool Presets Palette 19
Paragraph Palette 20, 145
Patch Tool 77
Patchwork 331
Path Selection Tools 13
Path Tools 14, 134-139
Paths 134, 137, 146, 150
Paths Palette 20, 137-138
Pattern Maker 343
Pattern Overlay 212

Pattern Stamp 79
Pencil 96
Pen Tool 135-136
Photocopy 318
Photo Filter 173, 175
Pinch 294
Pixelate Filters 302-306
   Color Halftone 303
   Crystallize 303
   Facet 304
   Fragment 304
   Mezzotint 305
   Mosaic 305
   Pointillize 306
Plaster 319
Plastic Wrap 276
Pointillize 306
Polar Coordinates 295
Poster Edges 276
Posterize 177

Q

Quick Mask 41

R

Radial Blur 284
Read Watermark 344
Render Filters 307-310
   Clouds 307
   Difference Clouds 307
   Fibers 308
   Lens Flare 308
   Lighting Effects 309
Replace Color 170-171
Reticulation 320
Retouching 113
Retouching Tools 76-81
RGB 165, 238-239
Ripple 296
Rough Pastels 277

S

Sampling and Measuring Tools 15
Satin 210
Saturation 16, 115, 168-169
Save Options 23-24
Saving 23-24

Screen Modes 15
Selection Tools 12, 32-38
Selecting the Color Mode 26
Selective Color 171-172
Select Menu 39
Shadow 166, 174-175
Shape 199
Shape Tools 15, 139-142
Sharpen 310
Sharpen Edges 311
Sharpen Filters 310-312
   Sharpen 311
   Sharpen Edges 311
   Sharpen More 311
   Unsharp Mask 312
Sharpen More 311
Sharpness 13, 113, 114, 165
Shear 296
Shortcut Keys 136
Sketch Filters 313-322
   Bas Relief 313
   Chalk and Charcoal 314
   Charcoal 314
   Chrome 315
   Conte Crayon 316
   Graphic Pen 316
   Halftone Pattern 317
   Note Paper 318
   Photocopy 318
   Plaster 319
   Reticulation 320
   Stamp 321
   Torn Edges 321
   Water Paper 322
Slice 17, 57
Smart Blur 285
Smudge 114
Smudge Stick 278
Solarize 326
Sponge 278
Spatter 289
Sprayed Strokes 290
Spherize 297
Spot Channels 240
Stained Glass 331
Stamp 320
Stroke 213
Stylize Filters 322-328
   Diffuse 323
   Extrude 324
   Find Edges 325
   Glowing Edges 325
   Solarize 326
   Tiles 326

Trace Contour 327
Wind 327
Styles Palette 19, 203-204
Sumi-e 291
Swatches Palette 19, 99

T

Text 199
Texture 210, 244, 250
Texturizer 332
Texture Filters 328-332
Craquelure 329
Grain 329
Mosaic Tiles 330
Patchwork 331
Stained Glass 331
Texturizer 332
Threshold 177
Tiles 326
Toolbox Summary 10-11
Adobe Online 18
Brightness Tools 16
Clone Tools 13
Color Swatches 15
Correction Tools 12
Crop Tool 12
Editing Modes 15
Edit in ImageReady 15
Eraser Tools 13
Fill Tools 16
History Brushes 16
Lasso Selection Tools 12
Magic Wand Tool 17
Move Tool 17
Notes Tools 14
Painting Tools 17
Path Selection Tools 13
Path Tools 14
Sampling and Measuring Tools 15
Saturation Tools 16
Screen Modes 15
Selection Tools 12
Shape Tools 15
Sharpness Tools 13
Slice Tools 17
Type Tools 16
Viewing Tools 14

Tool Presets Palette 19
Torn Edges 321
Trace Contour 327
Transform 58
Twirl 298
Type Tools 16, 142-145

U

Under Painting 279
Undoing Mistakes 23
Unsharp Mask 312

V

Variations 178
Video Filters 333-334
De-Interlace 333
NTSC colors 334
Viewing Tools 14

W

Warp Text 144
Watercolor 280
Water Paper 322
Wave 298
Wind 327

Z

ZigZag 299